Disability and Internati

MW00329106

Despite growing evidence of a close and complex relationship between disability and poverty, development policy, planning and programming have often failed to take full account of the concerns of disabled people. However, following the 2006 UN Convention on the Rights of Persons with Disabilities and the post-2015 Sustainable Development Agenda, which promises to 'leave no one behind', there have been increasing calls from governments and development agencies for disability to be mainstreamed into all development planning. *Disability and International Development* provides a comprehensive overview of key themes in the field of disability and development, including issues around identity, poverty, disability rights, education, health, livelihoods, disaster recovery and approaches to researching disability.

The book engages with relevant theory and draws on existing literature in the field, as well as the author's own research and teaching experience, to explore key issues using a range of examples taken from around the world. Written in an accessible and engaging style to suit both students and practitioners, the book also includes a wide range of reflection exercises, discussion questions and further reading suggestions, making it the perfect introduction to disability and international development.

David Cobley is a Teaching Fellow at the International Development Department, University of Birmingham, UK.

Rethinking Development

Rethinking Development offers accessible and thought-provoking overviews of contemporary topics in international development and aid. Providing original empirical and analytical insights, the books in this series push thinking in new directions by challenging current conceptualizations and developing new ones.

This is a dynamic and inspiring series for all those engaged with today's debates surrounding development issues, whether they be students, scholars, policy makers or practitioners internationally. These interdisciplinary books provide an invaluable resource for discussion in advanced undergraduate and postgraduate courses in development studies as well as in anthropology, economics, politics, geography, media studies and sociology.

Disability and International Development

A Guide for Students and Practitioners

David Cobley

Routledge
Taylor & Francis Group

LONDON AND NEW YORK

First published 2018
by Routledge
2 Park Square, Milton Park, Abingdon, Oxon OX14 4RN

and by Routledge
711 Third Avenue, New York, NY 10017

Routledge is an imprint of the Taylor & Francis Group, an informa business

British Library Cataloguing-in-Publication Data
A catalogue record for this book is available from the British Library

Library of Congress Cataloging-in-Publication Data
A catalog record for this book has been requested.

ISBN: 978-1-138-63190-8 (hbk)
ISBN: 978-1-138-63191-5 (pbk)
ISBN: 978-1-315-20855-8 (ebk)

Typeset in Sabon LT Std
by Swales & Willis Ltd, Exeter, Devon, UK

In memory of my father, Francis Cobley, who encouraged me to study

'*Disability and International Development* is a major contribution towards making the human rights of persons with disabilities, especially the right to be included in international cooperation, a reality. Cobley has provided a work that provides both a critical reading of disability and development theory and is immediately applicable in the concrete work of policymaking and program implementation.'

Stephen Meyers, Assistant Professor, Department of Law, Society and Justice/Jackson School of International Studies, University of Washington, USA

'David Cobley has written an excellent introductory textbook on disability and international development, that provides mandatory reading for all students studying development studies and disability studies. It positively combines a very good academic grounding in this ever-expanding field with excellent case studies that illustrate the practicalities of living with a disability in developing countries.'

Dr Raymond Lang, Senior Research Fellow, Leonard Cheshire Disability and Inclusive Development Centre, University College London, UK

'This book provides a great tool to generate interdisciplinary dialogue regarding the relevance of disability across sectors for inclusive, sustainable development. For all students, academics and researchers, the book tackles terminology and theories that inform approaches to inclusive policies and programmes. It addresses the complexity of service provision across sectors, which demonstrates the multiple transitions experienced by persons with disabilities and their families.'

Prof. Theresa Lorenzo, Programme Convenor for Disability Studies Doctoral Programme, Department of Health and Rehabilitation Sciences, Faculty of Health Sciences, University of Cape Town, South Africa

Contents

Figures, tables, boxes and case studies

Figures

Tables

Boxes

Case studies

Foreword

Disability has not been a high-profile issue in international development. But things are changing. Whereas it was not mentioned in the Millennium Development Goals, it is specifically mentioned in the Sustainable Development Goals, for example Goal 4 on inclusive and equitable education, Goal 8 on sustained, inclusive and sustainable economic growth, Goal 10 on reduction of inequality, Goal 11 on inclusive settlements and accessible transport and Goal 17 on data and monitoring. At the time of writing, 174 countries have ratified the Convention on the Rights of Persons with Disabilities, which sets out everything that needs to be done to promote, protect and ensure the rights and freedoms of all persons with disabilities.

This shift has largely been down to disabled people themselves. Not just in the developed world, but also across the Global South, disability rights movements have campaigned for access, inclusion and human rights. In my previous work for the World Health Organization, I was very struck by how effectively the International Disability Alliance mobilised the representative networks of self-organised groups, and how they worked together for the greater good of their community. This growth of human rights-based organisations, under the banner of 'nothing about us, without us', has also had impact on traditional NGOs working in this area. The voice of disabled people has been heard louder than ever.

An accessible introduction to these issues of disability and international development is long overdue, so I really welcome this excellent primer by David Cobley. Having worked in the field as well as knowing the academic literature, he is an excellent guide, not just for students but also for development workers who want to understand the key issues in working to promote the human rights of disabled people. I have found it very useful to have access to this clear and thorough introduction.

In welcoming this book, I want to stress two issues. One is clear from the data: although disabled people in developing countries experience multidimensional poverty and exclusion, it is sometimes not much worse than that experienced by non-disabled people. Extreme poverty is very equalising. The household is the unit of production, and everyone contributes. But when a country moves ahead on the path to development, it is likely that disabled people will lose out. Non-disabled people benefit from greater availability of wage labour and facilities such as education and healthcare. But disabled people may be left behind, because it is harder for them to get jobs in the formal economy, and because it is harder for them to travel to where the facilities are located. The people who supported them previously – children and women – may become incorporated in school and work. This trajectory echoes what happened to disabled people in the industrial revolution in developed countries. But now, with our greater knowledge and commitment to human rights, it is imperative that we ensure it does not happen again, because we have disability-inclusive development, not the disabling kind.

Second, when it comes to disability, we are talking about families, as much as individuals. Think of the parents of a disabled child. Think of the siblings or spouse of a disabled adult. Think of the children of an older person who becomes disabled. In my research with successful disabled people in southern Africa, over and again the respondent will talk of the mother who insisted he got a proper education, or the siblings who carried him 5 kilometres to school every day, or the uncle who helped him start his business. The individualistic emphasis of developed countries is very different from the more communitarian, family-based cultures of the Global South. However, families barely feature in the Convention on the Rights of Persons with Disabilities – in the preamble and in Article 23. This may be because many activists remember families being over-bearing and controlling, which is often the case. But just as often, families are the essential allies and supporters of disabled people achieving inclusion, and conversely, when disabled people are excluded, then the whole family can suffer.

My own research shows that disabled people can be successful. I knew this already, because of the many leaders and activists I have met from the Global South. In my project, I have interviewed civil servants and lawyers and teachers and farmers and shopkeepers and rice traders in four African countries. The key to their success, often, has been education. These are intelligent and resourceful people. But many times, they have also benefitted from a benefactor, or an NGO, or a DPO, or a government scholarship. Their stories show that disabled people are a good investment. Not just they, but also their siblings and their children benefit from their success. My participants have overcome barriers, after much striving. If only we could dismantle those barriers, it's clear that many more disabled people will achieve success on an equal basis to others.

I hope this book will help the practitioners of today and tomorrow to understand and work to remove barriers to inclusion and achievement of disabled people, in the countries of the South and of the North. I hope readers will end up with a commitment to hearing the voices of disabled people, and to working with us in partnership. That's the way to ensure that the human rights of persons with disabilities are realised.

Tom Shakespeare
Professor of Disability Research
University of East Anglia, UK

Preface

This book aims to provide readers with an overview of key themes within the relatively new field of disability and international development, encouraging them to reflect on how they understand and respond to disability. Since I am not a disabled person myself, some may question the authenticity of my attempts to describe and analyse the many complex challenges facing disabled people around the world today. As a practitioner in this field long before entering the world of academia, however, I have spent much of the past 30 years providing 'hands-on' support to disabled people in a variety of settings, allowing me some insight into their lived experiences and an awareness of the wide range of factors that create and reinforce disability. While this is no substitute for the true expertise that can only be gained from experiencing disability oneself, I do feel able to write on the subject from a perspective that is grounded in reality.

My academic motivations for writing this book stem from more recent experiences, over the past ten years or so, of studying, researching and teaching on disability and international development. During this time, I have become increasingly aware of the need for an introductory textbook-style book, exploring key topics and relevant theory, written in a style that is easily accessible to students, practitioners and development planners who are working on disability in an international or country context. Hopefully this book will go some way towards addressing that need. Given the growing calls for disability to be mainstreamed into all areas of development planning, it is also my hope that the book will serve as a valuable resource for those working or studying in the wider field of international development.

Acknowledgements

The support and assistance of many people has helped to make this book possible. Firstly, I would like to thank Helena Hurd, who planted the idea in my mind in the first place, and the editorial team at Routledge, including Margaret Farrelly and Matt Shobbrock. The external reviewers provided valuable feedback on the initial proposal and sample chapter. Gerard Genevois, Rosemary Tetteh-Wayoe, Joanna Cobley and John Cobley gave generously of their time to proofread the entire manuscript, while Gerard also assisted with the reproduction of illustrations. I would also like to acknowledge Stephen Meyers, Matt Schuelka and Paul Lynch for providing helpful feedback on individual chapters, and Tom Shakespeare, for kindly agreeing to write the foreword. Needless to say, I take full responsibility for any errors or omissions. My wife, Joanna, has been a constant source of encouragement and practical support, and I must also thank my two-year-old son, Benjamin, who had to put up with me disappearing into the study for 'work' far too often for his liking! Finally, I am indebted to many disabled people in various countries around the world who have contributed to research projects that I have instigated over the past ten years, providing the inspiration that has eventually led me to write this book.

Chapters 6 and 8 are derived in part from an article published in *Disability and Society* on 4 April 2012, available online: www.tandfonline.com/doi/full/10.1080/09687599.2012.654988

Abbreviations

ACHPR	African Charter on Human and People's Rights on the Rights of Persons with Disabilities in Africa
ADD	Action on Disability and Development
ADPI	Association of Disabled People Iloilo
AIHW	Australian Institute of Health and Welfare
APDK	Association for the Physically Disabled of Kenya
BDS	business development support
CBM	Christoffel Blinden Mission
CBR	community-based rehabilitation
CDD	Centre for Disability in Development (Bangladesh)
CIL	Center for Independent Living
CRC	Convention on the Rights of the Child
CRPD	Convention on the Rights of Persons with Disabilities
CSID	Centre for Services and Information on Disability (Bangladesh)
CV	curriculum vitae
DEC	Disasters Emergency Committee
DFID	Department for International Development (United Kingdom)
DPI	Disabled People's International
DPO	disabled people's organisation
DRM	disaster risk management
EFA	Education for All
ESCAP	Economic and Social Commission of Asia and the Pacific
GBS	Guillain–Barré syndrome
GDP	gross domestic product
GPDD	Global Partnership on Disability and Development
HCESC	House of Commons Education and Skills Committee
HIV/AIDS	human immunodeficiency virus infection and acquired immune deficiency syndrome
IAEG-SDGs	Inter-agency and Expert Group on Sustainable Development Goal Indicators
ICBL	International Campaign to Ban Landmines

ICCPR	International Covenant on Civil and Political Rights
ICESCR	International Covenant on Economic, Social and Cultural Rights
ICF	International Classification of Functioning, Disability and Health
ICIDH	International Classification of Impairments, Disabilities and Handicaps
ICT	information and communications technology
IDA	International Disability Alliance
IDDC	International Disability and Development Consortium
IDM	international disability movement
IFRC	International Federation of Red Cross and Red Crescent Societies
ILM	Independent Living Movement
ILO	International Labour Organization
Ksh	Kenyan shilling
MDG	Millennium Development Goal
NAB	National Institute for the Blind (India)
NCPEDP	National Centre for the Promotion of Employment of Disabled People
NDRRMC	National Disaster Risk Reduction and Management Council
NGO	non-governmental organisation
NUDIPU	National Union of Disabled Persons of Uganda
OECD	Organisation for Economic Co-operation and Development
OHCHR	Office of the High Commission on Human Rights
PAR	participatory action research
PLA	participatory learning and action
PRA	participatory rural appraisal
ROSCA	rotating savings and credit association
SDG	Sustainable Development Goal
SEN	special educational needs
SHG	self-help group
SHIA	Swedish Organizations of Disabled Persons International Aid Association
TTI	Technical Training Institute (Bangalore)
UDHR	Universal Declaration of Human Rights
UIS	UNESCO Institute for Statistics
UK	United Kingdom
UN	United Nations
UNDESA	United Nations Department of Economic and Social Affairs
UNESCO	United Nations Educational, Scientific and Cultural Organization
UNHCR	United Nations High Commissioner for Refugees
UNICEF	United Nations Children's Fund
UNISDR	United Nations Office for Disaster Risk Reduction

UPE	Universal Primary Education
UPIAS	Union of the Physically Impaired Against Segregation
US	United States
WDMC	Ward Disaster Management Committee (Bangladesh)
WFD	World Federation for the Deaf
WG	Washington Group
WHO	World Health Organization
WPA	World Programme of Action Concerning Disabled Persons
WRC	Women's Refugee Commission

1 Introduction

Disability has long been a neglected topic within the field of international development studies. However, with the growth of a coordinated and influential disability movement, together with increased international recognition of disability as a human rights issue, the need to respond to disability is now emerging as a development priority that can no longer be ignored. The most obvious indication of this was the adoption in 2006 of the United Nations Convention on the Rights of Persons with Disabilities (CRPD), widely heralded as a landmark achievement for the disability movement and a 'game-changer' in terms of raising awareness of disability rights on the international stage. The CRPD has now been ratified by the vast majority of nation states, signifying a near-global consensus on the need to remove the discriminatory barriers that hinder the full participation of disabled people in society. Governments around the world have followed up on this commitment by introducing a plethora of legislative and policy measures designed to foster more disability-inclusive societies. More recently, the post-2015 Sustainable Development Agenda, which boldly promises to 'leave no one behind', highlights the rising profile of disability through several explicit references, in stark contrast to the Millennium Framework's silence on the matter. Yet further evidence of the increased prominence of disability within mainstream development circles can be found in the Sendai Framework (United Nations, 2015),[1] adopted at the 2015 World Disasters Conference as a blueprint to guide disaster risk reduction and management processes until 2030. Crucially, this framework goes beyond recognising the vulnerability of disabled people when disasters occur to highlighting their potential to become active agents of disaster planning and recovery.

Despite these encouraging signs, many disabled people around the world continue to experience blatant discrimination, frequently reinforced by social exclusion and economic deprivation. Evidence of this can be found in the first ever *World Report on Disability*, jointly published by the World Health Organization (WHO) and World Bank in 2011, which estimates that disabled people, as a group, constitute around 15 per cent of the world's population, with the vast majority of them living in the Global South. The Report draws on evidence from around 70 countries to highlight the close links between disability and poverty, with disabled people often subject to stigma, disrespect, prejudice and even violence, as well as being particularly disadvantaged in terms of access to education, healthcare, employment and political participation.

The international development community has now clearly signalled its intention to confront the various forms of discrimination and injustice that create and reinforce disability. However, it is only by furthering our understanding of the issues and challenges facing disabled people on a daily basis that promises of a more inclusive society, in which disabled people are able to participate on an equal basis with others, can become a meaningful reality rather than empty rhetoric. This book aims to contribute to that process by providing a broad overview of various disability-related themes within this emerging field, drawing on an ever-growing body of empirical research that increasingly incorporates the perspectives of disabled people themselves.

Terminology

Disability is a complex phenomenon and its meaning is widely contested.[2] The lack of consensus on how disability should be defined is reflected in the CRPD, which describes disability as arising from 'the interaction between persons with impairments and attitudinal and environmental barriers' (United Nations, 2006, preamble (e)), but does not actually say what it is. This conceptual confusion is further reflected in disagreements among scholars within the field of disability studies over terminology. The issue is one of some significance, given that the choice of terminology can reflect the way in which disability is understood and how disabled people are perceived.

Historically, stigmatising and devaluing terms such as 'invalid', 'cripple' or 'retarded' have been commonplace, reinforcing notions of disabled people as weak, helpless and inferior. While such terms are now widely regarded as discriminatory and inappropriate, they 'can still remain present in all societies around the world' (Iriarte *et al.*, 2016, p. 8). The term 'people/persons with disabilities', used in the CRPD and most other recent international agreements that make reference to disability,[3] is perhaps now the most commonly used and widely accepted. This term is an example of 'person-first language', which recognises that disability is just one of many components to a person's identity. Singal (2010) argues that the use of person-first language is 'extremely importantly in societies, predominantly of the South, where disability continues to be highly stigmatising' (p. 417). However, many scholars prefer the term 'disabled people', which emphasises the role of society in creating and reinforcing disability, thus moving away from the medical model perspective in which disability arises solely from impairment. Perhaps the most influential advocate of this choice of terminology is Mike Oliver (1990), a giant in the field of disability studies and a disabled person himself, who argues that disability should not be viewed as an added appendage, as the term 'people with disabilities' might imply, but as an intrinsic part of one's identity.

While this book adopts the term 'disabled people', I recognise and fully respect that others will prefer person-first terminology. My advice to students is to choose whichever of these two terminology options they feel is most suitable, but to be mindful of the potential interpretations of the choice that they make. It also important to recognise that different expressions may be considered appropriate in different languages and cultures, so it is always advisable to ascertain the terminology preferences of disabled people themselves, wherever possible, when working or researching in different settings.

Another important terminology decision, in relation to this book, is reflected in the use of North–South terminology. The Global North is comprised of richer countries, such as those located in Western Europe and North America, that tend to dominate the global economy, while the Global South is made up of generally poorer countries that, in many cases, have historically been controlled, dominated or economically exploited by colonial powers, thus reinforcing their poverty and dependence (Meekosha, 2011). This is perhaps a rather simplistic way of distinguishing between richer and poorer countries, but I have adopted this terminology in preference to the use of terms such as 'developed' and 'developing', which tend to imply the superiority of one country over another, as well as ignoring the rather obvious fact that, in reality, all countries are 'developing' in one way or another. In referring to countries as part of the Global South or Global North, it is important to recognise that this does not imply homogeneity within either of these two blocs (Singal, 2010). All countries are characterised by a unique set of social, cultural, economic and political conditions that shape the experiences of those living within them, including disabled people.

Book structure and chapter summaries

Following this introductory chapter, the book is structured around nine further chapters which are briefly described below. While each of these chapters is self-contained, reading them sequentially will enable the reader to systematically build up an understanding of disability issues and related theoretical concepts that are frequently revisited in the chapters that follow. Each chapter includes a brief summary of key points, one or more reflection exercises and a short set of discussion questions, designed to facilitate self-reflection or group-based discussion among students and practitioners.

Chapter 2: Understanding, defining and measuring disability

This chapter introduces some of the main conceptual models of disability, including various individual models, the social model and the biopsychosocial model, each of which reflects a different way of understanding disability. These models are examined in terms of the perceptions that arise from them and their implications for policy and practice in relation to disability. There is a particular emphasis on the social model, which has contributed towards increased recognition of disability as a human rights issue but is sometimes questioned in terms of its relevance and applicability in the global context. The chapter also discusses the problems associated with measuring disability and presents a tool known as the 'Washington Group Short Set of Questions', underpinned by the WHO's (2001) International Classification of Functioning, Disability and Health (known as the ICF), which is designed to overcome some of these challenges.

Chapter 3: Disability, identity and shared experiences of poverty

Disabled people are individuals with multiple identities, rather than members of a homogeneous group. This chapter explores a wide range of factors that help to shape the identities of disabled people, both in a collective sense and individually, including differing perceptions arising from models of disability, impairment-related factors, personal circumstances, social differences and the cultural context. The chapter also explores the notion of a 'commonality of experience' among disabled people, based on shared experiences of discrimination and poverty, particularly in the Global South context. The close and complex relationship between disability and poverty is examined in conceptual terms, and also on the basis of a growing body of empirical evidence reflecting the real-life experiences of disabled people.

Chapter 4: International agreements on disability

The CRPD reflects a growing trend on the international stage for disability to be viewed as a human rights issue, rather than as a charity issue. This chapter starts by reviewing some significant international agreements that helped to pave the way for the CRPD, going right back to the 1948 Universal Declaration of Human Rights, before focusing on the content of the CRPD itself. This is followed by a discussion around some of the barriers to its implementation, particularly in the Global South context. The chapter also considers the extent to which the Sustainable Development Agenda takes account of disability, arguing that this framework presents a new opportunity for disability rights to be more fully recognised. Finally, the chapter reviews some important regional agreements, which reinforce the global agreements on disability while also taking account of more local concerns arising in different parts of the world.

Chapter 5: Disabled people's organisations and the international disability rights movement

The international disability rights movement, comprising individual disabled people's organisations (DPOs) operating at the grassroots level, district networks, national umbrella organisations and global coordinating bodies such as Disabled People's International, is one of the largest and most influential social movements in the world today. This chapter first examines the independent living movement, which began in the United States (US) in the 1960s, before describing the evolution of the broader disability rights movement that has been so successful in raising the profile of disability on the international stage. There is a particular focus on the key role played by DPOs within the movement and some of the challenges that they currently face. With the CRPD calling for DPOs to take a lead role in monitoring its implementation, the chapter discusses some of the dilemmas associated with the implementation of disability rights in practice, particularly where universal rights-based discourse may conflict with local-level priorities. Finally, the chapter explores the concept of disability mainstreaming, a strategy designed to ensure that development policies and programmes take full account of disability, and the closely associated twin-track approach, which is often seen as a solution to the perceived limitations of mainstreaming.

Chapter 6: Disability, health and rehabilitation

Disabled people are often denied access to health and rehabilitation services, as a result of which they tend to have higher levels of unmet health needs than the general population and are more vulnerable to poverty and social exclusion (WHO and World Bank, 2011). This chapter first identifies some of the health risk factors that are commonly associated with disability and discusses the evolving concept of rehabilitation. This is followed by an analysis of various issues that need to be addressed by development planners and practitioners in order to ensure that disabled people are able to access appropriate health and rehabilitation services, structured around the four key areas of accessibility, affordability, availability and quality. The chapter then explores the concept of community-based rehabilitation (CBR), a term that is used to describe strategies that involve drawing on community resources to meet the health and rehabilitation needs of disabled people and to empower them to live full and active lives within their communities.

Chapter 7: Access to education

It has been estimated that disabled children account for over a third of those children that do not attend school (Guernsey *et al.*, 2006), while those that do attend are frequently excluded within the classroom and less likely to complete their education (UNESCO, 2015). This chapter examines three strategic approaches to facilitating the education of disabled children – special education, integrated education and inclusive education. The chapter then reviews a series of international agreements that have underpinned initiatives such as Education for All (EFA) and Universal Primary Education (UPE), while increasingly encouraging governments around the world to embrace the concept of inclusive education. Finally, the chapter discusses some of the challenges associated with the implementation of inclusive education, particularly in resource-poor settings, and outlines a range of innovative strategies that have helped some schools to rise to these challenges.

Chapter 8: Pathways to economic participation

Economic participation is vital to reducing poverty among disabled people and enabling them to lead valued lives as productive members of society, while increased participation rates can also help to strengthen economies and build more inclusive societies. It is widely recognised, however, that disabled people are frequently excluded from the world of work (WHO and World Bank, 2011). This chapter begins with a review of important international agreements that establish and reinforce the rights of disabled people to economic participation, before going on to examine some of the environmental factors that often influence the economic opportunities that are open to them. The chapter then explores three particular pathways to economic participation – vocational skills development, waged employment and self-directed employment – identifying some of the barriers that exist in each of these areas and exploring various strategies designed to overcome them.

Chapter 9: Disability and disasters

This chapter explores the often disproportionate impact of major disasters, arising from natural hazards, human factors or a combination of both, on disabled people. The disaster management cycle is used as a framework to examine a range of disability issues, arising before, during and after the occurrence of disasters, which humanitarian agencies frequently fail to adequately address. Various ways of facilitating more disability-inclusive approaches are discussed, focusing particularly on the potentially vital role that DPOs can play. The chapter concludes with a brief review of international frameworks and guidance documents on disaster management, including the 2015 Sendai Framework, a new international blueprint for disaster risk reduction that explicitly identifies disabled people as key partners in the disaster planning and management process.

Chapter 10: Researching disability

There is a pressing need for more research on disability, particularly research that captures the voices of disabled people themselves, in order to support governments and development planners to understand the needs of disabled people and promote their rights to live as full members of society, in line with the CRPD. This chapter first examines concerns, often expressed by disabled people themselves, that much of the research on disability that has been carried out in the past has been disempowering and even oppressive, particularly when based on conventional research methods and underpinned by individual model perceptions of disability. The chapter then explores two particular research paradigms: participatory research and emancipatory research. Both have been increasingly favoured by disability researchers in response to growing calls for disabled people themselves to exert greater influence and control over research processes.

Notes

1 See Chapter 9 for more detailed discussion on the Sendai Framework.
2 See Chapter 2 for a discussion around the meaning of disability.
3 See Chapter 4 for a review of international agreements on disability.

References

Guernsey, K., Nicoli, M. and Ninio, A. (2006) *Making Inclusion Operational*. Washington, DC: World Bank.

Iriarte, E., McConkey, R. and McGilligan, R. (2016) 'Disability and Human Rights: Global Perspectives'. In Iriarte, E., McConkey, R. and Gilligan, R. (Eds.) (2016) *Disability and Human Rights: Global Perspectives*. London: Palgrave, 1–9.

Meekosha, H. (2011) 'Decolonizing disability: thinking and acting globally'. *Disability and Society* 26(6): 667–681.

Oliver, M. (1990) *The Politics of Disablement*. Basingstoke: Macmillan.

Singal, N. (2010) 'Doing disability research in a Southern context: challenges and possibilities'. *Disability and Society* 25(4), 415–426.

UNESCO (United Nations Educational, Scientific and Cultural Organization) (2015) *Education for All 2000–2015: Achievements and Challenges*. EFA Global Monitoring Report 2015. Paris: UNESCO.

United Nations (2006) *Convention on the Rights of Persons with Disabilities and Optional Protocol*. Washington, DC: United Nations.

United Nations (2015) *Transforming Our World: the 2030 Agenda for Sustainable Development*. Washington, DC: United Nations. Retrieved on 21 March 2017 from www.un.org/pga/wp-content/uploads/sites/3/2015/08/120815_outcome-document-of-Summit-for-adoption-of-the-post-2015-development-agenda.pdf

WHO (World Health Organization) (2001) *International Classification of Functioning, Disability and Health*. Geneva: WHO.

WHO and World Bank (2011) *World Report on Disability*. Geneva: WHO. Retrieved on 22 October 2016 from http://whqlibdoc.who.int/publications/2011/9789240685215_eng.pdf

2 Understanding, defining and measuring disability

Disability is understood, defined and measured in many different ways, with variations both within and between countries. Far from being a matter of academic interest only, the particular way in which the concept of disability is interpreted can determine how disabled people are perceived by others in society, and often has a direct impact on development policy and practice. Where disability is viewed primarily as a medical issue, for example, interventions designed to support disabled people are likely to centre on medical solutions. Alternatively, where disability is thought to arise from discriminatory practices, stigmatising beliefs and negative attitudes within society, interventions are more likely to focus on promoting disability rights and advocating for societal change.

This chapter presents some of the main conceptual models of disability, including individual models, the social model and the biopsychosocial model. These models are examined in terms of the perceptions and definitions of disability that arise from them and their influence in the global context. The chapter then moves on to consider the problem of how to measure the prevalence and extent of disability, in order to enable policymakers and service providers to plan interventions and allocate resources efficiently, as well as to facilitate international comparisons.

Individual models of disability

Individual models locate disability within the individual (Oliver, 1990), although they differ in terms of the socio-cultural and historical constructions that explain how disability arises and determine how disabled people are perceived. According to Oliver (1996), however, they are all underpinned by 'personal tragedy theory' which views disability as 'some terrible chance event which occurs at random to certain individuals' (p. 32). This section examines three distinct types of individual model – the religious model, the welfare model and the medical model.

Religious model

In this model, disability is the result of divine retribution for past sins or misdemeanours committed by disabled people themselves, their relatives or their ancestors. Disabled people are held accountable for these wrongdoings, and therefore considered to be deserving of their disabling impairments. This model is reinforced by spiritual principles such as 'karma', embraced by several Asian religions including Hinduism, Buddhism, Sikhism and Taoism, which relates to the future consequences of good or bad deeds, both in one's current life and in future lives. The concept originates from India, where it underpins negative perceptions of disability within general society that are often internalised by disabled people themselves and other household members (World Bank, 2009), but is influential throughout Asia.

Disability and karma

Karma guarantees retribution in the current life for unwholesome actions and thoughts in previous incarnations. From this perspective, disability is a form of repayment: the embodiment of demeritous (sic) deeds performed in past lives.

(Gartrell and Hoban, 2013, p. 201)

Welfare model

In this model, sometimes referred to as the 'charity model', disability is viewed in terms of 'suffering'. Disabled people are typically regarded as inferior, weaker or less productive members of society, dependent on the sympathy and assistance of others, who therefore represent a burden to society. Paul Hunt, a pioneer of the United Kingdom (UK) disability movement who lived for much of his life in residential institutions, alludes to this model in his classic article, 'A Critical Condition', where he describes society's perception of disabled people as 'unfortunate, useless, different, oppressed and sick' (1966, p. 3). The welfare model has been (and still is) very influential, especially in many countries of the Global South, where a long history of disability services being provided by charitable organisations and missionaries has often contributed to the creation of a 'culture of dependency' among disabled people (see, for example, dos Santos-Zingale and McColl, 2006; Cobley, 2012).

Medical model

In the medical model, disability arises from mental, physical or sensory impairments that are attributed to medical causes. The model views these impairments as biological or physiological defects which require medical treatment or rehabilitation in order to restore 'normal' functioning. This model became very prominent in the twentieth century, particularly in Western societies, with the advance of medical sciences and growing knowledge of the human body and how it works. The implication is that disabled people should be supported to conform to the norms of society, largely through medical treatment and rehabilitation, rather than society itself adapting to the needs of disabled people.

The medical model has attracted much criticism, particularly among disabled academics based in the Global North. Brisenden (1986), for example, points out that the model is 'one rooted in an undue emphasis on clinical diagnosis, the very nature of which is destined to lead to a partial and inhibiting view of the disabled individual' (p. 173). This clinical emphasis has led to diagnostic labels being attached to people with various impairments (often referred to as 'disabilities'), and disabled people being viewed as incapable of productive work, because their bodies do not work properly (Shakespeare, 1996). Medical professionals are therefore tasked with intervening to correct functional deficits, in order to enable disabled people to cope with the demands of mainstream society. Throughout much of the twentieth century, many disabled people were regarded as unable to make a useful contribution to society, and hence segregated into special institutions 'for their own good and to stop them being a burden on others' (Barnes and Mercer, 2003, p. 3).

Historically, the medical model has had a strong influence on official definitions of disability. In the 1970s, for example, the World Health Organization (WHO) developed the International Classification of Impairments, Disabilities and Handicaps (ICIDH), which defined disability in the following way:

Medical model definition of disability

Any restriction or lack (resulting from impairment) of ability to perform an activity in the manner or within the range considered normal for a human being.

(Wood, 1980, p. 27)

National legislation on disability has tended to reflect this understanding of disability in many countries around the world. The Zambian Persons with Disabilities Act of 1996, for example, refers to the ICIDH definition stated above, while in the Philippines the 1992 Republic Act 7277 (known as the Magna Carta for Disabled Persons) defines disability as 'a physical impairment that substantially limits one or more psychological, physiological or anatomical function of an individual or activities of such individual' (National Council for Disability Affairs, 2009).

Social model of disability

Increasing dissatisfaction, frequently expressed by disabled people themselves, with individual model perspectives has led to the rise of the social model of disability. The model has its origins within the UK disability movement of the 1970s, when a group of disabled people, including several that had been involved in protests against institutional practices at the Le Court Cheshire Home near Southampton,[1] came together to form the Union of the Physically Impaired Against Segregation (UPIAS). The Union provides an early example of an organisation *of* disabled people,[2] which created a platform for disabled people themselves to voice their concerns and opinions, rather than having them represented by others.

UPIAS viewed disability in terms of social repression. This understanding of disability, as distinct from impairment, was encapsulated in the Union's radical *Fundamental Principles of Disability* document, which contains the following statement:

Disability as social oppression

In our view, it is society which disables physically impaired people. Disability is something imposed on top of our impairments by the way we are unnecessarily isolated and excluded from participation in society. Disabled people are therefore an oppressed group in society.

(UPIAS, 1976, pp. 3–4)

The statement goes on to draw a clear distinction between disability and impairment:

Social model distinction between impairment and disability

thus we define impairment as lacking all or part of a limb, or having a defective limb, organism or mechanism of the body and disability as the disadvantage or restriction of activity caused by a contemporary social organisation which takes little or no account of people who have physical impairments and thus excludes them from participation in the mainstream of social activities.

(UPIAS, 1976, p. 14)

This definition, which was later widened to include sensory and intellectual impairments (Barnes, 1998), implies that society creates disability in two ways. Firstly, the structures of society, including families, communities, physical infrastructure, the economy and the political system, are not designed to fully accommodate people with certain physical and/or mental characteristics.[3] Secondly, society 'excludes' people with impairments through discriminatory attitudes, systems and practices.[4] In the early 1980s, this radical new way of conceptualising disability, encapsulated in the UPIAS document, gave rise to a feeling of optimism among disabled people that was captured by Allan Sutherland (1981, p. 1):

> Over the last few years, a new, more uncompromising mood has been springing up among people with disabilities. Increasingly, we are jettisoning passive acceptance of our situations, taking pride in our selves and our bodies, and coming to see ourselves as disabled, if we are disabled at all, not by the idiosyncrasies of our bodies but by a society which is not prepared to cater to our needs.

The growing feeling, among disabled people themselves, that social oppression and discrimination were the root cause of their disability was articulated in academic terms by Mike Oliver (1983) as the 'social model of disability', a new paradigm which would locate disability firmly within society, rather than within the individual. Oliver attributed the ideas behind the social model to the original distinction between impairment and disability drawn in the 1976 UPIAS document, and called for 'a switch away from focusing on the physical limitations of particular individuals to the way the physical and social environments impose limitations on certain groups and categories of people' (Oliver, 1983, p. 23).

The social model views disability, therefore, as created by the impact of environmental factors (or societal barriers) on people with impairments. In other words, disability arises from discrimination within society, rather than from impairment. The clear implication is that society itself should adapt to the needs of disabled people, rather than the other way around. Oliver (1990) points out that if disability is defined in social model terms, 'disabled people will be seen as the collective victims of an uncaring or unknowing society rather than as individual victims of circumstances' (p. 2).

Societal barriers

Societal barriers, which create and reinforce disability, can be described as 'all the things that impose restrictions on disabled people; ranging from individual prejudice to institutional discrimination, from inaccessible buildings to unusable transport systems, from segregated education to excluding work arrangements, and so on' (Oliver, 1996, p. 33). In social model terms, the removal of societal barriers is essential to reducing and

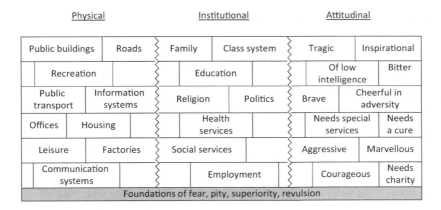

Figure 2.1 The wall of barriers

Source: Adapted from Harris and Enfield, 2003, p. 180

ultimately eradicating disability itself. While the contention that societal barriers actually create disability is contested, it is widely accepted that they greatly exacerbate the problems faced by disabled people and prevent them from accessing their rights to full and equal participation in society.

Harris and Enfield provide a useful conceptual framework, called 'The Wall of Barriers', which groups the societal barriers into three distinct categories: physical, institutional and attitudinal. This is illustrated in Figure 2.1.

The most obvious man-made physical barriers that disabled people have to contend with, in general, are those that relate to the built environment, such as badly designed public buildings and poorly maintained pavements, but there are also accessibility issues around transportation, technology and information sources. Merilainen and Helaakoski (2001) distinguish between 'access to' the built environment, or simply being able to reach and enter places, and 'accessibility of' the built environment, which is about being able to easily make use of the built environment without assistance. They argue that construction programmes in the Global South have lacked consideration of both of these required elements of a barrier-free built environment.

Institutional barriers are created by the segregation or exclusion of disabled people through the workings of key institutions, such as the family, the education system, health services, employment organisations or the political system. For disabled people, they arise when these institutions fail to take full account of their needs, or discriminate against them in various ways. A distinction is sometimes made between direct and indirect forms of institutional discrimination:

Institutional discrimination

it incorporates the extreme forms of prejudice and intolerance usually associated with individual or direct discrimination, as well as the more covert and unconscious attitudes which contribute to and maintain indirect and/or passive discriminatory practices within contemporary organisation.

(Barnes, 1991, p. 3)

Discriminatory job recruitment criteria, for example, may directly affect the chances of disabled people gaining employment, while discriminatory attitudes within workplaces may less directly (or indirectly) affect working conditions, job security and promotion chances.

Attitudinal barriers arise where descriptions or views of disabled people are based on negative or patronising generalisations, rather than on knowledge or appreciation of their individual strengths and weaknesses. The prevalence of negative attitudes, or 'fallacies of innate inferiority' (Chronic Poverty Research Centre, 2009, p. 76), in relation to disability is widely reported in the literature, as reflected in the following extract from the 2004–05 *Chronic Poverty Report*:

Discriminatory attitudes towards disabled people

Discrimination against disabled people is rooted in widely-shared attitudes, values and beliefs. People rationalise the exclusion and ostracism of disabled people and their families in many different ways. Beliefs that disability is associated with evil, witchcraft, bad omens or infidelity persist in many parts of the world. Disabled people also often experience suffocating overprotection and exclusion from everyday challenges.

(Chronic Poverty Research Centre, 2004–05, p. 20)

Reflection exercise 2.1

Use the 'Wall of Barriers' framework to identify the physical, institutional and attitudinal barriers that exist in a country with which you are familiar. How do these barriers prevent disabled people from fully participating in society? Consider participation in areas such as education, healthcare, employment and community activities.

Social model debates

While the social model has gained increasing recognition and acceptance, there have been growing debates over the interpretation and application of the model. In particular, concerns have been expressed that the model's strong focus on the disabling impact of society has led to the experience of specific impairments being ignored, dismissed or trivialised. Shakespeare and Watson (2002, p. 6) contend that some advocates of the social model have adopted a 'strong' version of the model, ignoring the significance of impairment, which is at odds with their private views:

> most activists concede that behind closed doors they talk about aches and pains and urinary tract infections, even while they deny any relevance of the body while they are out campaigning. Yet this inconsistency is surely wrong: if the rhetoric says one thing, while everyone behaves privately in a more complex way, then perhaps it is time to examine the rhetoric and speak more honestly.

They go on to argue that the clear line drawn between disability and impairment in the UPIAS (1976) statement creates a dichotomy which can oversimplify the complex relationship between the two. Moreover, they argue, denying the impact of impairment can create a risk that the need to avoid and reduce impairments may be underestimated. This is a particularly important observation in the context of the Global South, where disability often arises from 'disease, malnutrition or other treatable and preventable factors' (Singal, 2010, p. 422). It is important to emphasise that Shakespeare and Watson (2002) do stress that they 'entirely concur with the political imperative to remove disabling barriers' (p. 15). They do not argue against the need for social change, or the basic logic of the social model. They simply point out that by taking this logic to extremes, and underplaying the significance of impairments, there is a danger of undermining the whole argument.

These views have been echoed by several other scholars within the field of disability studies. Jenny Morris (1998), while acknowledging the value of the social model in terms of giving focus to the campaign against disabling barriers, points out that 'we have tended to push to one side the experience of our bodies' (p. 13). In a similar vein, Liz Crow (1996) argues that, by focusing so strongly on the impact of disabling barriers, 'we have tended to centre on disability as 'all'. Sometimes it feels as if this focus is so absolute that we are in danger of assuming that impairment has no part at all in determining our experiences' (p. 2). Crow goes on to call for a 'renewed social model', highlighting the ways in which disability and impairment work together. She does acknowledge, however, that 'the social model has never suggested that disability represents the total explanation or that impairment doesn't count – that has simply been the impression we have given by keeping our experiences of impairment private and failing to incorporate them into our public political analysis' (p. 9).

These quotations highlight a general concern that the social model's primary focus on the social causes of disability has led to a denial of the 'disabling' impact of impairment itself. Carol Thomas (2004) addresses this concern, to some extent, by referring back to the UPIAS (1976) statement on which the social model is based. While this statement associates disability with societal oppression, it does not deny that impairments can also cause suffering or restrict activities. It simply views disability in terms of the activity and participation restrictions that arise from society's reaction to people with impairments. Thomas goes on to suggest that the success and widespread acceptance of the social model has led to conceptual confusion, because the model itself tends to oversimplify the social relational aspect of the UPIAS view through its focus on societal barriers: 'It is only a short distance, and one that has been commonly travelled, from these blunt social modellist assertions to the proposition that 'all restrictions of activity are caused by social barriers' (p. 579). Thomas (1999) attributes many of the apparent criticisms of the social model to a loss of the social relational understanding of disability. In calling for a revival of this understanding, she proposes the following definition of disability:

Social relational definition of disability

> Disability is a form of social oppression involving the social imposition of restrictions of activity on people with impairments and the socially engendered undermining of their psycho-emotional wellbeing.
>
> (Thomas, 1999, p. 60)

Disability, according to this definition, relates only to those 'restrictions of activity' that arise from the social oppression of people with impairments. While impairments may well restrict activity as well, these impairment-related restrictions fall outside of the definition. Thomas's social relational definition also recognises the psychological aspects of disabled people's experiences, which are the most restricting aspects of disability for many disabled people (Reeve, 2004). The social model not only takes account of these psychological aspects but has helped many disabled people to cope with them by promoting a sense of self-worth and positive identity. Crow (1996) recognises this, bearing testament to the value of the social model to her personally in coping with the psychological aspects of her own experiences:

The psychological value of the social model

My life has two phases: before the social model of disability, and after it. Discovering this way of thinking about my experiences was the proverbial raft in stormy seas. It gave me an understanding of my life, shared with thousands, even millions, of other people around the world. I clung to it.

(Crow, 1996, p. 1)

The social model and the human rights framework

The social model provides a powerful alternative to traditional approaches based on the individual model. By highlighting the disabling role of society, disabled people themselves have encouraged governments and development agencies around the world to consider how societies can become more inclusive and accepting of diversity, in order to enable them to access their rights to full citizenship and participation in all aspects of life, rather than focusing solely on their medical needs. This approach is sometimes broadly referred to as the human rights model, framework or perspective, as explained below:

The human rights framework

A human rights framework is empowering. Where a model of individual pathology marginalises people with disabilities and forces them to attempt to conform to social contexts that do not account for their needs, a human rights approach insists that governments take measures to foster inclusive societies that anticipate and respond to variations in human characteristics that are inherent to the human condition.

(Rioux and Carbett, 2003, p. 11)

This perspective, in which the social creation of disability is viewed as a denial of human rights, is increasingly reflected in the language of international agreements in reference to disability.[5] The Convention on the Rights of Persons with Disabilities (CRPD), for example, calls for 'the protection and promotion of the human rights of persons with disabilities in all policies and programmes' (Article 4, paragraph 1b), while frequently referring to the environmental barriers that prevent many disabled people from accessing these rights. The human rights framework is now widely utilised by governments, development agencies and disability organisations as an ideological basis for strategies designed to remove the discriminatory barriers that hinder the inclusion and full participation of disabled people.

While the rights-based approach is increasingly viewed as offering a solution to problems that arise from disability, questions are sometimes raised as to the effectiveness this approach and its relevance to the everyday lives of disabled people, particularly those living in poverty. As Iriarte (2016) points out, many disabled people continue to face discrimination in all spheres of life, despite the passage of more than 60 years since the 1948 Universal Declaration of Human Rights (UDHR). Grech (2009) questions the wisdom of moving the focus away from impairment and functional limitations in countries where 'poor livelihoods (and ultimately survival) are often dependent on hard physical labour (e.g. agriculture), making a healthy body an imperative' (p. 776). He suggests that a focus on medical or rehabilitative solutions, aimed at enabling disabled people to cope better with their impairments, may reflect their immediate priorities more closely than strategies designed to bring about societal change in the longer term. Emma Stone faced similar dilemmas in her research on a community-based rehabilitation (CBR)[6] project in China, where she observed that 'In Shanlin County, the needs and aspirations expressed by research participants who had disabled children centred almost exclusively on western-style medical intervention' (1997, p. 222).

Yeo (2005) argues that promoting the social model agenda may sometimes put disability activists at odds with broader-based community movements that are fighting poverty. She gives an example of this from post-tsunami Sri Lanka, where disability organisations were lobbying for physical access to new hotels that were being built, while at the same time whole fishing communities were campaigning against their displacement if the hotels were built at all. She argues that disabled people living in those communities would have been better served if the disability organisations had added their weight to that broader campaign, rather than pursuing the social model agenda of focusing on the accessibility of the proposed new hotels. This is not an argument against the logic of the social model, or the need to make buildings accessible. Yeo's point is that the social model's strong focus on the role of society in creating disability, and implied 'call to action' on changing society, can sometimes lead to a diversion of resources which may be better employed in supporting poverty-focused community organisations that are trying to address the more immediate concerns of local people.[7]

Biopsychosocial model

The biopsychosocial model provides a conceptual basis for the WHO's International Classification of Functioning, Disability and Health (ICF), which was adopted by the World Health Assembly in 2001 as a framework for measuring health and disability at both the individual and national levels.

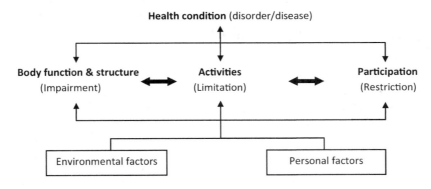

Figure 2.2 The biopsychosocial model
Source: WHO, 2002, p. 9

This hybrid model,[8] which incorporates environmental, biological and psychological factors, is illustrated in Figure 2.2.

Disability, within the ICF, is viewed in terms of functional limitations. As the diagram shows, there are three main aspects or components of functioning that are taken into consideration: body function and structure, activity limitations and participation restrictions. Body function and/or structure relates to functional limitations that arise from impairments, such as blindness or paralysis. Activity limitations are restrictions in carrying out everyday activities, such as eating, walking or getting dressed. Participation restrictions relate to aspects of community life, such as attending school, having a job or being involved in community organisations. The extent to which a disabled person experiences functional limitations in each of these three areas determines the extent of his or her disability. The model also incorporates various individual factors (such as a person's age, gender, economic circumstances or education levels) and environmental factors (such as inaccessible infrastructure or discriminatory attitudes) which may cause or reinforce functional limitations. Disability essentially arises from the interaction between these factors and a person with a health condition, as reflected in the definition below:

ICF definition of disability

The negative aspects of the interaction between an individual (with a health condition) and that individual's contextual factors (environmental and personal factors).

(WHO, 2001, p. 213)

This is a much broader definition than the other definitions highlighted in this chapter, because it views disability as arising both from the environment and from bodily impairment. Interactional definitions of disability, such as this, are increasingly reflected in international discourse and legal frameworks relating to disability. The CRPD, for example, describes disability as resulting from 'the interaction between persons with impairments and attitudinal and environmental barriers that hinders their full and effective participation in society on an equal basis with others' (United Nations, 2006, Preamble, (e)). In some countries, national legislation is also following this trend. In Uganda, for example, the 2006 Persons with Disabilities Act defines disability as 'a substantial functional limitation of daily life activities caused by physical or sensory impairment and environment barriers resulting in limited participation' (Government of Uganda, 2006, Section 2).

The ICF is not without its critics. Bakhshi and Trani (2006) point out that its main focus is still on the individual body and its limitations, rather than on the interactions between individuals and society, thus diminishing the role of the cultural context in determining the extent to which a functional limitation becomes a disability. Oliver and Sapey (2006) criticise the methodological approach for assuming 'that not only can the components of each level be reduced to numbers, so also can the complex relationships between them' (p. 60). They conclude that the ICF will be difficult to operationalise and is unlikely to contribute to improving the lives of disabled people.

Notwithstanding such criticisms, the ICF is viewed by many as a solution to the 'crude dualism' (Shakespeare, 2008) between socio-political and body-related issues that is sometimes reinforced by advocates of the 'strong' version of the social model. The biopsychosocial model is thus promoted in the *World Report on Disability* as representing a 'workable compromise between the medical and social models' (WHO and World Bank, 2011, p. 4). The report recommends adoption of the ICF as an international framework for assessing levels of disability, in order to guide the allocation of resources, set objectives, measure outcomes and evaluate services.[9]

Reflection exercise 2.2

Consider the following scenario:
  Pablo is a 62-year-old man who works as a delivery driver. He has recently been diagnosed with glaucoma, an eye condition which causes visual impairment, particularly if it is not treated at an early stage. Pablo is no longer able to see well enough to drive, so he asks his boss if he can be trained to do another job within the company. The boss does not feel that it is worth retraining him, as he is close to retirement anyway, so Pablo loses his job. As a result, he cannot

afford the treatment for glaucoma and his sight further deteriorates. Pablo feels that he is no longer valued by society, so he now spends most of his time at home and rarely sees his old colleagues and friends.

Describe Pablo's disability in terms of the three components of disability within the ICF:

- Body function and structure (impairment)
- Activities (limitations)
- Participation (restrictions)

Then use the ICF as a framework to analyse the various factors that create and reinforce disability in this case.

Measuring disability

Understanding the nature and extent of disability, within a country, is vitally important for enabling governments to make informed decisions about how best to design development policies and programmes that are disability-sensitive (UNESCO, 2012), in order to meet the needs of disabled people and to facilitate their increased participation in society. For most countries, disability prevalence rates are estimated on the basis of national censuses and household surveys. The results of these, however, depend very much on the particular questions that are asked and the ways in which they are asked. Under-reporting may occur, for example, when enumerators are poorly trained, or when survey respondents are unsure about the uses to which the data will be put (Filmer, 2008). Conducting surveys may also run the risk of raising expectations among disabled people. When visited by data collectors, it is natural for disabled people and their families to assume that their participation in the survey may lead to some direct support or benefit in the near future. As Ingstad (2001) observes, however, even when programmes and policies are introduced as a result of surveys they rarely benefit all those participating in the initial survey directly. Another problem associated with disability measurement is the impact of negative attitudes and certain cultural beliefs around disability in many societies, which can make some families reluctant to speak openly about disability. Mont (2007) observes the frequent under-reporting of disability in countries of the Global South, where the shame and stigma attached to disability leads to some households denying the existence of disabled family members altogether. Making international comparisons on disability prevalence presents even greater challenges, given the variety of definitions and understandings as to what actually constitutes disability, as well as inconsistent methods of data collection.

Measuring disability using the ICF

The *World Report on Disability* (WHO and World Bank, 2011) argues that measures of disability should extend beyond simply identifying those with particular impairment types. Environmental factors, such as the stigma attached to disability and the inclusivity of local community facilities, can have a huge impact on the lives of disabled people, and these factors often vary enormously between countries. Without taking these issues into account, the true nature and extent of disability can never be understood. The report advocates the use of the ICF as a basis for measuring disability in a holistic way, taking into account activity and participation restrictions, as well as bodily limitations.

The Washington Group (WG) was set up by the United Nations, in 2001, with a mandate to develop a standard tool, based on the ICF, for measuring the prevalence and extent of disability across the globe in an internationally comparable way. The tool that emerged was a short set of questions that would identify the majority of people, within a given population, experiencing difficulties in carrying out basic actions as a result of a health problem or condition (or impairment), thus restricting their ability to participate fully in society. The questions, shown in the Box 2.1, cover six functional domains (or basic activities): seeing, hearing, walking, cognition, self-care and communication.

Box 2.1   Washington Group Short Set of Questions

1   Do you have difficulty seeing, even if wearing glasses?
2   Do you have difficulty hearing, even if using a hearing aid?
3   Do you have difficulty walking or climbing steps?
4   Do you have difficulty remembering or concentrating?
5   Do you have difficulty (with self-care such as) washing all over or dressing?
6   Using your usual (customary) language, do you have difficulty communicating (for example, understanding or being understood by others)?

Each of these questions has four response categories, indicating the severity of the activity limitation:

• No difficulty
• Yes, some difficulty
• Yes, a lot of difficulty
• Cannot do at all

Several cut-off points can be used to measure the prevalence and extent of disability, based on responses to the questions. For example:

- At least *some difficulty* in at least *one* of the six domains
- At least *a lot of difficulty* in at least *one* of the six domains
- *Cannot do at all* in at least one of the six domains
- At least *a lot of difficulty* in at least *one* of the six domains **or** at least *some difficulty* in *two or more* domains.

Part of the rationale for basing questions on activity limitations, rather than on the impairment itself, is to avoid the risk of under-reporting due to negative stigma and connotations around disability. People with intellectual or psychological impairments, in particular, may fail to identify themselves, or be identified by others, as disabled or having a disability when asked the question directly. Focusing on activity limitations is thought to be more sensitive and socially acceptable, and thus likely to produce more accurate estimates of disability prevalence. There is also more flexibility in the WG approach, given the range of responses and cut-off options available. It is possible to focus on a particular domain of interest, for example, depending on the purposes of data collection. It is also possible to produce prevalence estimates that are disaggregated by domains, or be severity levels, thus providing a more nuanced picture of disability. Another advantage of the WG approach is the simplicity and non-ambiguity of the questions. Impairment-based survey approaches often require people to have some knowledge of their particular medical diagnosis or mental condition, or to make judgements as to whether their particular functional limitations qualify them as disabled, both of which could lead to under-reporting. Elderly people, for example, may interpret activity limitations as simply part of the ageing process, rather than the onset of disability.

Where the WG approach has been used, much higher prevalence rates have tended to emerge than in surveys where more traditional methods have been employed. For example, the 2000 Census in Zambia, which included the question 'Are you disabled in any way?', revealed a prevalence rate of 2.7 per cent. In contrast, much higher prevalence rates emerged from a 2006 Living Conditions Survey that made use of the WG short set of questions (Eide and Loeb, 2006). Where the cut-off point 'at least some difficulty in at least one of the six domains' was used, the resulting prevalence rate was 14.5 per cent. Choosing a more conservative cut-off point, 'at least a lot of difficulty in at least one of the six domains', still led to a prevalence rate of 8.5 per cent, more than three times the previous census-based estimate.

The *World Health Survey* (WHO, 2002–04), which covered 70 countries, represents perhaps the most ambitious attempt yet to measure disability across countries. Disability data were gathered from a weighted sample of respondents within each country, using a single questionnaire based on the ICF approach. The survey revealed an average prevalence rate of 15.6 per cent, across the 70 countries, ranging from 11.8 per cent in high-income countries to 18 per cent in low-income countries. The *World Report on Disability* (WHO and World Bank, 2011) uses data from this survey, together with the Global Burden of Disease survey conducted between 2000 and 2004, to estimate the current worldwide disability prevalence rate at 15 per cent. This equates to over one billion people, or nearly one sixth of the world's population. The report acknowledges, however, that both of the surveys on which these estimates are based had significant limitations, including the arbitrariness of where to set the threshold for disability and differences between countries in terms of the extent to which respondents were willing to report difficulties in functioning, partly due to differing cultural expectations around how disabled people should live their lives.

Summary of key points

- Models of disability play an important role in shaping perceptions of disability and thus influencing both policy and practice in the field of disability and development.
- Individual models locate disability within the impaired body and are underpinned by notions of disability as a personal tragedy. The religious model, the welfare model and the medical model are examples of individual models.
- The social model locates disability firmly within society. Within this model, disability arises from the failure of society to adapt to the diverse needs of disabled people. The growing influence of the social model has encouraged disabled people to value themselves more highly and to seek justice as citizens within an unfair society. There are debates, however, around the extent to which this model adequately takes account of the disabling impact of impairment, particularly in the Global South context.
- The human rights framework, which is underpinned by the social model, has been increasingly adopted by governments, development agencies and disability organisations on the international stage as a basis for promoting the full participation of disabled people within mainstream society.
- The ICF is a biopsychosocial model of disability, incorporating elements of the medical model and social model. This model views disability in terms of functional limitations in three core areas: body function and structure, activities and participation. The ICF has provided a basis for the development of the WG questions, a flexible tool designed to measure disability in a way that facilitates international comparisons and reduces the impact of stigma on the data collection process.

Discussion questions

1   How is disability understood in the country where you live or work? Which models of disability are reflected in these perceptions? How have perceptions changed over time?

2 How are models of disability reflected in the various linguistic terms that are used in relation to disability and disabled people?
3 What are the advantages and disadvantages of using the WG questions as a tool for measuring disability?

Notes

1 See Chapter 10 for further discussion on this case.
2 Organisations *of* disabled people, as opposed to organisations *for* disabled people, are usually referred to as disabled people's organisations (DPOs). Chapter 5 focuses on some of the issues and challenges facing DPOs today.
3 This is consistent with the 'human variation model', which defines disability as the 'systematic mismatch between physical and mental attributes of individuals and the present (but not potential) ability of social institutions to accommodate those attributes' (Schriner and Scotch, 2001, p. 100).
4 This is consistent with the 'minority group model', which identifies disabled people as members of a minority group subject to stigmatisation, discrimination and exclusion, in much the same way as certain ethnic minority groups.
5 See Chapter 4 for a review of major international agreements on disability.
6 See Chapter 6 for an explanation of the CBR approach.
7 Debates around the relevance and applicability of the human rights framework in the local context are further explored in Chapters 4 and 5.
8 There are a number of other hybrid models, such as the cultural model, the defectology model and the Columbian model. Iriarte (2016) (see Suggested further reading) provides a useful explanation of these three models.
9 Chapter 6 examines the use of the ICF as a framework to guide rehabilitation processes.

Suggested further reading

Grech, S. (2009) 'Disability, poverty and development: critical reflections on the majority world debate'. *Disability and Society* 24(6), 771–784.
Iriarte, E. (2016) 'Models of Disability'. In Iriarte, E., McConkey, R. and Gilligan, R. (Eds.) (2016) *Disability and Human Rights: Global Perspectives*. London: Palgrave, 10–32.
Shakespeare, T. and Watson, N. (2002) 'The social model of disability: an outdated ideology?'. *Research in Social Science and Disability* 2, 9–28. Retrieved on 12 March 2017 from http://disability-studies.leeds.ac.uk/files/library/Shakespeare-social-model-of-disability.pdf

References

Bakhshi, P. and Trani, J. (2006) 'The Capability Approach to Understanding Disability: Increasing Comparability, Defining Efficient Programs'. In Reboud, V. (Ed.) *Capabilities and Public Policies*. Paris: French Agency for Development, 1–14.
Barnes, C. (1991) *Disabled People in Britain and Discrimination: A Case for Anti-discrimination Legislation*. London: Hurst & Co.
Barnes, C. (1998) 'The Social Model of Disability: A Sociological Phenomenon Ignored by Sociologists'. In Shakespeare, T. (Ed.) *The Disability Reader*. London: Continuum, 65–78.

Barnes, C. and Mercer, G. (2003) *Disability*. Cambridge: Polity Press.

Brisenden, S. (1986) 'Independent Living and the Medical Model of Disability'. In Shakespeare, T. (Ed.) (1998) *The Disability Reader*. London: Continuum, 20–27.

Chronic Poverty Research Centre (2004–05) *The Chronic Poverty Report 2004–05*. Manchester: The Chronic Poverty Research Centre. Retrieved on 21 February 2017 from www.chronicpoverty.org/uploads/publication_files/CPR1_ReportFull.pdf

Chronic Poverty Research Centre (2009) *The Chronic Poverty Report 2008–09: Escaping Poverty Traps*. Manchester: The Chronic Poverty Research Centre. Retrieved on 21 February 2017 from www.chronicpoverty.org/uploads/publication_files/CPR2_ReportFull.pdf

Cobley, D.S. (2012) 'Towards economic empowerment: segregation versus inclusion in the Kenyan context'. *Disability and Society* 27(3), 371–384.

Crow, L. (1996) 'Including All of Our Lives: Renewing the Social Model of Disability'. In Barnes, C. and Mercer, G. (Eds.) *Exploring the Divide: Illness and Disability*. Leeds: Disability Press, 55–72.

dos Santos-Zingale, M. and McColl, M.A. (2006) 'Disability and participation in post-conflict situations: the case of Sierra Leone'. *Disability and Society* 21(3), 243–257.

Eide, A. and Loeb, M. (2006) *Living Conditions among People with Activity Limitations in Zambia: A National Representative Study*. Oslo: SINTEF. Retrieved on 27 April 2017 from 'www.sintef.no/upload/Helse/Levek%C3%A5r%20 og%20tjenester/ZambiaLCweb.pdf

Filmer, D. (2008) 'Disability, poverty and schooling in developing countries: results from 14 household surveys'. *The World Bank Economic Review* 22(1), 141–163. Retrieved on 1 May 2017 from https://openknowledge.worldbank.org/bitstream/handle/10986/4475/wber_22_1_141.pdf?sequence=1

Gartrell, A. and Hoban, E. (2013) 'Structural vulnerability, disability and access to non-governmental organisation services in rural Cambodia'. *Journal of Social Work in Disability & Rehabilitation* 12(3), 194–212.

Government of Uganda (2006) *Persons with Disabilities Act 2006*. Retrieved on 21 May 2017 from www.ilo.org/wcmsp5/groups/public/---ed_protect/---protrav/---ilo_aids/documents/legaldocument/wcms_232181.pdf

Grech, S. (2009) 'Disability, poverty and development: critical reflections on the majority world debate'. *Disability and Society* 9(2), 343–358.

Harris, A and Enfield, S. (2003) *Disability, Equality and Human Rights: A Training Manual for Development and Humanitarian Organisations*. Oxford: Oxfam Publishing.

Hunt, P. (1966) 'A Critical Condition'. In Shakespeare, T. (Ed.) *The Disability Reader*. London: Continuum, 7–19.

Ingstad, B. (2001) 'Disability in the Developing World'. In Albrect, G.L., Seelman, K. and Bury, M. (Eds.) *Handbook of Disability Studies*. London: Sage, 772–792.

Iriarte, E. (2016) 'Models of Disability'. In Iriarte, E., McConkey, R. and Gilligan, R. (Eds.) (2016) *Disability and Human Rights: Global Perspectives*. London: Palgrave, 10–32.

Merilainen, A. and Helaakoski, R. (2001) *Transport, Poverty and Disability in Developing Countries*. Washington, DC: World Bank.

Mont, D. (2007) *Measuring Disability Prevalence*. Washington, DC: World Bank. Retrieved on 11 April 2017 from http://siteresources.worldbank.org/DISABILITY/Resources/Data/MontPrevalence.pdf

Morris, J. (1998) 'Feminism, Gender and Disability'. Paper presented at seminar in Sydney, Australia, February 1998. Retrieved on 6 November 2016 from www. leeds.ac.uk/disability-studies/archiveuk/morris/gender%20and%20disability.pdf

National Council for Disability Affairs (2009) *Republic Act 7277*. Manila: NCDA.

Oliver, M. (1983) *Social Work with Disabled People*. Basingstoke: Macmillan.

Oliver, M. (1990) *The Politics of Disablement*. Basingstoke: Macmillan.

Oliver, M. (1996) *Understanding Disability: From Theory to Practice*. Basingstoke: Macmillan.

Oliver, M. and Sapey, R. (2006) *Social Work with Disabled People*. Third Edition. Basingstoke: Macmillan.

Reeve, D. (2004) 'Psycho-emotional Dimensions of Disability and the Social Model'. In Barnes, C. and Mercer, G. (Eds.) *Implementing the Social Model of Disability: Theory and Research*. Leeds: The Disability Press, 83–100.

Rioux and Carbett (2003) 'Human rights and disability: the international context'. *Journal of Development Disabilities* 10(2), 1–13.

Schriner, K. and Scotch, R. (2001) 'Disability and institutional change: a human variation perspective on overcoming oppressions'. *Journal of Disability Policy Studies* 12(2), 100–107.

Shakespeare, T. (1996) 'Disability, Identity and Difference'. In Barnes, C. and Mercer, G. (Eds.) *Exploring the Divide*. Leeds: The Disability Press, 3–15.

Shakespeare, T. (2008) 'Debating disability'. *Journal of Medical Ethics* 34, 11–14.

Shakespeare, T. and Watson, N. (2002) 'The social model of disability: an outdated ideology?'. *Research in Social Science and Disability* 2, 9–28.

Singal, N. (2010) 'Doing disability research in a Southern context: challenges and possibilities'. *Disability and Society* 25(4), 415–426.

Stone, E. (1997) 'From the Research Notes of a Foreign Devil: Disability Research in China'. In Shakespeare, T. (Ed.) *The Disability Reader*. London: Continuum, 207–227.

Sutherland, A. (1981) *Disabled We Stand*. London: Souvenir Press.

Thomas, C. (1999) *Female Forms: Experiencing and Understanding Disability*. Buckingham: Open University Press.

Thomas, C. (2004) 'How is disability understood? An examination of sociological approaches'. *Disability and Society* 19(6), 569–583.

UNESCO (United Nations Economic and Social Council (2012) *Mainstreaming Disability in the Development Agenda*, Draft Resolution E/CN.5/2012/L.6 submitted by the Commission for Social Development. Retrieved on 28 October 2017 from www.un.org/disabilities/documents/csocd/draft_res_e_cn_5_2012_l6.pdf

United Nations (2006) *Convention on the Rights of Persons with Disabilities and Optional Protocol*. Washington, DC: United Nations.

UPIAS (Union of the Physically Impaired Against Segregation) (1976) *Fundamental Principles of Disability*. London: UPIAS. Retrieved on 24 April 2016 from www.leeds.ac.uk/disability-studies/archiveuk/UPIAS/fundamental%20 principles.pdf

WHO (World Health Organization) (2001) *International Classification of Functioning, Disability and Health*. Geneva: WHO.

WHO (2002) *Towards a Common Language for Functioning, Disability and Health: ICF*. Geneva: WHO.

WHO (2002–04) *World Health Survey*. Geneva: WHO.

WHO and World Bank (2011) *World Report on Disability*. Geneva: WHO. Retrieved on 22 October 2016 from http://whqlibdoc.who.int/publications/2011/9789240685215_eng.pdf

Wood, P. (1980) *International Classification of Impairments, Disabilities and Handicaps*. Geneva: WHO.

World Bank (2009) *People with Disabilities in India: From Commitments to Outcomes*. Human Development Unit, South Asia Region. Washington, DC: World Bank.

Yeo, R. (2005) *Disability, Poverty and the New Development Agenda*. London: DFID. Retrieved on 4 May 2016 from www.dfid.gov.uk/r4d/PDF/Outputs/Disability/RedPov_agenda.pdf

3   Disability, identity and shared experiences of poverty

The term 'identity', in the social context, relates to the various ways in which individuals or groups view and understand themselves. In simple terms, having a sense of identity means 'knowing who you are' (Kidd and Teagle, 2012, p. 25). Social identity is determined, to some extent, by the social roles that people perform, such as being a parent or having a particular job, and the social groups or categories to which they belong. Disability itself is the basis of one such social group, but disabled people may also identify with a number of other social groups, defined on the basis of shared characteristics such as gender, ethnicity, class, religion, sexual orientation, socio-economic status, occupation or a common interest. It is clear, therefore, that disabled people do not constitute a homogenous group, and that the process of identity forming is likely to vary greatly from one individual to another. As Simon Brisenden (1986) points out:

Disability and individuality

It is important that we do not allow ourselves to be dismissed as if we all come under this one great metaphysical category 'the disabled'. The effect of this is a depersonalization, a sweeping dismissal of our individuality, and a denial of our right to be seen as people with our own uniqueness, rather than as the anonymous constituents of a category or group.

(Brisenden, 1986, p. 21)

In the global context the differences are magnified. Perceptions of disability differ considerably, due to the various ways in which the concept of disability has been socially and historically constructed, as does the social, political, economic and cultural context within which disabled people live. Despite these differences, however, some commentators have referred to a 'commonality of experience' among disabled people, particularly those living in countries of the Global South, predominantly brought about through exposure to multi-dimensional poverty, discrimination and injustice. Barnes (2001), for example, points to testimonials drawn from over 3,500 responses to a global survey conducted for the World Health Organization's (WHO) Disability and Rehabilitation team in 2000, the vast majority of which came directly from disabled people themselves, revealing shared experiences of economic, political and social deprivation. The rapid growth of the international disability movement[1] is partly founded on this commonality of experience.

This chapter discusses a range of factors that play a role in shaping the identities of disabled people, both collectively and individually, influencing their experiences, aspirations and sense of self-worth, as well as how others view them and interact with them. These include the perceptions arising from models of disability, impairment-related factors, social difference and the cultural context. The chapter then focuses on the close relationship between disability and poverty, highlighting some of the mechanisms that are believed to cause and reinforce the widespread economic and social exclusion of disabled people, particularly those living in the Global South.

Models of disability

Historically, the collective identity of disabled people as a social group has often been strongly influenced by non-disabled people, based on individual model perspectives of disability. Medical and rehabilitation professionals, for example, have tended to identify disabled people as deficient in terms of functioning and hence incapable of conforming fully to the norms of society, while others have projected disabled people as victims of tragic circumstances or as needy recipients of charity (Oliver, 1983). Negative stereotypes have arisen from ill-informed assumptions about what disabled people are capable of, thus reinforcing perceptions of disability based on sweeping generalisations rather than recognition of uniqueness and individuality (Murugami, 2009). These negative identities are often internalised by disabled people themselves, as Morris (1998) explains:

Negative messages internalised

The messages we receive are very strong and clear and we have little access to different values which may place a more positive value on our bodies, ourselves and our lives. Our self-image is thus dominated by the non-disabled world's reaction to us.

(Morris, 1998, p. 28)

The rise of the social model of disability has played an important role in empowering disabled people to reshape their identities. The social model emphasises the disabling impact of society, thus shifting attention from individual deficits to the inadequacies of society. This reconceptualisation of disability has encouraged disabled people to value themselves more and to reject the negative identities that are sometimes imposed on them by society. This is sometimes easier within a collective environment, and the growth of the disability movement has helped to make this increasingly possible. The movement has challenged perceptions of disabled people as incapable and passive, instead highlighting their potential to fulfil more valued social roles as experts on disability and agents of change. In projecting a collective identity, however, there is a danger that differences among disabled people may be downplayed, or even ignored altogether. Shakespeare (1996), for example, points out that disabled people within Asian or Islamic societies may tend to prioritise the importance of family ties and mutual solidarity, rather than the 'very individualistic model of liberation' (p. 108) that is often embraced by disability rights campaigners in Western societies.[2]

Impairment-related factors

Disability is often categorised according to different types of impairment, such as physical, intellectual, hearing or visual. A person with a hearing impairment, for example, is thought to have a different type of disability to someone with an intellectual impairment. When disability is viewed in social model terms, however, the categorisation of disability according to impairment types makes less sense. As Oliver (1990) points out, all disabled people experience disability as social restriction, in one form or another, regardless of the type (or types) of impairment that they have. Nonetheless, the impact of impairment on the experiences of disabled people cannot be denied, and each type of impairment, or combination of impairment types, is associated with a different set of needs and experiences. Powers (2008), for example, outlines the differing needs that disabled people may have, depending on their impairment type, in order to participate fully in the workplace: people with hearing impairments may need sign language interpreters; those with mobility impairments may have physical accessibility needs; those with intellectual impairments may need job tasks to be broken down into a series of steps that are easier to follow. The type and severity of impairment that a disabled person has can also have a significant impact on the levels of discrimination that he or she faces. Those with intellectual impairments or mental health conditions, for example, are particularly vulnerable to discrimination in many settings (WHO and World Bank, 2011), while Grech's (2008) study on disability and poverty in rural Guatemala found that those with more severe impairments were 'disadvantaged in terms of employment, social relationships and the costs incurred' (p. 5).

The visibility of impairment can have a significant impact on the extent to which a person develops a strong sense of identity as a disabled person. A person with a clearly visible impairment is likely to be labelled by others as 'disabled', and hence may find it easier to access support services that enable him or her to participate more fully in society, thus boosting self-esteem and the forming of a positive identity. However, this labelling process may cause the impairment to become central to the person's identity, overshadowing other elements of self and leading others to see only the impairment, rather than the person (Dunn and Burcaw, 2013). Those with less visible impairments face a different set of challenges. They are less likely to be labelled as 'disabled' by others, at least initially, and may also be less willing to identify as disabled people themselves, thus denying themselves the opportunity to develop a positive sense of disability identity and possibly exposing themselves to the stress that arises from the threat of potential discovery (Pachankis, 2007).

Social difference

Disabled people can be differentiated by a multiplicity of social identities, each of which may potentially intersect with disability itself to reinforce marginalisation and discrimination. For example, many disabled people experience additional exclusion in several domains, including health, education and employment, as they grow older, particularly in the Global South (Ghosh et al., 2016). The Convention on the Rights of Persons with Disabilities (CRPD)[3] recognises the potential impact of social difference, pointing out that disabled people may be 'subject to multiple or aggravated forms of discrimination on the basis of race, colour, sex, language, religion, political or other opinion, national, ethnic, indigenous or social origin, property, birth, age or other status' (United Nations, 2006, Preamble, (p)), while paying particular attention to gender discrimination (Article 6) and discrimination against children (Article 7).

Historically, much of the academic literature on disability has failed to pay adequate attention to gender issues (Meekosha, 1998). However, there is growing evidence to suggest that disabled women and girls frequently face a double burden of inequality and discrimination in both their public and private lives. Erb and Harris-White (2002) carried out anthropological studies in three Indian villages which revealed that disabled girls typically received less care than disabled boys, leading to higher mortality rates among girls. A more recent study exploring the experiences of disabled women in Ethiopia (Katsui and Mojtahedi, 2015) showed that the intersection between disability and gender tends to lead to a denial of opportunities and choices, particularly in the areas of education and employment, largely due to societal expectations that disabled women will fulfil traditional gender roles within the household. Similarly, Nagata (2003) observes that disabled women living in Arab countries face double discrimination in various spheres of life, such as education and employment, and that they are far less likely to marry than non-disabled women. In Malawi, a qualitative study (Braathen and Kvam, 2008) involving 23 disabled women highlighted a range of obstacles to marriage, including a perception among some men that marriage to a disabled woman would bring bad luck to their families. Only five of the participants were married at the time of the study, with nine divorced (left alone, in most cases, to look after the children), one widowed and eight never having been married. Some of those that were married reported discrimination and ill-treatment within their marriages, on account of being both disabled and female:

Gender discrimination within marriage

A women with a disability is never taken out by her [able-bodied] husband, but often a disabled man is seen out with his able-bodied woman . . . The woman is always controlled by the man. If she borrows money to make some business the man will take the money and use it for other things. If the woman is disabled, maybe he will use the money to go out with able-bodied women.

(Braathen and Kvam, 2008, p. 467)

Marginalisation, oppression and discrimination can occur among disabled people themselves, as well as within society more widely. In the United Kingdom (UK) context, for example, the disability movement has received some criticism for failing to take account of the multiple forms of oppression that many disabled people experience:

Discrimination within the disability movement

Disabled people and their organisations are no more exempt from racism, sexism and heterosexism than non-disabled people and their organisations . . . Both women and ethnic minorities are distinctly under-represented and issues around racism, sexism and sexuality have tended to be avoided.

(Morris, 1991, p. 178)

The marginalisation of certain social groupings within the disability movement has also been referred to in the global context. The World Bank (2007), for example, has reported that disabled people's organisations (DPOs) are often 'dominated by disabled men, for whom the concerns of women and children and the rural disabled are low priority' (p. 36).[4] Vernon (1998) points out that most disabled people around the world experience multiple forms of oppression due to certain aspects of their social identity, besides their impairments, that are regarded as inferior within the particular context in which they live. She argues, therefore, that the disability movement should take account of all forms of social oppression and recognise, in particular, how the lives of disabled people may be affected by discrimination on the basis of social difference even within the disability community.

Cultural context

Culture can be defined as 'the set of attitudes, values, beliefs and behaviours shared by a group of people, but different for each individual, communicated from one generation to the next' (Matsumoto, 1996, p. 16). Given that disability itself is a socially constructed concept (Bickenbach, 2009), it follows that experiences of disability are greatly dependent on the nature of the cultural context in which disabled people live. This section considers how various cultural factors influence the lives and identities of disabled people.

Local beliefs systems and disability-related stigma can have a profound influence on perceptions of disabled people. Beliefs about karma within Asian societies, for example, have led many to perceive disability as the result of divine justice, meted out by the Gods as a punishment for sins committed in previous lives. One study (Lang, 2001) involving interviews with around 70 disabled people living in the South Indian state of Karnataka found that, as a result of such beliefs, some respondents felt that they 'had become objects of pity, derision, and should be shut away and cared for by their parents' (p. 296). However, Lang's study did reveal some differences between attitudes in rural and urban areas, with those living in rural areas strongly associating disability with karma, while those in urban areas were more likely to acknowledge the medical causes of impairments.

In parts of Africa, disability is often associated with witchcraft, as explained through the testimony of one disabled woman in Malawi:

Disability and witchcraft

I became physically disabled when I was about . . . years old. I was feeling pain on my waist, especially the left leg, and then I could not walk. I stayed in hospital for three months, and later I was told that my left leg has been affected by polio. My parents could not believe it, so they took me to a witchdoctor, who said that I had stepped on something which was put by a certain woman who was not happy with me. He said I had been bewitched . . . Other people regard my disability as witchcraft. They say that I fell from a witchcraft airplane at night while going to bewitch other people.

(Braathen and Kvam, 2008, p. 465)

Stigmatising beliefs and perceptions are present in all societies, and can easily be internalised by disabled people themselves. This was illustrated by a qualitative study (Munsaka and Charnley, 2013) involving 20 disabled participants living in a rural district of north-west Zimbabwe, over half of whom 'understood that the cause of their impairments was linked to witchcraft or the power of ancestral spirits' (p. 760).[5]

Cultural understandings and attitudes are often reflected in language, while language itself plays a role in shaping culture (Underhill, 2012). The use of negative or demeaning linguistic terms in relation to disability, for example, is likely to reinforce cultural attitudes that justify the social exclusion of disabled people (Gargett *et al.*, 2016). Charlton (1998) provides a powerful example of this in his iconic book *Nothing About Us Without Us*, in which he includes the following quotation from a representative of the National Council of Disabled Persons of Zimbabwe:

Disability and language

In Africa, in our culture, we do not even use the awful term 'cripple'. It's even worse. In Shona, the word is '*chirma*', which means totally useless, a failure. So a person with disability begins life as a *chirma*.
(Charlton, 1998, p. 66)

Cultural influences are not always negative. Many originate from legends, folklore and religious texts, which often send out mixed messages. Miles (1999) describes how some snippets of classical Hindu and Buddhist literature ridicule disabled people, while others elevate them to a higher status. For example, the Jataka stories in Buddhism include disabled characters such as the blind sea pilot, who sees more with his hands than others see with their two eyes. It is important, therefore, to avoid making sweeping generalisations when discussing attitudes towards disability around the world. Ingstad (2001) takes up this point, challenging 'the myth that people in non-Western societies hide, abuse and even kill their disabled family members' (p. 774). While not denying that these abhorrent practices may occur from time to time, she argues that most families are very motivated to provide the best care that they can for their disabled family members, and that premature deaths of disabled people are more often associated with general poverty and poor health care than wilful neglect. She also observes that there are sometimes significant variations between how disability is perceived, and how people actually act towards disabled people, referring to a study conducted by Robert Edgerton (1970) among American Indians and East African tribal communities, which revealed that local people often acted towards disabled people in a way that ran contrary to local beliefs and customs.

A collection of articles edited by Ingstad and Whyte (1995) highlight the concept of personhood, which relates to being valued by others as a human being, as crucial to understanding how disabled people are viewed (and view themselves) within particular societies. These essays draw on empirical evidence from a wide range of settings to show how the acceptance of disabled people is often dependent on the extent to which they conform to the defining characteristics of personhood within the particular society in which they live. In countries of the Global South, this notion of personhood is often linked to community identity, reinforced by the strength of kinship ties and the ability to play an important role within one's family and community, rather than depending greatly on individual abilities and attributes.

Economic and political factors can also play an important role in shaping the cultural context. For example, the nature of local economies can have an impact on the extent to which disabled people are viewed as capable of making a productive contribution to society. People with intellectual impairments, for example, may face greater barriers to economic participation in societies where jobs require high levels of literacy and information technology skills, and consequently may be viewed by many as 'less competent' than those with similar impairments living in societies where manual skills are more in demand (World Bank, 2007). Political institutions influence the cultural context through legislation and policies. In Myanmar, for example, political and institutional frameworks have promoted the view of disabled employees as 'special cases', requiring extra leeway in terms of meeting productivity and performance standards, thus promoting a view of disabled people as less productive and even unemployable (Gargett *et al.*, 2016).[6] In many countries, national laws continue to define disability in medical terms, thus reinforcing the view of impairment as the cause of disability, and therefore medical solutions as the appropriate societal response.

Culture is a dynamic concept, and the cultural context in which disabled people live is constantly evolving. With increasing international recognition of disability rights and understanding of the social factors that create and reinforce disability, it is to be hoped that the evolving cultural context in many countries will increasingly shape the identities of disabled people in a positive way. There is some evidence to suggest that this process has already begun. For example, the following observation was made during a focus group discussion involving representatives of a disability-focused organisation in the Indian city of Chennai:

Cultural change in South India

There has been a sea-change in attitudes over the last fifteen years. Parents now believe that if their children are educated then there will be job opportunities for them . . . disabled people are starting to have aspirations. They are aiming higher.

(Cobley, 2013, p. 273)

This participant also identified a greater awareness of disability rights, which was gradually challenging a deep-rooted culture of charity-oriented attitudes to disability in India. She attributed this partly to an increase in media coverage, with disability now being treated as a hard issue rather than a human interest story, and more respectful language being used. Another participant agreed, pointing out that the Indian film industry was now portraying disability in a much more positive way, rather than presenting characters as comic or tragic diversions.

Reflection exercise 3.1

List some of the cultural factors that influence the identities of disabled people, within a country or region that you are familiar with. How has the cultural context changed over the past ten years or so, and to what effect?

Shared experiences of poverty

The CRPD acknowledges the apparent connection between disability and poverty, stating that 'the majority of persons with disabilities live in conditions of poverty' (United Nations, 2006, Preamble (t)) and calling for greater recognition of the rights of disabled people to 'an adequate standard of living for themselves and their families' (Article 28, Paragraph 1). This close association between disability and poverty, particularly evident in the context of the Global South, has long been recognised, as revealed in a much-quoted literature survey (Elwan, 1999) that was published by the World Bank as a background paper for the 2000/2001 *World Development Report*:

Disability and poverty

Disabled people are estimated to make up 15 to 20 per cent of poor people in developing countries. In some communities, the disabled are regarded as the most disadvantaged by others in the community, and it is frequently observed that in low-income countries, the disabled poor are among the poorest of the poor.

(Elwan, 1999, pp. 15–16)

Elwan herself acknowledges a lack of empirical evidence with which to verify these claims at the time that this article was written. While there is now a larger body of research on the linkages between disability and poverty in the global context, some of which will be examined later in this chapter, there is still a need for a much deeper understanding of the complex mechanisms that create and reinforce these linkages (Groce *et al.*, 2011).

Conceptualising the relationship

Some analysts have referred to a 'vicious cycle of poverty and disability', as illustrated by Figure 3.1. The diagram shows how disability and poverty tend to cause and reinforce each other. Disabled people often experience social exclusion, discrimination and a lack of opportunities for economic, social and human development, thus increasing the likelihood that they will fall into poverty. Conversely, poverty increases vulnerability and the risk of ill-health, through factors such as poor nutrition and sanitation, lack of access to health services, including vaccination programmes, and dangerous working conditions, thus increasing the likelihood of disability (DFID, 2000). Ghai (2001) highlights the disabling impact of poverty in India, for example, noting that the prevalence of polio and blindness is 'four times higher among those who are below the poverty line than those who are above it' (p. 29). In the African context, a study on disability and malaria in

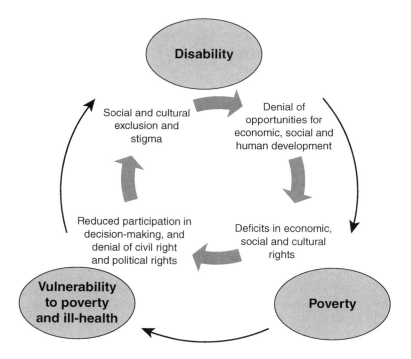

Figure 3.1 The vicious cycle of poverty and disability

Source: Adapted from DFID, 2000, p. 4

Malawi (Ingstad *et al.*, 2012) reveals that many poor people are vulnerable to the disabling after-effects of malaria because they lack the means to pay for treatment and transport to health centres.

An alternative conceptualisation is offered by Rebecca Yeo (2005), who observes that disability and poverty have much in common, and suggests that the vicious cycle diagram tends to obscure the common factors that characterise both disability and poverty due to its emphasis on the two-way causal link. She points out that processes of social and economic exclusion that apply to disabled people, such as limited access to education, employment and basic health services, are very similar to those that apply to poor people in general. For many disabled people, she argues, these issues around poverty, exclusion and discrimination are more pressing than impairment-related concerns. This view was supported by a survey of 108 disabled people in Sri Lanka, conducted in the aftermath of the Asian tsunami, in which the vast majority of those questioned prioritised issues relating to housing, land, livelihoods, education and sanitation, rather than the need for impairment-related aids and appliances (Kett *et al.*, 2005). Given this common ground between disability and poverty, Yeo suggests that the relationship between the two would be better represented by the diagram shown in Figure 3.2.

This diagram shows how processes of marginalisation, isolation and deprivation, as well as lack of access to many aspects of community life, are common to both the disabled and non-disabled poor. When the commonalities between disability and poverty are highlighted in this way, the implication is that any initiatives designed to reduce poverty in general are likely to benefit disabled people who are poor. Yeo concludes that the dis-

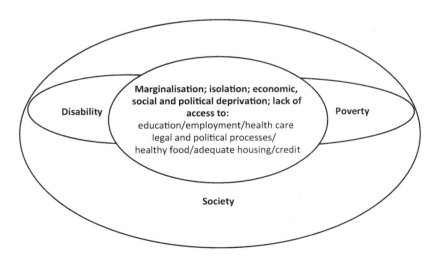

Figure 3.2 The relationship between the characteristics of poverty and disability

Source: Adapted from Yeo, 2005, p. 21

ability movement should strive to forge alliances with general campaigns to reduce poverty.[7]

Capability and the conversion handicap

The strength of the relationship between disability and poverty becomes clearer when one considers poverty from the perspective of 'capability', defined by Amartya Sen as 'the freedom to do the things one has reason to value' (1999, p. 18). According to Sen, poverty is not simply a lack of material wealth, but a lack of capability to attain the various components, or 'substantive freedoms', that constitute an acceptable standard of living. These are determined by individual priorities but may include, for example, adequate shelter, nourishment, social status, educational achievement, political freedom or being able to form and maintain a family. In other words, levels of poverty are determined not only by the resources that people have but by their ability to use those resources to live the kind of lives that they choose to value. Disabled people are more likely to be considered poor when poverty is viewed from a capability perspective, because they are often at a disadvantage in terms of their ability to convert a given level of resources into desired outcomes. For example, when people with mobility impairments need to travel (or choose to travel) they may well have to use a greater proportion of their income to attain this freedom than would be necessary for the general population, due to the extra travel costs that they face, particularly where public transport is inaccessible. Sen (2004) refers to this disadvantage, or the extra cost faced by disabled people in converting a given level of income into well-being, as the 'conversion handicap'. The capability perspective is a useful concept in that it broadens our understanding of poverty to take account of the opportunities and choices that people have in life. Disabled people are often denied access to opportunities and the freedom to make choices, thus deepening their poverty. The concept of a 'conversion handicap' highlights this injustice and places a moral responsibility on society to ensure that disabled people are afforded the various forms of additional support necessary to ensure that they have the same freedom as others to live their lives to the full.

Empirical evidence on poverty and disability

There is a growing body of quantitative and qualitative research on the economic and social status of disabled people in countries of the Global South. Most of these studies conclude that disabled people are at a significant disadvantage, compared with non-disabled people, in terms of access to education and employment (see, for example, Hoogeveen, 2005; World Bank, 2009). The evidence is less conclusive, however, when other dimensions of poverty, such as asset ownership and living conditions, are taken into consideration.

For example, a study based on a national survey of living conditions among disabled people in Zambia (Eide and Loeb, 2006) found no significant differences in the number of household possessions, for households with and without disabled family members, in all but one of the provinces included in the study. The exception was Lusaka, where households with disabled family members had slightly fewer possessions. In a separate study (Trani and Loeb, 2010), the findings of the Zambian survey are compared with the findings from a similar survey in Afghanistan, again suggesting little difference between the assets and living conditions of disabled and non-disabled people. These findings imply that, in countries where poverty is widespread, the differences in household wealth between households with and without disabled family members may be less than is sometimes assumed. However, this does not deny the overall impact of disability on poverty, given that both of these studies highlight significant disparities between disabled people and the general population in terms of access to employment, education and health services.

Filmer (2008) conducted a desk-based analysis of household surveys conducted between 1992 and 2004 in 13 countries (Bolivia, Cambodia, Chad, Columbia, India, Jamaica, Romania, Burundi, Mongolia, Indonesia, Mozambique, South Africa and Zambia). Her study concludes that disabled adults are generally more likely to live in poorer households within these countries, although disabled children aged between 6 and 17 were not, on average, found to be living in poorer or wealthier households than other people of their age. Filmer attributes the correlation between disability and poverty for disabled adults to low educational attainment, due to prior exclusion from schooling. She acknowledges, however, that the validity of her findings is limited by the extremely low disability prevalence rates (typically less than 2 per cent) revealed by the surveys on which she bases her analysis. Given that worldwide disability prevalence is now estimated at around 15 per cent (WHO and World Bank, 2011), it is likely that the surveys failed to identify the majority of disabled people living in these countries.

Another desk-based study (Mitra *et al.*, 2012) analyses data from the 2002–04 *World Health Survey* in order to examine the economic status of working age disabled people living in 15 low and middle-income countries across Asia, sub-Saharan Africa, Latin America and the Caribbean. Their analysis revealed that disabled people were experiencing higher levels of multi-dimensional poverty than non-disabled people in most of these countries, although the types of economic deprivation that they faced varied from one country to another. Disability was found to be associated with lack of educational attainment in 14 of the countries, lack of employment in 9 of the countries and increased healthcare expenditures in 9 of the countries. When poverty was examined in terms of household assets, such as ownership of a car or truck, domestic appliances or electrical goods, households with disabled family members were at a disadvantage in 12 of the 15 countries, although the gap was statistically significant in just 4 of these countries. Interestingly, the study also found that the differences in economic welfare between disabled people and the general population were greater in the middle-income countries than in the low-income countries, despite the existence of financial safety nets in some of the middle-income countries. This suggests, as the authors acknowledge, the possibility of an 'adverse relation between economic growth and the disability/poverty association' (p. 11).

A number of smaller-scale qualitative studies provide further evidence of strong linkages between disability and poverty. One such study (Ingstad and Grut, 2007) was based on 92 interviews conducted across various ethnic groups located in urban and rural areas of Kenya. The findings highlighted several mechanisms by which poverty leads to disability, such as the high frequency of accidents among poorer people, who often travel in overloaded vehicles. Similarly, mechanisms by which disability leads to poverty, such as the tendency for young disabled people to be exploited when they move away from their families, were identified. These findings reinforce the vicious circle conceptualisation of the relationship between poverty and disability, illustrated in Figure 3.1. Grech's (2008) study on disability and poverty in rural Guatemala finds that disability has a negative impact on all livelihood assets, reducing the choice of livelihood strategies open to disabled people and leading to multi-dimensional impoverishment, with a knock-on effect for their whole families. This is also illustrated by Case Study 3.1 from Bangladesh, which shows how a range of disabling factors, from unaffordable medical treatment to discriminatory attitudes, reinforce household poverty.

Case study 3.1   Discrimination against disability as a cause of impoverishment in Bangladesh

At the age of 21, Bidhan developed a degenerative condition called Guillain–Barré syndrome (GBS). This auto-immune disease results in acute paralysis in the lower body, which progresses towards the upper limbs and the face. The treatment cost 400,000 to 500,000 taka per year (roughly $5,160 to $6,450), which was completely unaffordable for his family. Bidhan started to become completely dependent on other people as he couldn't even go to the toilet, dress or bath himself without assistance.

In the early days of his illness his family members were very supportive and sympathetic. But when the financial condition of the family worsened, they grew tired of looking after him and compassion fatigue set in. Their finances became so bad that they had to move to his sister's house in

Sajahanpur to reduce their costs, where six of his family members lived in one small room. It was not easy to find any other room for rent: when landlords learned about Bidhan's disability they refused to rent rooms to the family. Bidhan said: 'The landlords did not want to rent their rooms to our family because they thought we would not be able to pay the house rent since I am disabled. The landlords were also afraid about their rent because they saw I have no income – I did not even beg. On the other hand they thought that a disabled person would need much water and therefore the landlord would have less profit'.

Bidhan's dependency on others grew and, at the same time, his elder brother got married and moved to his in-laws. Once he had his own child he was no longer able to help Bidhan as much as he once did. Bidhan's sister and brother-in-law have very little income and they have to pay the house rent. Their only son (Bidhan's nephew) is at school and they want to him to complete his studies, but he is Bidhan's main caregiver in the absence of other family members, which is hampering his schoolwork.

Bidhan's brother and sister can't afford to care for Bidhan any longer and want him to leave – even telling him to commit suicide when they are angry. They also feel that the investment they are making in their son going to school is becoming worthless, as caring for Bidhan distracts him from his studies.

Source: Chronic Poverty Advisory Network (2014, p. 22)

Until now, much of the empirical research on disability and poverty appears to have been conducted by those who specialise in disability research and advocacy. Groce (2010) calls for more attention to be paid to this issue within the wider international development community, so that disability research can be included within wider theoretical debates and studies around poverty reduction. Broadening and deepening the body of empirical evidence on the relationship between disability and poverty, in order to increase our understanding of the mechanisms that create and reinforce this relationship, is a vital step towards the realisation of international poverty reduction targets, such as those set out in the Sustainable Development Agenda.[8] This framework, together with the CRPD, provides clear guidance to governments and development agencies on the need to ensure that development processes recognise the diverse needs and aspirations of disabled people while also acknowledging and addressing their shared experiences of poverty.

Reflection exercise 3.2

Describe some of the mechanisms that create and strengthen the linkages between disability and poverty in a country with which you are familiar. What kind of policies and programmes are needed to break these linkages?

Summary of key points

- Historically, the identities of disabled people have been strongly influenced by non-disabled people, based on negative stereotypes associated with individual model perspectives of disability. The social model has played an important role in terms of empowering disabled people to adopt more positive identities.
- While some commentators refer to a 'commonality of experience among disabled people', based on shared experiences of economic and social deprivation, it should also be recognised that disabled people are individuals with multiple identities. To support disabled people effectively it is necessary to address common areas of concern, in line with the objectives of the disability movement, while also recognising the diverse needs, experiences and priorities of disabled people.
- The relationship between disability and poverty has been conceptualised as a mutually reinforcing vicious cycle, while others have highlighted the common ground shared by disabled and non-disabled poor people.
- Sen's capability perspective provides a useful theoretical framework for understanding poverty in terms of a denial of rights and opportunities. Many disabled people experience a 'conversion handicap', which relates to the extra costs that they face in converting material resources into desired outcomes.
- While there is a growing body of evidence on the existence of a close relationship between poverty and disability, there is a need for further research to explain the mechanisms that create and reinforce this relationship.

Discussion questions

1   How can disabled people be supported to formulate their own positive identities, in a context where negative stereotypes are prevalent and decisions are often made for them?
2   How can the disability movement take account of differing views and priorities among disabled people, while retaining a sense of unity and collective identity?
3   This chapter has presented two diagrammatic representations of the relationship between disability and poverty. Which of these best illustrates the relationship and why?

Notes

1 See Chapter 5 for further discussion around the growth of the disability movement.
2 See Suggested further reading.
3 The CRPD is further analysed in Chapter 4.
4 DPOs are examined more closely in Chapter 5.
5 See Suggested further reading.
6 See Suggested further reading.
7 An example of such an alliance is given in Case Study 5.1, Chapter 5.
8 The Sustainable Development Agenda is examined in Chapter 4.

Suggested further reading

Gargett, A., Barton, R., Llewellyn, G., Tsaputra, A., Soe, S. and Tawake, S. (2016) 'Global cultures and understandings of disability'. In Iriarte, E., McConkey, R. and Gilligan, R. (Eds.) (2016) *Disability and Human Rights: Global Perspectives*. London: Palgrave, 68–80.
Munsaka, E. and Charnley, H. (2013) 'We do not have chiefs who are disabled: disability, development and culture in a continuing complex emergency'. *Disability and Society* 28(6), 756–769.
Shakespeare, T. (1996) 'Disability, identity and difference'. In Barnes, C. and Mercer, G. (Eds.) *Exploring the Divide*. Leeds: The Disability Press, 3–15.

References

Barnes, C. (2001) *Rethinking Care from the Perspective of Disabled People*. Conference Report and Recommendations. WHO Disability and Rehabilitation Team. Retrieved on 17 April 2017 from http://whqlibdoc.who.int/hq/2001/a78624.pdf
Bickenbach, J. (2009) 'Disability, culture and the UN Convention'. *Disability and Rehabilitation* 31(4), 1111–1124.
Braathen, S.H. and Kvam, M.H. (2008) 'Can anything good come out of this mouth? Female experiences of disability in Malawi'. *Disability and Society* 23(5), 461–474.
Brisenden, S. (1986) 'Independent Living and the Medical Model of Disability'. In Shakespeare, T. (Ed.) (1998) *The Disability Reader*. London: Continuum, 20–27.
Charlton, J. (1998) *Nothing About US Without Us*. Berkeley: University of California Press.
Chronic Poverty Advisory Network (2014) *The Chronic Poverty Report 2014–15: The Road to Zero Extreme Poverty*. London: Overseas Development Institute. Retrieved on 21 May 2017 from www.odi.org/sites/odi.org.uk/files/odi-assets/publications-opinion-files/8834.pdf
Cobley, D. (2013) *Disability and Economic Empowerment in Kenya and India*. Saarbrucken: Lambert Academic Publishing Ltd.
DFID (Department for International Development) (2000) *Disability, Poverty and Development*. London: DFID.
Dunn, D.S. and Burcaw, S. (2013) 'Disability identity: exploring narrative accounts of disability'. *Rehabilitation Psychology* 58(2), 148–157.
Edgerton, R. (1970) 'Mental Retardation in Non-Western Societies: Towards a Cross-cultural Perspective on Incompetence'. In Haywood, H. (Ed.) *Sociocultural Aspects of Mental Retardation*. New York: Century Crofts, 227–237.

Eide, A. and Loeb, M. (Eds.) (2006) *Living Conditions Among People with Activity Limitations in Zambia: A National Representative Study*. Oslo: SINTEF. Retrieved on 8 May 2017 from .www.sintef.no/upload/Helse/Levek%C3%A5r%20og%20 tjenester/ZambiaLCweb.pdf

Elwan, A. (1999) *Poverty and Disability: A Survey of the Literature*. SP Discussion Paper No. 992 Washington, DC: World Bank.

Erb, S. and Harris-White, B. (2002) *Outcast from Social Welfare: Disability in Rural India*. London: Sage.

Filmer, D. (2008) 'Disability, poverty and schooling in developing countries: results from 14 household surveys'. *The World Bank Economic Review* 22(1), 141–163. Retrieved on 1 May 2017 from https://openknowledge.worldbank.org/bitstream/ handle/10986/4475/wber_22_1_141.pdf?sequence=1

Gargett, A., Barton, R., Llewellyn, G., Tsaputra, A., Soe, S. and Tawake, S. (2016) 'Global Cultures and Understandings of Disability'. In Iriarte, E., McConkey, R. and Gilligan, R. (Eds.) (2016) *Disability and Human Rights: Global Perspectives*. London: Palgrave, 68–80.

Ghai, A. (2001) 'Marginalisation and Disability: Experiences from the Third World'. In Priestley, M. (Ed.) *Disability and the Life Course: Global Perspectives*. Cambridge: Cambridge University Press, 26–37.

Ghosh, S., Dababnah, S., Parish, S. and Igdalsky, I. (2016) 'Disability, Social Exclusion and Poverty'. In Iriarte, E., McConkey, R. and Gilligan, R. (Eds.) (2016) *Disability and Human Rights: Global Perspectives*. London: Palgrave, 81–97.

Grech, S. (2008) 'Living with disability in rural Guatemala: exploring connections and impacts on poverty'. *International Journal of Disability, Community and Rehabilitation* 7(2). Retrieved on 30 January 2017 from www.ijdcr.ca/ VOL07_02_CAN/articles/grech.shtml

Groce, N. (2010) 'Foreward'. In Barron, T. and Ncube, J. (Eds.) *Poverty and Disability*. London: Leonard Cheshire Disability, 1–3.

Groce, N., Kembhavi, G., Wirz, S., Lang, R., Trani, J-F. and Kett, M. (2011) *Poverty and Disability: A Critical Review of the Literature in Low and Middle Income Countries*. London: Leonard Cheshire Disability. Retrieved on 22 December 2016 from www.ucl.ac.uk/lc-ccr/centrepublications/workingpapers/WP16_Poverty_ and_Disability_review.pdf

Hoogeveen, J. (2005) 'Measuring welfare for small but vulnerable groups: poverty and disability in Uganda'. *Journal of African Economies* 14(4), 603–631.

Ingstad, B. (2001) 'Disability in the Developing World'. In Albrect, G.L., Seelman, K. and Bury, M. (Eds.) *Handbook of Disability Studies*. London: Sage, 772–792.

Ingstad, B. and Grut, L. (2007) *See Me, and Do Not Forget Me: People with Disabilities in Kenya*. Washington, DC: World Bank. Retrieved on 16 February 2017 from http://siteresources.worldbank.org/DISABILITY/Resources/Regions/ Africa/LCKenya2.pdf

Ingstad, B. and Whyte, S. (Eds.) (1995) *Culture and Disability*. Berkeley and Los Angeles: University of California Press.

Ingstad, B., Munthali, A., Braathen, S. and Grut, L. (2012) 'The evil circle of poverty: a qualitative study of malaria and disability'. *Malaria Journal* 11, 15.

Katsui, H. and Mojtahedi, M. (2015) 'Intersection of disability and gender: multi-layered experiences of Ethiopian women with disabilities'. *Development in Practice* 25(4), 563–573.

Kett, M., Stubbs, S. and Yeo, R. (2005) *Disability in Conflict and Emergency Situations: Focus on Tsunami-affected Areas*. IDDC Research Report. Disability Knowledge and Research Programme. Retrieved on 13 December 2016 from http://iddcconsortium. net/sites/default/files/resources-tools/files/kar_tsunami_paper_05.pdf

Kidd, W. and Teagle, A. (2012) *Culture & Identity*. Second Edition. Basingstoke: Palgrave Macmillan.

Lang, R. (2001) 'Understanding disability from a South Indian perspective'. Paper presented at the 14th Annual Meeting of the Disability Studies Association, Winnipeg, Canada. Retrieved on 1 April 2017 from www.ucl.ac.uk/lc-ccr/ lccstaff/raymond-lang/understanding_disability_in_india.pdf

Matsumoto, D. (1996) *Culture and Psychology*. Pacific Grove, CA: Brooks/Cole.

Meekosha, H. (1998) 'Body Battles: Bodies, Gender and Disability'. In Shakespeare, T. (Ed.) *The Disability Reader*. London: Continuum, 163–180.

Miles, M. (1999) 'Can Formal Disability Services be Developed with South Asian Historical and Conceptual Foundations'. In Stone, E. (Ed.) (1999) *Disability and Development: Learning from Action and Research on Disability in the Majority World*. Leeds: The Disability Press, 228–256.

Mitra, S., Posarac, A. and Vick, B. (2012) *Disability and Poverty in Developing Countries: A Multidimensional Study*. Washington, DC: World Bank. Retrieved on 17 March 2017 from www.addc.org.au/documents/resources/disability-and-poverty-in-developing-countries-a-multidimensional-study_578.pdf

Morris, J. (1991) *Pride Against Prejudice: Transforming Attitudes to Disability*. London: The Women's Press.

Morris, J. (1998) 'Feminism, gender and disability'. Paper presented at seminar in Sydney, Australia, February 1998. Retrieved on 6 November 2016 from www. leeds.ac.uk/disability-studies/archiveuk/morris/gender%20and%20disability.pdf

Munsaka, E. and Charnley, H. (2013) 'We do not have chiefs who are disabled: disability, development and culture in a continuing complex emergency'. *Disability and Society* 28(6), 756–769.

Murugami, M. (2009) 'Disability and identity'. In *Disability Studies Quarterly* 29(4). Retrieved on 4 April 2017 from http://dsq-sds.org/article/view/979/1173

Nagata, K. (2003) 'Gender and disability in the Arab world: the challenges in the new millennium. *Asia Pacific Disability Rehabilitation Journal* 14(1), 10–17. Retrieved on 21 March 2017 from www.aifo.it/english/resources/online/apdrj/ apdrj103/arab-region.pdf

Oliver, M. (1983) *Social Work with Disabled People*. Basingstoke: Macmillan.

Oliver, M. (1990) *The Politics of Disablement*. Basingstoke: Macmillan.

Pachankis, J.E. (2007) The psychological implications of concealing a stigma: a cognitive-affective-behavioural model'. *Psychological Bulletin* 133(2), 328–345.

Powers, T. (2008) *Recognising Ability: The Skills and Productivity of Persons with Disabilities*. Employment Working Paper No. 3 Geneva: ILO. Retrieved on 27 October 2017 from www.ilo.org/public/english/employment/download/wpaper/ wp3.pdf

Sen, A. (1999) *Development as Freedom*. Oxford: Oxford University Press.

Sen, A. (2004) *Disability and Justice*. Keynote Speech. 2nd International Disability Conference, World Bank. Retrieved on 14 October 2016 from http://info.worldbank. org/etools/bSPAN/PresentationView.asp?PID=1355&EID=667

Shakespeare, T. (1996) 'Disability, Identity and Difference'. In Barnes, C. and Mercer, G. (Eds.) *Exploring the Divide*. Leeds: The Disability Press, 3–15.

Trani, J. and Loeb, M. (2010) 'Poverty and disability: a vicious circle? Evidence from Afghanistan and Zambia'. *Journal of International Development* 24, S19–S52.

Underhill, J. (2012) *Ethnolinguistics and Cultural Concepts: Truth, Love, Hate and War*. Cambridge: Cambridge University Press.

United Nations (2006) *Convention on the Rights of Persons with Disabilities and Optional Protocol*. Washington, DC: United Nations.

Vernon, A. (1998) 'Multiple Oppression and the Disabled People's Movement'. In Shakespeare, T. (Ed.) *The Disability Reader*. London: Continuum, 201–210.

World Bank (2007) *Social Analysis and Disability: A Guidance Note*. Washington, DC: World Bank. Retrieved on 12 October 2016 from http://hpod.org/pdf/SAnalysisDis.pdf

World Bank (2009) *People with Disabilities in India: From Commitments to Outcomes*. Human Development Unit, South Asia Region. Washington, DC: World Bank.

WHO (World Health Organization) and World Bank (2011) *World Report on Disability*. Geneva: WHO. Retrieved on 22 October 2016 from http://whqlibdoc.who.int/publications/2011/9789240685215_eng.pdf

Yeo, R. (2005) *Disability, Poverty and the New Development Agenda*. London: DFID. Retrieved on 4 May 2016 from www.dfid.gov.uk/r4d/PDF/Outputs/Disability/RedPov_agenda.pdf

4   International agreements on disability

The Convention on the Rights of Persons with Disabilities (CRPD) was adopted by the United Nations (UN) General Assembly on 13 December 2006 and came into force on 3 May 2008. This marked the culmination of a long struggle, led by the international disability movement (IDM), for a legally binding international treaty that would promote and protect the rights of disabled people to participate in society on an equal basis with others. The CRPD represents a landmark achievement for the disability movement, reflecting a growing understanding that, despite the prior existence of international human rights treaties that implicitly included disabled people, as well as a number of non-binding agreements and declarations on disability, disabled people around the world continued to experience widespread discrimination and a lack of respect for their human rights.

This chapter has a particular focus on the CRPD, including a discussion around some of the implementation challenges that it faces. The chapter also reviews a series of other important international agreements in relation to disability, from the 1948 Universal Declaration of Human Rights (UDHR) to the Sustainable Development Agenda, a framework built around the Sustainable Development Goals (SDGs) that is designed to guide mainstream development objectives and priorities until 2030. Finally, some important regional agreements on disability are reviewed. The international agreements and events that are covered in the chapter are set out in Table 4.1.

Universal Declaration of Human Rights (1948)

The 1948 UDHR was the first major global declaration on the basic rights to which all are entitled. This famous declaration makes only one specific reference to disability, proclaiming the right to security 'in the event of unemployment, sickness, disability . . .' (United Nations, 1948, Article 25). While the other articles do not refer to disability, they clearly do not exclude disabled people either. Article 23, for example, declares that '*everyone* has the right to work, to free choice of employment, to just and favourable conditions of work and to protection against unemployment'. The implicit inclusion of disabled people in the UDHR is underlined by the following

Table 4.1 Timeline of international agreements and events

1948	Universal Declaration of Human Rights
1966	International Bill of Human Rights
1971	UN Declaration on the Rights of Mentally Retarded Persons
1975	Declaration on the Rights of Disabled Persons
1981	International Year of Disabled Persons
1982	World Programme of Action
1983–92	UN Decade of the Disabled
1992	UN Standard Rules on the Equalization of Opportunities for Persons with Disabilities
1995	Copenhagen Declaration on Social Development
1997	Ottawa Treaty (Landmines)
1999	Inter-American Convention for the Elimination of All Forms of Discrimination against Persons with Disabilities
2000	UN Resolution 2000/51
2000	Millennium Development Goals
2002	Sapporo Declaration
2004	Global Partnership on Disability and Development
2006	UN Convention on the Rights of Persons with Disabilities and Optional Protocol
2012	Incheon Strategy
2015	2015 Addis Ababa Financing Agenda
2015	Sustainable Development Agenda
2016	Draft Protocol on the Rights of Persons with Disabilities in Africa

statement from Bengt Lindqvist, a stalwart of the international disability movement and the UN's special rapporteur on disability from 1994 to 2002:

Disability and human rights

Disability is a human rights issue. So long as people with disabilities are denied the opportunity to participate fully in society, no one can claim that the objectives of the Universal Declaration of Human Rights have been achieved.

(DFID, 2000, p. 5)

In 1966, the UDHR became part of the International Bill of Human Rights, alongside the International Covenant on Civil and Political Rights (ICCPR) and the International Covenant on Economic, Social and Cultural Rights (ICESCR). These two covenants were legally binding treaties providing greater detail on the rights set out in the UDHR, again emphasising the universality of human rights and thus the implicit inclusion of disabled people.

The ICCPR, for example, states that 'recognition of the inherent dignity and of the equal and inalienable rights of *all* members of the human family is the foundation of freedom, justice and peace in the world' (my emphasis, United Nations, 1966, Preamble).

United Nations Declaration on the Rights of Mentally Retarded Persons (1971)

This was the first international agreement to specifically address the rights of people with intellectual impairments and mental health issues, referred to using the now outdated terminology of 'mentally retarded persons'. The declaration recognised that 'the mentally retarded person should have, to the maximum degree of feasibility, the same rights as all other human beings' (United Nations, 1971, Paragraph 1). Importantly, these rights extended to those requiring institutional care, which 'should be provided in surroundings and other circumstances as close as possible to those of normal life' (Paragraph 4).

United Nations Declaration on the Rights of Disabled Persons (1975)

This declaration promoted the political and civil rights of all disabled people, while also highlighting the need to consult with disabled people's organisations (DPOs) 'in all matters regarding the rights of disabled persons' (United Nations, 1975, Point 12). This provided an indication that the principle of actually involving disabled people themselves in the process of promoting and protecting disability rights was beginning to achieve international recognition.

World Programme of Action (1982)

Following the International Year of Disabled Persons in 1981, which was marked by various research projects, conferences and policy recommendations, the UN adopted the World Programme of Action Concerning Disabled Persons (WPA) in December 1982. This programme effectively restructured disability policy into three broad areas – prevention, rehabilitation and equalisation of opportunities – and advocated long-term, multi-sectoral strategies that could be integrated into national policies (United Nations, 1983). The UN General Assembly also stipulated that 1983–92 would be known as the UN Decade of Disabled Persons, in which member states would be encouraged to implement the WPA.

The WPA represents an important landmark because it was the first major international agreement to view disability from a social model perspective, emphasising the role of societal barriers in creating and reinforcing disability. The guiding principle of the WPA was the concept of 'equalisation of opportunities', which was about promoting the full participation of disabled people in all aspects of economic and social life, in order to achieve equality. This declaration represented mainstream acceptance of a newly perceived reality – that medical solutions alone would not be sufficient to meet the needs and aspirations of disabled people, and that 'societies have to identify and remove obstacles to their full participation' (United Nations, 1983, Paragraph 22).

United Nations Standard Rules (1993)

The UN Decade of Disabled Persons (1983–92) culminated in the introduction of the 'UN Standard Rules on the Equalisation of Opportunities for Persons with Disabilities'. This set of guidelines was designed to 'ensure that girls, boys, women and men with disabilities, as members of societies, may exercise the same rights and obligations as others' (United Nations, 1993, Paragraph 15). Based on the same guiding principles as the WPA, the aim was essentially to promote inclusion and eliminate all forms of disability discrimination. The 22 rules included 4 relating to 'preconditions' for equal opportunities (such as awareness raising), 8 relating to target areas for equal participation (such as education and employment) and 10 relating to implementation measures (such as information and research, economic policies and international cooperation). The UN also appointed a new special rapporteur, Bengt Lindqvist, to monitor implementation and provide regular reports.

The Standard Rules were not compulsory, although the UN envisaged that they would become 'international customary rules when they are applied by a great number of states with the intention of respecting a rule in international law' (Paragraph 14). Their importance was also underlined by a later UN resolution (2000/51), which stated that 'any violation of the fundamental principle of equality or any discrimination or other negative differential treatment of persons with disabilities inconsistent with the United Nations Standard Rules on the Equalisation of Opportunities for Persons with Disabilities is an infringement of the human rights of persons with disabilities' (United Nations, 2000a, Paragraph 1).

Some positive outcomes in relation to the Standard Rules were highlighted by Lindqvist (1998) in a statement to the General Assembly, in which he summarised the findings of two global surveys that had been conducted under his supervision. He reported that 'a considerable number of governments have adopted new legislation, made plans of action or otherwise initiated a further development of their policies, based on the Standard Rules', but also acknowledged that disabled people were still facing discrimination in many areas of life. Lindqvist refrained from calling for discussions on a 'special convention' on disability, however, arguing that more time was needed for strengthening disability rights through existing channels (O'Reilly, 2007).

Copenhagen Declaration on Social Development (1995)

The 1995 World Summit for Social Development was attended by 117 'heads of states' or governments, making it the largest gathering of world leaders that had ever taken place up until then. The conference ended with the adoption of the Copenhagen Declaration and Programme of Action, which set out a range of social development objectives to be achieved through sustainable policies that promoted human rights and the empowerment of vulnerable groups. The tone of the declaration was set in the introduction, with the acknowledgement that 'in both economic and social terms, the most productive policies and investments are those that empower people to maximise their capacities, resources and opportunities' (United Nations, 1995, Paragraph 7). The declaration had a clear disability dimension, recognising that disabled people are 'too often forced into poverty, unemployment and social isolation' (United Nations, 1995, Paragraph 16(h)), and the Programme of Action recommended specific measures to promote the participation of disabled people in areas such as education, employment, independent living and access to assistive technology. The World Bank (2004) has acknowledged the contribution of the Copenhagen Declaration in helping to ensure that its poverty reduction programmes place an emphasis on vulnerable groups, including disabled people.

Ottawa Treaty (1997)

The 1997 Convention on the Prohibition of the Use, Stockpiling, Production and Transfer of Anti-Personnel Mines and on their Destruction (also known as the Ottawa Treaty or the Mine Ban Treaty), which entered into force in 1999, imposed a complete ban on the use of anti-personnel landmines on ratifying states, as well as calling for the destruction of stockpiled and emplaced mines. Anti-personnel landmines are weapons of 'mass and indiscriminate destruction' (Thakur and Malley, 1999, p. 278), killing and maiming both soldiers and civilians, often long after conflicts have ended. They also hamper the distribution of humanitarian aid, disrupt the movement of refugees during times of conflict and deprive communities of safe access to land and vital infrastructure.

The Ottawa Treaty was much heralded for the involvement of civil society, led by the International Campaign to Ban Landmines (ICBL), in rapidly negotiating its terms. The ICBL was a fairly loose transnational coalition of governmental and non-governmental organisations (NGOs), including disability-focused NGOs such as Handicap International, which was established in 1992 with the aim of freeing the world of antipersonnel landmines and advocating on behalf of landmine survivors. The campaign's coordinator and main spokesperson, Jody Williams, declared that ICBL's influential role in the Ottawa Process confirmed civil society as the 'world's new superpower' (Axworthy, 1998, p. 5). However, Short (1999) contends that civil society participation was actually quite 'narrow and centralised' (p. 495), with the ICBL usually represented by the single voice of its spokesperson and the vast majority of NGOs involved in the Treaty Signing Forum representing Western, industrialised nations.

While the Ottawa Process may have benefitted from being a media-friendly issue, successfully framed by the ICBL as a humanitarian crisis rather than a military issue, there is no doubt as to its significance in terms of addressing one of the most devastating human causes of impairment. The treaty has now been signed and ratified by more than 80 per cent of the world's countries (ICBL website, undated), thus representing a broad international consensus. However, there are no verification or compliance mechanisms (Thakur and Malley, 1999) and key players such as the United States (US) and Russia are yet to sign up to its terms. With insurgent and terrorist groups also outside the reach of the treaty, and unexploded munitions creating new hazards in conflict areas on a daily basis, the landmine threat is still very real.

Millennium Declaration (2000)

This famous declaration, adopted by all 189 UN member states, set out a blueprint for a global partnership aimed at ensuring that 'globalisation becomes a positive force for all the world's people' (United Nations, 2000b, Paragraph 5). This global partnership would focus on promoting peace and reducing poverty by working towards the achievement of the eight Millennium Development Goal (MDGs), shown in Box 4.1, by 2015.

Box 4.1   The Millennium Development Goals

1   Goal 1: Eradicate extreme poverty and hunger
2   Goal 2: Achieve universal primary education
3   Goal 3: Promote gender equality
4   Goal 4: Reduce child mortality
5   Goal 5: Improve maternal health
6   Goal 6: Combat HIV, malaria and other diseases
7   Goal 7: Ensure environmental sustainability
8   Goal 8: Develop a global partnership for development

While the declaration refers to various vulnerable social groups, including women, children and people with HIV/AIDS, there is no specific mention of disability. Former UN Secretary-General Ban Ki-Moon has acknowledged the error of ignoring disability in the wording of the Millennium Declaration, and its accompanying guidelines, pointing out that, 'as a consequence, periodic reviews of the MDGs that are under way within the UN do not include reference to disability issues' (United Nations, 2009, p. 3). His report concludes that these omissions, together with the difficulties in obtaining sufficient data on the disability situation in many countries, have made it very difficult to assess the impact of the MDGs on disabled people.

Sapporo Declaration (2002)

In 2002, Disabled People's International (DPI)[1] held a gathering in Sapporo, Japan, involving over 3,000 delegates representing 109 countries. This conference resulted in the release of the Sapporo Declaration, which highlighted various forms of discrimination and deprivation experienced by disabled people around the world, while also noting that 'rights under existing UN Conventions are generally ignored or marginalised in monitoring procedures' (DPI, 2002). Significantly, this declaration also called for a new rights-based convention that would be formulated with the full involvement of disabled people, as highlighted in Box 4.2.

Box 4.2   Excerpt from the Sapporo Declaration

- We demand a specific international convention as an instrument of binding norms to protect and respect the full enjoyment of our human rights. This convention must be human rights in nature and not economic and social based.
- Disabled people demand a voice of our own in the development of this instrument. We must be consulted at all levels on all matters that concern us.
- We urge all countries to support the formulation and adoption of this convention and we encourage all disabled people and their organizations to educate the public and their political representatives on the need and benefits of a convention.
- In addition: We demand that every country adopt and implement anti-discrimination legislation and policies that ensures the equalization of opportunity for disabled people.

Source: DPI, 2002

United Nations Convention on the Rights of Persons with Disabilities (2006)

The first major human rights treaty of the twenty-first century places legal obligations on ratifying states to promote and protect the rights of disabled people. It is important to emphasise here that, in general, these are not *new*

Table 4.2 Human rights treaties protecting the rights of vulnerable groups

1965	Anti-Racism Convention
1979	Women's Rights Convention
1984	Convention Against Torture and Other Inhumane or Degrading Treatment or Punishment
1989	Convention on the Rights of Children
1990	Convention on the Rights of Migrant Workers
2006	Convention on the Rights of Persons with Disabilities

rights.[2] However, the introduction, for the first time, of a legally binding instrument to promote the universal inclusion of disabled people provided an opportunity for real progress to be made in terms of enabling disabled people to access their rights, and for putting into practice some of the recommendations made in previous agreements. The CRPD has taken its place alongside other important UN treaties protecting the human rights of vulnerable social groups, as shown in Table 4.2.

Preparations for the CRPD began in 2001, when the Mexican government submitted a draft text and proposed the formation of an ad hoc committee, which was formally established later in the same year with a mandate to consider the proposed convention and to oversee the drafting process. An important feature of this process was the involvement of civil society, including a large number of DPOs and disability-focused NGOs that joined forces to form the International Disability Caucus. This coalition participated as an equal partner throughout the negotiation process and was also present at subsequent events, such as the signing ceremony in 2007 (Schulze, 2010).

The CRPD consists of 50 articles that address an array of civil, economic, social, cultural and political rights, as summarised in Box 4.3.

Box 4.3   Disability rights covered by the CRPD

- Equality before the law without discrimination (Article 5)
- Rights to life, liberty and security (Articles 10 and 14)
- Equal recognition before the law and legal capacity (Article 12)
- Freedom from torture (Article 15)
- Freedom from exploitation, violence and abuse (Article 16)
- Right to respect physical and mental integrity abuse (Article 17)
- Freedom of movement and nationality (Article 18)
- Right to live in the community (Article 19)
- Freedom of expression and opinion (Article 21)
- Respect for privacy (Article 22)
- Respect for home and the family (Article 23)

- Right to education (Article 24)
- Right to health (Article 25)
- Right to work (Article 27)
- Right to adequate standard of living (Article 28)
- Right to participate in political and public (Article 29)
- Right to participation in cultural life (Article 30)

Source: United Nations, 2006

These basic human rights are founded on eight general principles, set out in Article 3, as shown in Box 4.4.

Box 4.4   CRPD general principles (Article 3)

- Respect for inherent dignity, individual autonomy including the freedom to make one's own choices, and independence of persons;
- Non-discrimination;
- Full and effective participation and inclusion in society;
- Respect for difference and acceptance of persons with disabilities as part of human diversity and humanity;
- Equality of opportunity;
- Accessibility;
- Equality between men and women;
- Respect for the evolving capacities of children with disabilities and respect for the right of children with disabilities to preserve their identities.

Source: United Nations, 2006

As the wording of these general principles implies, the CRPD reflects the trend, established in previous international agreements, of framing disability as a human rights issue, thus challenging perceptions of disabled people as a medical problem or as needy recipients of charity. The social model of disability[3] is not explicitly referred to, but its influence is plain to see. Disability is described as arising from 'the interaction between persons with impairments and attitudinal and environmental barriers' (Preamble (e)), and the treaty places a firm obligation on governments to take the necessary steps to remove the societal barriers that hinder the participation of disabled people. Article 8 (Awareness-raising), for example, calls on State Parties to tackle the 'stereotypes, prejudices and harmful practices' (Paragraph 1(b)) that exist within society.

The CRPD has now been signed and ratified by the vast majority of nation states, representing a near-global consensus. Signatory of the CRPD means that governments are committed to the principles of the treaty, although they are not legally required to adhere to them. Ratification, by contrast, means that the treaty has been approved through an appropriate national process, signifying its acceptance as a binding piece of international law. Ratifying countries thus have a legally binding commitment to facilitate the implementation of the CRPD within their own boundaries. This implementation process involves ensuring that national legislation is in place that reflects the principles of the CRPD and the formulation of appropriate policies, programmes and evaluation mechanisms, as well as the mainstreaming of disability[4] into existing policies and programmes.

The CRPD recognises that some countries may require various kinds of assistance to support the implement process, either through international development programmes or general cooperation between states. Article 32, entitled 'International Cooperation', addresses this issue, calling for measures such as 'providing, as appropriate, technical and economic assistance, by facilitating access to and sharing of accessible and assistive technologies, and through the transfer of technologies' (Paragraph 1(d)). This article provides a clear framework for the donor community, including international development agencies and the governments of the Global North, to support and encourage governments of the Global South to sign, ratify and implement the Convention.

One example of international cooperation, originally launched in 2004 but since refocused to support implementation of the CRPD, is the World Bank's Global Partnership on Disability and Development (GPDD). This partnership aims to raise awareness on disability and strengthen cooperation among various stakeholders, including governments of the Global South, donor agencies, UN agencies, NGOs, DPOs and academic institutions. These stakeholders were brought together in an informal coordinating mechanism, specifying clear roles for each within a framework designed to advance the inclusion of disability issues in mainstream social and economic development (Coleridge, 2007). The GPDD is backed by a multi-donor trust fund which was set up to support stakeholders in the implementation of various initiatives, including networking forums, theme-based e-discussions, knowledge sharing, research studies and capacity building projects (Lord *et al.*, 2010).

Optional Protocol

In order to monitor the global implementation of the CRPD, and to deal with issues relating to non-compliance, the UN also established the Committee on the Rights of Persons with Disabilities. The working procedures of this Committee are set out in an Optional Protocol, accompanying the main Convention, which requires State Parties to recognise the competence of the Committee to pass judgment on any perceived violations of the CRPD within their own countries. Individuals or groups within those countries that have ratified the Optional Protocol are, therefore, provided with an avenue for bringing their grievances to the Committee, once 'all available domestic remedies' (Article 2, Paragraph (d)) have been exhausted. It should be noted, however, that countries that have ratified the CRPD have a right to make 'declarations', which relates to how they interpret particular terms of the agreement, or 'reservations', which means that they can effectively opt out of certain clauses. This means that any investigation of perceived violations would need to take account of these declarations and reservations. The United Kingdom (UK), for example, has reserved the right not to apply obligations in relation to equal treatment in employment, under the terms of the CRPD, to admission to the armed forces.

The establishment of the Committee provides a useful focal point within the UN system for monitoring the implementation of the CRPD and drawing attention to compliance issues within member states. The Optional Protocol provides no details of any significant penalties for non-compliance, however, other than a commitment on behalf of the Committee to 'forward its suggestions and recommendations, if any, to the State Party concerned and to the petitioner' (Article 5).

Implementation barriers

As with all human rights treaties, the task of ensuring that agreements on paper make a real and lasting difference to the lives of ordinary people, particularly those who are poor and marginalised, is hugely challenging. This section outlines some of the key challenges facing governments, development agencies and disability organisations as they work towards effective implementation of the CRPD.

Lack of adequate data

The CRPD acknowledges a widespread lack of statistical and research data on disability, calling for State Parties to collect new data to support its implementation (Article 31). Several years after it came into force, the monitoring committee established by the Optional Protocol continued to raise concerns about 'absent, outdated or inconsistent disaggregated data collected on persons with disabilities' (United Nations, 2015a, p. 23). National data collection is hampered by differing understandings around the meaning of disability itself, flawed approaches to collecting data and stigma surrounding disability (Mont, 2007).[5] Estimates of disability prevalence, particularly those produced by national censuses, are often unrealistically low, thus weakening the case for governments to make adequate budget allocations. A lack of baseline data on particular disability issues (such as the number of disabled children excluded from schooling, for example) makes the task of monitoring progress on these issues extremely difficult.

Lack of political will

Nation states that have ratified the CRPD have a clear duty to take the steps necessary to ensure effective implementation. However, the most recent sessional report of the Committee on the Rights of Persons with Disabilities (United Nations, 2015a) lists a number of failures on the part of governments in relation to these necessary steps. The report notes that many states have failed to define an implementation mechanism, and that where mechanisms have been established they are often under-resourced and do not function properly. Additionally, the report notes that many governments continue to define disability in medical terms, have failed to set up appropriate mechanisms for consulting with DPOs and have failed to establish effective procedures to combat disability discrimination. Meekosha and Soldatic (2011)[6] observe that many states are guilty of abusing human rights themselves, or simply ignoring them, thus raising further doubts over the extent to which the governments of such states can be expected to fulfil the role of upholding human rights.

Weak governance structures

Where governance structures are weak, the capacity of states to implement rights-based laws may be undermined, even when political will is present. In the Ghanaian context, for example, Grischow (2015) describes how those in power often demand 'under-the-table' payments in order to exercise their duties, thus creating financial barriers that may prevent many disabled people, who are typically among the poorest members of society, from accessing their rights. He goes on to argue that, in the absence of a social transformation that would break the reliance of weaker members of society on connections with more powerful patrons, the existence of instruments such as the CRPD and national disability legislation will 'not automatically produce equal access to entitlements for all disabled Ghanaians' (2015, p. 110).

Lack of DPO capacity

DPOs have played an unprecedented role in negotiating the terms of the CRPD, and perhaps have an even more important role to play in monitoring its implementation, as set out in Article 33 (National Implementation and Monitoring). Some have risen to this challenge admirably. In the Philippines, for example, a coalition comprised of over 20 DPOs and disability-focused NGOs has engaged closely with local and national government agencies on various disability issues, particularly around legislative reform and budget allocations, while also producing an excellent independent report on the state of implementation of the CRPD, highlighting numerous areas of concern

(Philippines Coalition, 2013). However, many national DPOs lack the necessary capacity to effectively lobby their own governments and hold them to account due to a lack of leadership skills and resources (Mittler, 2016) as well as, in many cases, a limited understanding of legal and policy-making processes (Lang *et al.*, 2011).[7]

Charity outlook

Despite increased international recognition of disability as a rights-based issue, as reflected in the CRPD, the recognition of disability rights in everyday life is still hampered by a deep-rooted charity or welfare culture in many countries. The activities of civil society organisations, including some DPOs, often reflect this approach and even politicians that use rights-based rhetoric do not always fully understand disability from a right-based perspective (Lang *et al.*, 2011). In some countries, a long history of missionary and charity-based service delivery has led to a culture of dependency among disabled people themselves (Cobley, 2012; dos Santos-Zingale and McColl, 2006), thus reinforcing their reliance on welfare-based approaches.

Lack of awareness and negative attitudes

Where negative attitudes and disability-related stigma continue to prevail, the task of implementing legislation and policies designed to facilitate the full and equal participation of disabled people becomes immeasurably harder. For example, a study on disability and development conducted in Binga, an impoverished district of north-west Zimbabwe, draws on empirical evidence to show that 'despite the existence of pro-disability legislation and policy in Zimbabwe, disabled participants in Binga experienced systematic exclusion from community life, predicated on cultural beliefs about the meaning of disability' (Munsaka and Charnley, 2013, p. 767).

Reflection exercise 4.1

List some of the barriers to the effective implementation of the CRPD in your own country, or a country with which you are familiar. Then make a list of measures that could be taken to tackle these barriers. For each of these measures, consider which stakeholders could be involved in planning and implementing them (for example, DPOs, disability-focused NGOs, community organisations, traditional institutions, government departments, donor agencies, employers, academic institutions or the media) and the roles that each might play.

Addis Ababa Financing Agenda (2015)

This important agreement, which emerged from an international conference in Addis Ababa involving representatives of 193 UN member states, laid some important foundations for the forthcoming Sustainable Development Agenda. The agreement covered a wide range of measures designed to improve global finance practices and stimulate the necessary financial investment for effective implementation of the SDGs. There was also a renewed commitment to overseas development aid, particularly for the poorest countries of the world, and a pledge to increase South–South cooperation (UNDESA, 2015). Significantly, the Financing Agenda contains several explicit references to disability, including commitments to disability-sensitive education facilities, promoting the participation of disabled people in formal labour markets, accessible technology and the increased use of data disaggregated by disability (United Nations, 2015b).

Sustainable Development Agenda

Given the widely acknowledged failure of the Millennium Declaration to take account of disability, preparations for the post-2015 Sustainable Development Agenda were punctuated by calls from international and national development agencies, as well as the disability sector, for the new framework to explicitly incorporate disability concerns. This was reflected in an official report by Secretary-General Ban-Ki Moon (United Nations, 2013), entitled *The Way Forward: A Disability-Inclusive Development Agenda Towards 2015 and Beyond*. The report highlighted some encouraging progress in terms of mainstreaming disability as a cross-cutting development issue, while concluding that progress overall had been patchy, both within and between countries, and that the development of international frameworks for action, particularly the CRPD, had not yet been matched by action on the ground. It goes on to outline a series of proposals designed to promote a more disability-inclusive mainstream development agenda, such as including disabled people in the implementation of the SDGs, improving the accessibility of the built environment and building closer partnerships between development agencies and DPOs.

The Sustainable Development Agenda (United Nations, 2015c), built around the SDGs, was unveiled in September 2015. One of the guiding principles of this new development framework was 'to leave no one behind', a clear sign that the inclusion of vulnerable populations groups, including disabled people, would be prioritised. Each of the 17 SDGs was accompanied by a set of targets, 169 in total, with seven of these targets making explicit reference to disability.[8] These disability-related targets are shown in Table 4.3.

Table 4.3 Disability in the SDGs

Goal 4	Ensure inclusive and equitable quality education and promote life-long learning opportunities for all	
	Target 4.5	By 2030, eliminate gender disparities in education and ensure equal access to all levels of education and vocational training for the vulnerable, including **persons with disabilities**, indigenous peoples and children in vulnerable situations
	Target 4.8	Build and upgrade education facilities that are child, **disability** and gender sensitive and provide safe, non-violent, inclusive and effective learning environments for all
Goal 8	Promote sustained, inclusive and sustainable economic growth, full and productive employment and decent work for all	
	Target 8.5	By 2030, achieve full and productive employment and decent work for all women and men, including for young people and **persons with disabilities**, and equal pay for work of equal value
Goal 10	Reduce inequality within and among countries	
	Target 10.2	By 2030 empower and promote the social, economic and political inclusion of all irrespective of age, sex, **disability**, race, ethnicity, origin, religion or economic or other status
Goal 11	Make cities and human settlements inclusive, safe, resilient and sustainable	
	Target 11.2	By 2030, provide access to safe, affordable, accessible and sustainable transport systems for all, improving road safety, notably by expanding public transport, with special attention to the needs of those in vulnerable situations, women, children, **persons with disabilities** and older persons
	Target 11.7	By 2030, provide universal access to safe, inclusive and accessible, green and public spaces, in particular for women and children, older persons and persons with disabilities
Goal 17	Strengthen the means of implementation and revitalize the global partnership for sustainable development	
	Target 17.18	By 2020, enhance capacity building support to developing countries, including for LDCs and SIDS, to increase significantly the **availability of high quality, timely and reliable data disaggregated** by income, gender, age, race, ethnicity, migratory status, **disability**, geographic location and other characteristics relevant in national contexts

Following the adoption of the Sustainable Development Agenda, work continued on the crucial task of developing a global indicator framework for the SDGs and their corresponding targets. The Inter-agency and Expert Group on SDG Indicators (IAEG-SDGs), which was the focal point for the new indicator framework, proposed nine indicators explicitly referring to disability, linked to six of the SDGs (UNESCO, 2015). The report also called for data disaggregation by disability, where relevant, as well as highlighting the need to improve both international and national data collection mechanisms, and to expand international guidelines on collecting reliable and comparable data. The proposed global indicator framework, incorporating these recommendations, was agreed and adopted by the UN Statistical Commission in March 2016. In relation to Goal 1 on poverty reduction, for example, Indicator 1.3.1 requires data to be collected on the proportion of people covered by social protection schemes, disaggregated by various population groups, including disabled people.[9]

By incorporating disability-related targets and indicators into its framework, the Sustainable Development Agenda appears to have answered calls for disability to be mainstreamed into development planning. The challenge that lies ahead for governments and development agencies, as well as disabled people themselves and the organisations that represent them, is to ensure that this opportunity to foster greater recognition of disability rights and more inclusive societies is not lost.

Regional agreements

Various regional agreements have reinforced the international legal framework in relation to disability, while also drawing attention to the importance of local issues and contextual differences. Some of the most significant ones are reviewed in this section.

Regional decades

Following the original UN Decade of the Disabled (1983–92), which achieved some success in terms of raising awareness on disability and strengthening the international disability movement, most regions of the world have implemented similar initiatives. In 1992, for example, the UN Economic and Social Commission of Asia and the Pacific (ESCAP) announced the first Asia and Pacific Decade of Disabled Persons (1993–2002), reinforced by the adoption of the Proclamation on the Full Participation and Equality of People with Disabilities. This was followed by a second decade (2003–12) and then a third (2013–22). The onset of this latest Asia and Pacific Decade was marked by the adoption of the Incheon Strategy, entitled 'To Make Right Real', which comprises the first set of regionally-agreed disability-inclusive development goals, designed to build on the CRPD and to 'promote a barrier-free and rights-based society for persons with disabilities in Asia and the Pacific'

(ESCAP, 2012, Abstract). The proliferation of regional decades reflects a growing sense that global approaches to solving the problems associated with disability do not always reflect the priorities of disabled people in different parts of the world. Thus the regional decades support more localised approaches to addressing these priorities.

Inter-American Convention for the Elimination of All Forms of Discrimination against Persons with Disabilities (1999)

This Convention, which entered into force in 2001, has now been ratified by 19 states within the Organization of American States.[10] The Convention advocates a range of measures designed to promote independence, quality of life and inclusion, calling on governments within the region to adopt 'legislative, social, educational, labour-related, or any other measures needed to eliminate discrimination against persons with disabilities and to promote their full integration into society' (Organization of American States, 1999, Article III).

Draft Protocol to the African Charter on Human and People's Rights on the Rights of Persons with Disabilities in Africa (2016)

The African Decade of Disabled Persons was launched in 1999, with the aim of promoting the full participation, equality and empowerment of disabled people in Africa. The African Union's focus on disability rights during the course of the decade was guided by a Continental Plan of Action and followed up by the adoption, in 2016, of the Draft Protocol on the Rights of Persons with Disabilities in Africa. This document draws on the CRPD but also addresses issues thought to be specific to the African continent, particularly in relation to conditions of extreme poverty in which many disabled people live and the damaging impact of certain beliefs and practices. For example, the Protocol expresses concern at the 'maiming and killing of persons with albinism in many parts of the continent' (ACHPR, 2016, Preamble), while Article 6 calls on State Parties to 'eliminate harmful practices perpetrated on persons with disabilities, including witchcraft, abandonment, concealment, ritual killings or the association of disability with omens' (Paragraph 1).

Summary of key points

- There is now a raft of international agreements in place that are designed to protect the rights of disabled people and promote their full inclusion in society. The language of these agreements has increasingly reflected a perception of disability that takes into account the disabling role of society and the need to remove societal barriers, so that disabled people can enjoy the rights and freedoms to which they are entitled.

- The CRPD is the first major human rights treaty of the twenty-first century, taking its place in a family of human rights treaties protecting vulnerable social groups and providing a legal basis to support the implementation of previous international agreements on disability. The Convention is considered a landmark achievement for the international disability movement, which was fully involved in the drafting process and has an important role to play in monitoring its implementation.
- With the vast majority of UN member states now having signed and ratified the CRPD, disability rights are widely recognised in law throughout the world. However, there are a range of barriers to the effective implementation of the CRPD, including inadequate data, weak governance structures, lack of political will, limited DPO capacity and a prevailing charity outlook on disability in many countries.
- While the 2000 Millennium Framework was disappointingly silent on disability, the new Sustainable Development Agenda aims to 'leave no one behind' and contains several explicit references to disability, underlining the rising profile of disability as a mainstream development priority and presenting a new opportunity for disabled people to be recognised as citizens with rights to full participation in society.
- A number of important regional agreements have reinforced global treaties, such as the CRPD, while also reflecting more localised concerns, thus emphasising the need to ensure that international agreements take account of contextual realities in different parts of the world.

Discussion questions

1   The international agreements highlighted in this chapter reflect the increasing adoption of a rights-based perspective on disability, despite a long history of charity or welfare approaches to disability in many countries. To what extent have disability practices changed to reflect the rights-based perspective in your own country, or a country with which you are familiar?
2   The CRPD promotes principles such as inclusion, participation, individuality and independence, which are sometimes viewed as Western values. To what extent do you view the adoption of these principles or values as appropriate in the global context?
3   How does the Sustainable Development Agenda differ from the Millennium Framework in relation to disability, and what difference do you think that the SDGs will make to the lives of disabled people in the coming years?

Notes

1 The role of DPI as a focal point for the international disability movement is discussed in Chapter 5.
2 Most of the rights referred to in the CRPD were covered by previous international treaties, although it could be argued that the CRPD has actually expanded the

disability rights framework to include, for example, rights to social protection and inclusion in mainstream development programmes (Kayess and French, 2008).
3 See Chapter 2 for an explanation of the social model.
4 See Chapter 5 for a discussion on disability mainstreaming.
5 See Chapter 2 for further discussion on the issues around disability data collection.
6 See Suggested further reading.
7 DPO constraints are further explored in Chapter 5.
8 Several other targets make reference to vulnerable persons or persons in vulnerable situations.
9 The full list of indicators can be viewed at http://unstats.un.org/sdgs/indicators/database/
10 The US is a notable exception.

Suggested further reading

Ingstad, B. (2007) 'Seeing Disability and Human Rights in the Local Context: Botswana Revisited' In Ingstad, B. and Whyte, S. (Eds.) *Disability in Local and Global Worlds*. Berkeley: University of California Press, 237–258.

Meekosha, H. and Soldatic, K. (2011) 'Human rights and the Global South: the case of disability'. *Third World Quarterly* 32(8), 1383–1398.

Mittler, P. (2016) 'The UN Convention on the Rights of Persons with Disabilities'. In Iriarte, E., McConkey, R. and Gilligan, R. (Eds.) (2016) *Disability and Human Rights: Global Perspectives*. London: Palgrave, 33–48.

Schulze, M. (2010) *Understanding the UN Convention on the Rights of Persons with Disabilities and Optional Protocol*. Third Edition. London: Handicap International. Retrieved on 12 June 2017 from www.hiproweb.org/uploads/tx_hidrtdocs/HICRPDManual2010.pdf

References

ACHPR (African Commission on Human and People's Rights) (2016) *Draft Protocol to the African Charter on Human and People's Rights on the Rights of Persons with Disabilities in Africa*. Retrieved on 22 April 2017 from www.achpr.org/files/news/2016/04/d216/disability_protocol.pdf

Axworthy, L. (1998) 'A Ban of the people: the landmines campaign and the new diplomacy'. Cambridge University Conference on Global Governance, 9 May 1998.

Cobley, D.S. (2012) 'Towards economic empowerment: segregation versus inclusion in the Kenyan context'. *Disability and Society* 27(3), 371–384.

Coleridge, P. (2007) 'Economic Empowerment'. In Barron, T. and Amerena, P. (Eds.) *Disability and Inclusive Development*. London: Leonard Cheshire International, 111–154.

DFID (Department for International Development) (2000) *Disability, Poverty and Development*. London: DFID.

dos Santos-Zingale, M. and McColl, M.A. (2006) 'Disability and participation in post-conflict situations: the case of Sierra Leone'. *Disability and Society* 21(3), 243–257.

DPI (Disabled People's International) (2002) *Sapporo Declaration*. Retrieved on 26 April 2017 from http://dpi.org/document/world-assemblies-declaratio/cairo-declaration/index.html

ESCAP (Economic and Social Commission for Asia and the Pacific) (2012) *Incheon Strategy 'To Make The Right Real' for Persons with Disabilities in Asia and the Pacific*. Retrieved on 6 March 2017 from www.unescap.org/resources/incheon-strategy-%E2%80%9Cmake-right-real%E2%80%9D-persons-disabilities-asia-and-pacific

Grischow, J. (2015) '"I nearly lost my work": chance encounters, legal empowerment and the struggle for disability rights in Ghana'. *Disability and Society* 30(1), 101–113.

ICBL (International Campaign to Ban Landmines) (undated) *Treaty Status*. Retrieved on 6 May 2017 from www.icbl.org/en-gb/the-treaty/treaty-status.aspx

Kayess, R. and French, P. (2008) 'Out of darkness into light? Introducing the Convention on the Rights of Persons with Disabilities'. *Human Rights Law Review* 8(1), 1–34.

Lang, R., Kett, M., Groce, N. and Trani, J.F. (2011) 'Implementing the United Nations Convention on the Rights of Persons with Disabilities: principles, implications, practice and limitations'. *European Journal of Disability Research* 5(3), 206–220.

Lindqvist, B. (1998) *Statement by Mr. Bengt Lindqvist, Special Rapporteur of the UN Commission for Social Development*. UN Commission on Human Rights. 54th Session, Agenda Item 15. Washington, DC: United Nations.

Lindqvist, B. (1999) *World Disability Report*. Geneva: International Disability Foundation.

Lord, J., Posarac, A., Nicoli, M., Peffley, K., McClain-Nhlapo, C. and Keogh, M. (2010) *Disability and International Cooperation and Development: A Review of Policies and Practices*. Retrieved on 12 March 2017 from http://siteresources.worldbank.org/DISABILITY/Resources/Publications-Reports/Disability_and_Intl_Cooperation.pdf

Meekosha, H. and Soldatic, K. (2011) 'Human rights and the Global South: the case of disability'. *Third World Quarterly* 32(8), 1383–1398.

Mittler, P. (2016) 'The UN Convention on the Rights of Persons with Disabilities'. In Iriarte, E., McConkey, R. and Gilligan, R. (Eds.) *Disability and Human Rights: Global Perspectives*. London: Palgrave, 33–48.

Mont, D. (2007) *Measuring Disability Prevalence*. Washington, DC: World Bank. Retrieved on 11 April 2017 from http://siteresources.worldbank.org/DISABILITY/Resources/Data/MontPrevalence.pdf

Munsaka, E. and Charnley, H. (2013) 'We do not have chiefs who are disabled: disability, development and culture in a continuing complex emergency'. *Disability and Society* 28(6), 756–769.

O'Reilly, A. (2007) *The Right to Decent Work of Persons with Disabilities*. Geneva: ILO.

Organization of American States (1999) *Inter-American Convention for the Elimination of All Forms of Discrimination against Persons with Disabilities*. AG/RES. 1608 (XXIX 0/99). Retrieved on 15 March 2017 from www.oas.org/juridico/english/treaties/a-65.html

Philippines Coalition (2013) *UN Convention on the Rights of Persons with Disabilities: A Parallel Report Submitted to the Committee on the Rights of Persons with Disabilities on the Implementation of the Convention in the Republic of the Philippines from 2008–2013*. Retrieved on 2 May 2017 from http://crpdparallelreport.net.ph/wp-content/uploads/2015/01/2013-CRPD-Parallel-Rept-of-Phil-Coalition.pdf

Schulze, M. (2010) *Understanding the UN Convention on the Rights of Persons with Disabilities and Optional Protocol.* Third Edition. London: Handicap International. Retrieved on 12 June 2017 from www.hiproweb.org/uploads/tx_hidrtdocs/HICRPDManual2010.pdf

Short, N. (1999) 'The role of NGOs in the Ottawa process to ban landmines'. *International Negotiation* 4, 481–500.

Thakur, R. and Malley, W. (1999) 'The Ottawa Convention on Landmines: a landmark humanitarian treaty in arms control?'. *Global Governance* 5, 273–302.

UNDESA (United Nations Department of Economic and Social Affairs) (2015) *Countries Reach Historic Agreement to Generate Financing for New Sustainable Development Agenda.* United Nations Department of Economic and Social Affairs Press Release. Retrieved on 4 June 2017 from www.un.org/esa/ffd/ffd3/press-release/countries-reach-historic-agreement.html

UNESCO (United Nations Educational, Scientific and Cultural Organization) (2015) *Report of the Inter-agency and Expert Group on SDG Indicators.* Retrieved on 28 October 2017 from www.un.org/disabilities/documents/sdgs/iaeg_report.pdf

United Nations (1948) *Universal Declaration of Human Rights.* Retrieved on 28 January 2017 from www.un.org/en/documents/udhr/

United Nations (1966) *International Covenant on Civil and Political Rights.* Retrieved on 28 January 2017 from https://treaties.un.org/doc/publication/unts/volume%20999/volume-999-i-14668-english.pdf

United Nations (1971) *Declaration on the Rights of Mentally Retarded Persons, G.A. Res 2856 (XXVI).* Retrieved on 31 January 2017 from www2.ohchr.org/english/law/res2856.htm

United Nations (1975) *Declaration on the Rights of Disabled Persons, G.A. Res 3447 (XXX).* Retrieved on 31 January 2017 from www.un-documents.net/a30r3447.htm

United Nations (1983) *World Programme of Action Concerning Disabled Persons.* Retrieved on 3 February 2017 from www.leeds.ac.uk/disability-studies/archiveuk/united%20nations/world%20programme.pdf

United Nations (1993) *Standard Rules on Equalization of Opportunities for Persons with Disabilities.* Retrieved on 3 February 2017 from www.un.org/esa/socdev/enable/dissre00.htm

United Nations (1995) *Copenhagen Declaration on Social Development and Programme of Action.* Retrieved on 7 February 2017 from www.unesco.org/education/pdf/COPENHAG.PDF

United Nations (2000a) *Resolution 2000/51.* UN Commission on Human Rights DocE/CN.4?Res/2000/51. Retrieved on 14 February 2017 from http://ap.ohchr.org/documents/E/CHR/resolutions/E-CN_4-RES-2000-51.doc

United Nations (2000b) *Millennium Declaration.* Retrieved on 13 February 2017 from www.un.org/millennium/declaration/ares552e.htm

United Nations (2006) *Convention on the Rights of Persons with Disabilities and Optional Protocol.* Washington, DC: United Nations.

United Nations (2009) *Realizing the MDGs for Persons with Disabilities through the Implementation of the WPA and the UNCRPD.* Report of the Secretary-General A/RES/63/150. Retrieved on 20 February 2017 from www.un.org/disabilities/default.asp?id=1463

United Nations (2013) *The Way Forward: A Disability-Inclusive Development Agenda Towards 2015 and Beyond.* Report of the Secretary-General A/68/95. Retrieved on 20 February 2017 from www.un.org/disabilities/default.asp?id=1590

United Nations (2015a) *Report of the Committee on the Rights of Persons with Disabilities* Seventieth Session. Supplement No. 55 (A/70/55). Retrieved on 17 March 2017 from https://documents-dds-ny.un.org/doc/UNDOC/GEN/G15/095/26/PDF/G1509526.pdf?OpenElement

United Nations (2015b) *Addis Ababa Action Agenda of the Third International Conference on Financing for Development*. Outcome Document adopted at Third International Conference on Financing for Development (Addis Ababa, Ethiopia, 13–16 July 2015) and endorsed by General Assembly in Resolution 69/313 on 27 July 2015. Retrieved on 3 June 2017 from www.un.org/esa/ffd/wp-content/uploads/2015/08/AAAA_Outcome.pdf

United Nations (2015c) *Transforming our World: the 2030 Agenda for Sustainable Development*. Retrieved on 21 March 2017 from www.un.org/pga/wp-content/uploads/sites/3/2015/08/120815_outcome-document-of-Summit-for-adoption-of-the-post-2015-development-agenda.pdf

World Bank (2004) *The World Bank and the Copenhagen Declaration Ten Years After*. Social Development Department. Retrieved on 3 April 2017 from http://siteresources.worldbank.org/EXTSOCIALDEVELOPMENT/Resources/World+Bank+and+Copenhagen+Commitments+Final092004.pdf

5   Disabled people's organisations and the international disability rights movement

It is largely due to the actions of disabled people themselves, in articulating their own experiences and challenging society to be more accommodating, that disability rights are now widely recognised in international law. The Convention on the Rights of Persons with Disabilities (CRPD) in particular, with its emphasis on the removal of disabling barriers and promotion of full participation, represents a major shift in thinking from an individual model perspective, in which disabled people are required to adapt to the norms of a society that is not designed to include them, to an approach which values and respects disabled people as citizens with equal rights. This rights-based approach to disability can bring benefits to the whole of society, as reflected in the following statement from the CRPD:

Rights-based perspective in the CRPD

the promotion of the full enjoyment by persons with disabilities of their human rights and fundamental freedoms and of full participation by persons with disabilities will result in their enhanced sense of belonging and in significant advances in the human, social and economic development of society and the eradication of poverty.

(United Nations, 2006, Preamble (m))

This chapter begins by looking at the independent living movement (ILM) in the United States (US), an early example of disabled people coming together to articulate their concerns and campaign for greater freedoms within mainstream society, before describing the growth of the democratic and coordinated international disability rights movement that exists today. There is a particular focus on the critical role of disabled people's organisations (DPOs) within the movement, and some of the challenges that they currently face.

This is followed by a discussion around the extent to which a rights-based approach to disability policy and practice is truly reflective of the needs and priorities of disabled people around the world, particularly those living in poverty. The chapter concludes with an explanation of the disability mainstreaming approach, a strategy designed to operationalise the rights-based approach by ensuring that mainstream development planning takes full account of disability.

Independent living movement

Triggered by the actions of a small group of disabled students at the University of Berkeley in California, the ILM arose in the late 1960s against the backdrop of the American civil rights movement. Despite being housed in a local hospital wing, due to the severity of their physical impairments, these students were determined to live their student lives to the full (Hurst, 2000). Led by the charismatic figure of Ed Roberts, sometimes referred to as the 'father of disability rights' (Carson, 2013), they set up an organisation on campus to campaign for accessibility improvements and the provision of disability support services, such as personal assistants. On completing their degrees, they continued to work together to uphold the rights of disabled people to self-determination and independence, leading to the founding of the first Center for Independent Living (CIL) in Berkeley in 1972, with Ed Roberts serving as executive director. In line with its main objective of supporting disabled people to live full and independent lives within mainstream society, the CIL provided core services in five main areas, as shown in Box 5.1.

Box 5.1   Core CIL services

- Housing
- Personal assistance
- Transport
- Access
- Peer counselling and support.

The ILM spread rapidly and within ten years there were over 200 CILs across the US, all run by disabled people and inclusive of people with all types of impairment. Some of them added additional services to the original core services, such as information, employment and education support, in order to combat social exclusion and poverty among disabled people. There are now CILs in many countries around the world, supporting disabled people to live full and independent lives within mainstream society. Case Study 5.1 describes the work of one such organisation called Life Haven, based in Manila, which provides core services in line with original CIL model and has also achieved notable success in its advocacy work.

Case study 5.1   Life Haven

Based on the ILM philosophy Life Haven campaigns for personal assistant services to enable disabled people to live more independently, as well as raising awareness more generally on disability issues within the Philippines.

Life Haven recently joined Social Watch Philippines, a federation of civil society organisations which campaigns to improve policies and service delivery, and has close links with the government. By linking up with Social Watch, members of Life Haven have been able to participate in consultation clusters that advise the government on budget priorities in areas such as education, health, employment, the environment and social protection. Life Haven's president, Abner Manlapaz, recalled that before joining Social Watch they were occasionally invited to join workshops organised by non-governmental organisations (NGOs) or government agencies. Now they were able to engage directly with government committees on a regular basis, even influencing decision making at Congress, the highest level of government. There was also more awareness on disability within Social Watch itself as a result of the partnership, he observed, with disability issues sometimes being raised at cluster meetings even when Life Haven representatives were not present.

The opportunity for Life Haven to influence government policy making and planning at the highest levels came about through its willingness to form an alliance with poverty-focused organisations within civil society. This approach shows an awareness of the commonalities between disability and poverty and reflects Yeo's (2005) call for the disability movement to forge horizontal alliances with more general campaigns to reduce poverty.

Source: Adapted from Cobley, 2015

Disabled People's International and the international disability movement

The international disability movement (IDM) really took off with the birth of Disabled People's International (DPI) in 1981, which was designated by the United Nations (UN) as the 'International Year of Disabled People'.

The creation of DPI was triggered by events that took place in 1980 at a conference in Canada organised by Rehabilitation International, an organisation run mainly by non-disabled rehabilitation professionals, to which a number of prominent disabled people from around the world were invited. During the conference, a charter was proposed that included the aim 'to take all necessary steps to ensure the fullest possible integration of and participation by disabled people in all aspects of the life of their communities' (Rehabilitation International, 1980, p. 647).

Some of the disabled delegates that were present proposed that Rehabilitation International should put these words into action by actually becoming a DPO itself, allowing disabled people to take control of the organisation (Oliver, 1990). This proposal was rejected, leading to many of the disabled delegates staging a walk-out and holding their own side-conference in the same hotel, at which they decided to set up an international movement that would give disabled people a voice and enable them to access their rights to equal participation. Some of those present agreed to set up national umbrella organisations of DPOs in their own countries, which led to the formation of bodies such as the British Council of Organisations for Disabled People and the National Council of Disabled People of Zimbabwe. In 1981, the group met again in Singapore, where DPI was founded with the aim of promoting disability rights and the equalisation of opportunities for disabled people worldwide. Driedger (1989) describes the early history of DPI, arguing that its establishment marked the beginning of a coordinated struggle for the recognition of human rights for disabled people around the world.

DPI now consists of over 130 national assemblies (DPI website, undated). The organisation's adopted slogan, 'nothing about us without us', is based on the title of James Charlton's (1998) remarkable study of disability oppression and empowerment, which draws on interviews conducted with disability activists around the world over a ten-year period. This slogan has become a rallying call for the movement, implying that disabled people, and the organisations that represent them, need to be involved in all decisions that affect their lives. They need to be at the forefront of their own development and empowerment, if real social change is to take place.

DPI itself has been very focused on ensuring that the voices of disabled people are heard on the international stage when important decisions are made. They have worked closely with the UN, in particular, and have had a significant impact on the drafting of several major international agreements, including the World Programme of Action, the Copenhagen Declaration and the CRPD.[1] In fact, the advocacy and lobbying efforts that led up to the adoption of the CRPD, in which DPI played a major role as a key member of the International Disability Alliance (IDA), is now widely viewed as the 'most important accomplishment of the Disability Rights Movement' (Malinga and Gumbo, 2016, p. 64).

Disabled people's organisations

There is a long history of organisations *for* disabled people, set up to pro-mote the welfare of disabled people and provide services to them. In the United Kingdom (UK), for example, the Royal National Institute for the Blind was established in 1868, while in France the Institut Nacional des Jeunes Aveugles (National Institution for the Young Blind) was estab-lished by Valentine Hauy in 1784 and later attended by Louis Braille, the inventor of the braille reading and writing system. On the international stage, Rehabilitation International was founded in 1922, while the World Federation for the Deaf was established in 1951. Both are now global organ-isations with member organisations in over 100 countries around the world.

DPOs are a far more recent phenomenon. They differ from the disability organisations described above in that they are predominantly run by disa-bled people themselves.[2] Oliver (1990) attributes the rise of DPOs in the UK to disillusionment among disabled people at the charity model outlook of many traditional organisations for disabled people, their failure to assume that disabled people were capable of taking control of their own lives and the tendency of key individuals within these organisations to serve their own interests. Among the early DPOs in the UK was the Union of the Physically Impaired Against Segregation (UPIAS), formed in the 1970s. UPIAS created a platform for disabled people themselves to voice their concerns and opin-ions, and used this platform to articulate the ideas that formed the basis of Oliver's (1983) social model.[3]

As in the UK and US, disability activists and advocates around the world have increasingly campaigned for the rights of disabled people to represent themselves and participate in their own development, rather than being repre-sented by other organisations, such as charities and NGOs. This has led to the spread of DPOs across the globe, from small local self-help groups to regional and national networks of DPO that have formed to facilitate cohesion among local groups and to coordinate advocacy campaigns. In Uganda, for example, the National Union of Disabled Persons of Uganda (NUDIPU), an umbrella body of DPOs, has been credited with winning unique constitutional rights for disabled people, who are now represented at every level of government, and having a positive influence on national legislation (Dube *et al.*, 2005).

Box 5.2   Typical DPO roles

- Building solidarity and companionship among disabled people (reducing isolation);
- Providing members with opportunities to articulate their own needs and experiences of disability;

(continued)

(continued)

- Sharing information among members;
- Providing services (such as revolving savings schemes, vocational training programmes and business development support);
- Advocating on behalf of individual members;
- Campaigning for improved access to society and increased recognition of disability rights;
- Challenging societal attitudes and negative beliefs/stigmas around disability.

DPOs carry out a wide range of functions, as summarised in Box 5.2. In addition to these typical roles, many run their own income-generating projects, providing members with valuable livelihood opportunities. For example, the Githunguri Disabled Self-help Group, located in Kenya's Central Province, runs a small rural production workshop where curios are produced from banana fibres and tree seedlings, which are in abundance locally and usually donated to the project by locals, with products being sold via agents at trade fairs across Kenya. Members that are unable to reach the workshop are able to work at home, since products are made by hand. The group has also worked hard to integrate with the local community through various initiatives, such as regular drama productions showing how natural resources can be put to productive use. Maxwell Mbygua, the Group chairman, claimed that these initiatives have altered community perceptions from 'seeing the group as a "charity case" to a self-reliant organisation' (Cobley, 2012, p. 379).

Challenges facing disabled people's organisations

Box 5.3   Recognition of DPOs in the CRPD

Article 4 (Paragraph 3), General Obligations:

In the development and implementation of legislation and policies to implement the present Convention . . . State Parties shall closely consult with and actively involve persons with disabilities, including children with disabilities, through their representative organisations.

Article 29 (Paragraph 3), on 'Participation in political and public life':

Promote actively an environment in which persons with disabilities can effectively and fully participate in the conduct of public affairs . . . including . . . (ii) Forming and joining organisations of persons with disabilities to represent persons with disabilities at international, national, regional and local levels.

Article 33 (Paragraph 3), on 'National Implementation and Monitoring':

Civil society, in particular persons with disabilities and their representative organisations, shall be involved and participate fully in the monitoring process.

The CRPD recognises the vital role of DPOs as representative organisations for disabled people, as shown in Box 5.3, effectively institutionalising them as the primary interpreters and monitors of the Convention within nation states (Stein and Lord, 2012). There are some doubts, however, as to whether DPOs have the capacity, or even the willingness, to fulfil this role effectively, given the resource constraints that they often face, with many relying mainly on member contributions. Rachel Hurst (2000), a leading figure within the IDM, observes that donor funding, when it can be accessed at all, tends to be earmarked for running projects or services, rather than for covering core running costs, and she also identifies a need for leadership training and support within many DPOs. A desk-based review (Young *et al.*, 2016) of 11 peer-reviewed studies on DPOs found that most of them referred to financial and human resource limitations. On a cautionary note, however, Thomas (2005) points out that, while DPOs often value the support of Northern NGOs, particularly in terms of engaging with donor agencies on their behalf, 'the perception that DPOs lack capacity is not always well-founded and is in danger of becoming a self-fulfilling prophecy' (p. 14).

There are also questions over the extent to which DPOs are truly representative of disabled people, with some controlled by one or more dominant individuals who may not adequately represent the views of less powerful members. Yeo (2005) points out that the most articulate and vociferous members of DPOs, who often rise to become leaders, are rarely the most marginalised. She argues, therefore, that leaders should be trained to listen to others and try to understand their situations, so that they can accurately represent their views. Even if DPOs are able to effectively represent the views of their own members, there is a danger that they may not represent the wider community of disabled people, particularly those living in rural areas. A study in Nigeria (Lang and Upah, 2008), for example, revealed a complete lack of awareness of disability rights within a rural community of people with epilepsy, which the researchers viewed as 'a classic example of how, from an historic perspective, DPOs have systematically failed to engage with disabled people living in rural areas' (p. 21).

A further challenge, with the potential to undermine the ability of DPOs to effectively represent the best interests of disabled people, is the risk of fragmentation and conflict. DPOs often cater for members with a diverse range of impairments, abilities and social backgrounds, so the task of ensuring that the opinions, needs and priorities of all members are taken into account is a difficult one. There may be conflicting aims and objectives, particularly when resource limitations require difficult choices to be made between alternative courses of action. Conflict between DPOs can also occur, especially where different groups are competing for limited donor funds. Sometimes fragmentation within groups causes them to split and effectively function as rival groups. This was the case in Botswana, for example, where two DPOs for people with visual and physical impairments engaged in a power struggle for many years, preventing them from uniting to present their needs to the government (Ingstad, 2001).

Tensions may also exist between the global human rights discourse, as reflected in the CRPD, and the priorities of local DPOs. Since the advent of the CRPD there has been a marked increase in the implementation of capacity-building programmes, often instigated by donor agencies, disability-focused NGOs and global DPO networks, such as DPI and the IDA, designed to enable DPOs to fulfil their CRPD monitoring role effectively (Meyers, 2016). Unfortunately, as Meyers points out, these activities often pressurise local DPOs to realign their objectives and divert resources away from existing activities which, though they may be highly valued by members, do not appear to reflect the rights-based agenda. In the process, there is a danger that this shift in priorities may mean that local DPOs themselves become less relevant to their members and quickly lose support. This problem was illustrated by a study conducted by Meyers (2014)[4] in Nicaragua, where he spent 18 months observing the activities of seven local disability associations belonging to a city-wide disability rights coalition. One of the coalition leaders expressed frustration at the pressure placed on them by international donors to engage in advocacy work, in conflict with priorities that they had identified themselves:

Global versus local priorities

Sometimes we find that we are financed for certain objectives in a particular way that is a bad use of money, you understand? That is to say they want to pour more into promoting awareness, but we want to strengthen the associations internally. Because, look, how are you going to believe in those associations if they have no real capacity (Interview, August 17, 2012).

(Meyers, 2014, p. 467)

Ironically, the association with the strongest advocacy focus had experienced a dramatic decline in active membership, to the point where decisions often could not be made at meetings because association rules required a 50 per cent quorum, and the researcher attributes this decline to the tendency of group leaders to pay insufficient attention to issues raised by members that did not align with the externally driven rights-based agenda. Meyers concludes that donor organisations, including the global DPO networks that head up the IDM, need to build creative partnerships with local DPOs that build on existing capacities, value local knowledge and allow space for the expression of views and priorities that might differ from the global right-based perspective that broadly underpins the IDM.

Rights-based approach in practice

While the principles of participation, empowerment and inclusion have gained increasing acceptance within the international development community, questions are sometimes raised as to how rights-based rhetoric relates, in practice, to the everyday lives of those living in poverty, many of whom may regard such rhetoric as irrelevant. Mikkelsen (2005), for example, observes that many development organisations claim to have adopted the rights-based approach without actually having developed their methodologies and capacities in order to fully operationalise such an approach. Uvin goes further, arguing that development agencies have tended to adopt the rights-based perspective in order to 'benefit from the moral authority and political appeal of the human rights discourse' (2002, p. 4). He implies that, given fierce levels of competition for development funding, this approach is driven by a need to protect reputations and attract donor funding, rather than any genuine desire to challenge the power structures that lead to inequality and injustice. Uvin even criticises Sen, on whose work much human rights discourse is based, for failing to complement his broad philosophical insights with some consideration of the practical implications of trying to apply them to development interventions. Uvin's criticisms are broadly based on the premise that the language of human rights is the sole preserve of the Western-dominated development establishment. However, as Slim (2002) points out, the rights-based approach has also been adopted by grassroots movements around the world in order to bring about social change and justice for under-privileged groups. He describes, for example, how the language of human rights has played an important role in struggles against political repression in Latin America, apartheid in South Africa and injustices around land rights in South Asia. Slim concludes that the rights-based approach has the potential to bring about real change in the lives of oppressed people, as long as those that represent them at the local level are fully engaged in the change process.

Slim's argument has particular resonance for the IDM, within which disabled people in various parts of the world have joined together to redefine their identities, articulate their own experiences of disability and campaign for recognition of their rights to full participation. However, as Meyer's (2014) study in Nicaragua also illustrates, the genuine and meaningful involvement of disabled people at the grassroots level in this process is vital to its continued success. The potential of disabled people to transform their own lives and bring about real social change, rather than having change imposed on them, is illustrated by the rapid spread of self-help groups (SHGs) in India. Based on the well-established model of women's SHGs in India, these are small groups comprised of disabled people who have joined together to share information and work towards common goals, often with the support of development agencies. Case Study 5.2 describes how this grassroots movement has enabled ordinary disabled people to take responsibility for their own personal development and empowerment.

Case study 5.2   Self-help groups in India

Initially these groups were issue-based and neither handled savings nor operated loans. Their primary concern was to obtain the benefits to which disabled people are entitled under the law from the state: medical certificates, bus passes, help with buying aids and appliances, income supplements (pensions) and scholarships for education. While these benefits are statutory entitlements, most of the disabled individuals and their families were not aware of them. The few who were aware and attempted to access them met with apathy, insensitivity and corruption in the government system. Meeting and negotiating with government officials needs courage and self-confidence, which an individual disabled person often did not have. SHGs provided both. The identity of an SHG as a community-based organisation provided the minimal degree of power that was imperative for meeting and negotiating with officials. While one individual with a disability was easily dismissed or ignored, a group could not be.

Experience has shown that these groups have revolutionised the way disabled people think about themselves, and also the way they are regarded in their communities. Forming a group makes them more visible in the community, showing that they are as capable as anyone else of managing their affairs. They come together for the purpose of solving their common problems through mutual help and collective actions. Members can support one another by sharing information on the availability of services and resources. They reach a better understanding of disability, discrimination and human rights. They provide a means for disabled people to be part of the community decision-making process. Most of all, membership of the group gives a disabled person the experience of being a contributor rather than a passive receiver, which is the first essential step to personal empowerment.

Source: Coleridge and Venkatesh, 2010, pp. 185–186

Disability mainstreaming and the twin-track approach

National governments and international development agencies, as well as supranational institutions such as the World Bank and the International Labour Organization (ILO), have increasingly responded to calls for development planning and programming to take account of disability, emanating mainly from the disability movement, by adopting an approach that is referred to as 'disability mainstreaming'. This can be defined as follows:

Disability mainstreaming

the process of assessing the implications for disabled people of any planned action, including legislation, policies and programmes, in all areas and at all levels. It is a strategy for making disabled people's concerns and experiences an integral dimension of the design, implementation, monitoring and evaluation of policies and programmes in all political, economic and societal spheres so that disabled people benefit equally and inequality is not perpetuated. The ultimate goal is to achieve disability equality.

(Albert *et al.*, 2005, p. 2)

As this statement implies, disability mainstreaming is underpinned by the belief that disabled people should be enabled to access the same rights and opportunities as others, thus reflecting the rights-based approach. The United Nations (2011) has published a collection of case studies from across the globe, illustrating best practice criteria in relation to disability mainstreaming and demonstrating how this approach can be instrumental to the effective implementation of the CRPD. These criteria are summarised in Box 5.4.

Box 5.4   Best practice criteria for mainstreaming disability initiatives

- Adopt a rights-based approach. This, in turn, means that each mainstreaming initiative must:

  o   Ensure equality and be non-discriminatory, allowing people to participate regardless of their disability, level of education, age, social and life skills, religion or ethnicity;

  o   Recognize the interaction between gender and disability; in this regard, data should be disaggregated by sex and by type of disability;

  o   Promote accessibility (built environment, information and communications technology, institutional, economic, social);

  o   Be participatory, actively and meaningfully involving people with disability in all matters concerning them in the process of forming policies and programmes. DPOs are key players in this process and development agencies need to consider investing in capacity-building and capacity development initiatives for its promotion;

  o   Be accountable to persons with disabilities, involving them directly in the decision-making process in projects/programmes and policies and creating accountability mechanisms for monitoring, complaint and feedback;

- Increase awareness and understanding of disability at organizational, community and institutional levels so as to promote positive attitudes towards disability;

- Be results-based and produce a measurable change that contributes to the improvement of quality of life of people with disability;

- Be appropriately resourced, financially and in terms of human resources;

- Be sustainable, socially, culturally, economically, politically and environmentally;

- Be replicable, able to show how the product and/or process can be reproduced or adapted in other countries and contexts; replicability should be assessed taking into consideration context-specificity, since it is important to recognize that some practices in one country or context are not necessarily valid or transferable to the circumstances of another;

- Involve effective partnerships that show commitment of organizations, including government, academia, media, the UN, NGOs etc.; inter-agency and inter-organizational efforts should be emphasized with the full involvement of DPOs and local governments to assure ownership of the initiative.

Source: Adapted from United Nations, 2011, pp. 7–8

Disability mainstreaming is now the dominant strategy for promoting inclusion and equality for disabled people (WHO and World Bank, 2011). In practice, however, the effectiveness of this approach may be reduced if the necessary conditions are not in place to support the participation of disabled people as equal partners in development. This was illustrated by a study of an NGO programme designed to promote the social and economic rehabilitation of disabled people in a rural district of Cambodia (Gartrell and Hoban, 2013). The research found that discriminatory attitudes among NGO staff, reinforced by the low status of disabled people within Cambodia's traditional hierarchy of social relations, often left programme participants feeling disempowered. Furthermore, they frequently faced significant cost barriers to participation in the programme and sometimes received inappropriate forms of assistance due to the conviction among some staff that disabled people did not know what was best for themselves. As the researchers conclude, this highlights the need for 'government and development NGOs to address stigmatising social cultural perceptions and attitudes' (p. 208), and for disabled people to be fully involved in decision-making processes during both the planning and implementation of mainstreaming initiatives.

Case study 5.3   Mainstreaming in East Africa

The ILO's 'Developing Entrepreneurship among Women with Disabilities' project, implemented between 2005 and 2007, was aimed at helping disabled women to access mainstream entrepreneurship development activities in Ethiopia, Tanzania, Uganda and Zambia. Through this initiative, disabled women were supported to participate in business skills training sessions designed for women entrepreneurs in general. Training sessions covered entrepreneurial skills, product design and marketing strategies.

A progress assessment, carried out in all four countries during 2006, revealed that virtually all disabled and non-disabled participants felt that integrated provision had great benefits, and was preferable to segregated provision, despite some difficulties in relation to the accessibility of buildings and training materials. One typical comment was 'the non-disabled women were very cooperative, and in the end it was very fruitful, because we are all just people'. The integrated approach was thought to have helped disabled entrepreneurs to forge strong bonds with non-disabled entrepreneurs, leading to potential social and business support networks for the future. These views were shared by programme partner organisations. Representatives of local women entrepreneur associations, for example, noted that disabled women

(continued)

(continued)

entrepreneurs that were previously reluctant to join, due to fear of rejection, were now clamouring to join.

It was also noted, however, that some of the disabled entrepreneurs were limited by low confidence and a lack of literacy skills, and would have benefited from some support in these areas, prior to their participation in the mainstream programme. Although the programme had enabled around 450 disabled women to access business skills training, the assessment concluded that the integrated training would have worked even better if trainers and organisers had received more practical support and guidance on how to make reasonable accommodations for disabled participants.

Source: Adapted from Gilbert, 2007

Case Study 5.3 describes an apparently successful initiative in East Africa designed to support disabled women to participate in mainstream business skills development. While this is a positive example of disability mainstreaming in practice, it does illustrate the importance of ensuring that necessary adaptations are made to the environment in which mainstreaming occurs, as well as drawing attention to the frequent need for specialist support to be provided – in this case to support potential beneficiaries in acquiring the skills and confidence to make the most of the mainstream training provision. This dual focus on mainstreaming and the provision of specialist support is sometimes referred to as the twin-track approach, as illustrated by Figure 5.1.

The twin-track approach entails mainstreaming disability into all areas of development planning, while simultaneously supporting more focused initiatives designed to empower disabled people and their representative organisations. The aim is to promote social inclusion and rights to equal participation for disabled people, without neglecting the need to ensure that they receive the necessary support systems and services to enable them to make the most of the mainstream opportunities available to them. These support systems may range from the provision of basic skills training and information services for individual disabled people to leadership training and capacity-building for DPOs. The value of the twin-track approach is now widely recognised by international development agencies. The International Disability and Development Consortium (IDDC), for example, has declared that 'the full human rights of disabled persons will not be realised without a twin-track approach to inclusive development' (2004, p. 3).

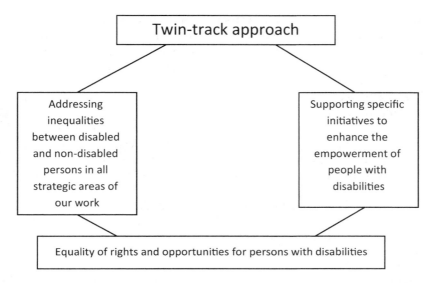

Figure 5.1 A twin-track approach to disability and development
Source: Adapted from DFID, 2000, p. 11

Reflection exercise 5.1

Disability mainstreaming aims to promote equality and enable disabled people to enjoy equal access to development opportunities, in areas such as education, employment, recreation, health and rehabilitation. Consider just one of these areas in the context of your own country, or a country with which you are familiar, and then list the barriers to effective disability mainstreaming that may exist.

Consider how a twin-track approach might enable policy makers and/or practitioners to overcome the barriers that you have listed.

Summary of key points

- Disabled people themselves have played a key role in ensuring that their rights to full and equal participation in society are widely recognised on the international stage.
- The independent living movement which began in the US and has spread around the world, provides an early example of disabled people coming together to campaign for greater freedoms within mainstream society.

- The international disability movement has grown into a structured, global civil rights movement, with democratic structures in place from the grassroots level upwards. International networks, such as DPI, have played a key role in coordinating the movement and representing the voices of disabled people on the international stage.
- The CRPD has created a mandate for DPOs to play a central role in monitoring its implementation. However, DPOs face a number of challenges, including resource limitations, lack of capacity and the risk of fragmentation, both within and between groups. As a result, they may not always adequately represent the views of their own members, let alone the broader community of disabled people.
- It should not be assumed that donor funding and capacity-building initiatives will necessarily strengthen local organisations, particularly if these initiatives fail to take account of the views and priorities of the disabled people for whom they exist, and on whom they often depend for their survival.
- Governments and development agencies are increasingly attempting to mainstream disability into their policies and programmes in order to promote equality and full participation in line with the CRPD.
- The twin-track approach has gained increasing international acceptance as a means of ensuring that disabled people, as well as the organisations that represent them, receive the specialist support necessary to ensure that they are able to fully benefit from the opportunities that disability mainstreaming initiatives may create.

Discussion questions

1   How realistic is it to expect DPOs to take responsibility for monitoring the implementation of the CRPD, and how can they be supported to fulfil this role more effectively?
2   How can DPOs balance the need to satisfy donor expectations while also being responsive to the needs and priorities of their own members?
3   How relevant is the universal language of human rights, as reflected in the CRPD, to the everyday lives of disabled people that are living in extreme poverty?

Notes

1 See Chapter 4 for more discussion on these three international agreements.
2 Organisations led by parents of disabled children, or by relatives of people with intellectual or multi-sensory impairments, are also commonly referred to as DPOs.
3 See Chapter 2 for more discussion on UPIAS and the ideas presented in its 1976 statement entitled 'The Fundamental Principles of Disability'.
4 See Suggested further reading.

Suggested further reading

Barnes, C. and Sheldon, A. (2010) 'Disability, politics and poverty in a majority world context'. *Disability and Society* 25(7), 771–782.

Malinga, J. and Gumbo, T. (2016) 'Advocacy and Lobbying: The Road Map from Charity to Human Rights'. In Iriarte, E., McConkey, R. and Gilligan, R. (Eds.) (2016) *Disability and Human Rights: Global Perspectives*. London: Palgrave, 49–67.

Meyers, S. (2014) 'Global civil society as megaphone or echo chamber? Voice in the international disability rights movement'. *International Journal of Politics, Culture and Society* 27, 459–476.

Whyte, S. and Muyinda, H. (2007) 'Wheels and New Legs: Mobilization in Uganda'. In Ingstad, B. and Whyte, S. (Eds.) *Disability in Local and Global Worlds*. Berkeley: University of California Press, 287–310.

References

Albert, B., Dube, A and Riis-Hansen, T. (2005) *Has Disability Been Mainstreamed into Development Cooperation*. DFID Knowledge and Research Project.

Carson, D. (2013) *Ed Roberts: Father of Disability Rights*. Indianapolis, IN: Dog Ear Publishing.

Charlton, J. (1998) *Nothing About US Without Us*. Berkeley: University of California Press.

Cobley, D.S. (2012) 'Towards economic empowerment: segregation versus inclusion in the Kenyan context'. *Disability and Society* 27(3), 371–384.

Cobley, D.S. (2015) 'Typhoon Haiyan one year on: disability, poverty and participation in the Philippines'. *Disability and the Global South* 2(3), 686–707.

Coleridge, P. and Venkatesh, B. (2010) 'Community Approaches to Livelihood Development: Self-help groups in India'. In Barron, T. and Ncube, J. (Eds.) *Poverty and Disability*. London: Leonard Cheshire Disability, 177–213.

DFID (Department for International Development) (2000) *Disability, Poverty and Development*. London: DFID.

Driedger, D, (1989) *The Last Civil Rights Movement: Disabled People's International*. London: Hurst & Co Ltd.

Dube, A., Hurst, R., Light, R. and Malinga, J. (2005) *Promoting Inclusion? Disabled People, Legislation and Public Policy*. London: DFID. Retrieved on 11 June 2017 from www.dfid.gov.uk/r4d/PDF/Outputs/Disability/thematic_legis.pdf

Gartrell, A. and Hoban, E. (2013) 'Structural vulnerability, disability and access to non-governmental organisation services in rural Cambodia'. *Journal of Social Work in Disability & Rehabilitation* 12(3), 194–212.

Gilbert (2007) *Link and Learn: Inclusion of Women with Disabilities in the ILO WEDGE Programme. Progress Assessment in Four African countries*. Geneva: International Labour Organization. Retrieved on 10 January 2017 from www.voced.edu.au/content/ngv%3A32049

Hurst, R. (2000) 'The International Disability Rights Movement'. Text of public lecture given on 11 October 2000 at the Centre for Disability Studies, University of Leeds. Retrieved on 31 March 2017 from http://disability-studies.leeds.ac.uk/files/library/Hurst-Disability-Rights.pdf

IDDC (International Disability and Development Consortium) (2004) *Inclusive Development and the UN Convention*. IDDC Reflection Paper. Retrieved on 30 March 2017 from www.un.org/esa/socdev/enable/rights/ahc3iddc.pdf

Ingstad, B. (2001) 'Disability in the Developing World'. In Albrect, G.L., Seelman, K. and Bury, M. (Eds.) *Handbook of Disability Studies*. London: Sage, 772–792.

Lang, R. and Upah, L. (2008) *Scoping Study: Disability Issues in Nigeria*. DFID-commissioned final report. Retrieved on 31 July 2017 from www.ucl.ac.uk/lc-ccr/downloads/scopingstudies/dfid_nigeriareport

Malinga, J. and Gumbo, T. (2016) 'Advocacy and Lobbying: The Road Map from Charity to Human Rights'. In Iriarte, E., McConkey, R. and Gilligan, R. (Eds.) *Disability and Human Rights: Global Perspectives*. London: Palgrave, 49–67.

Meyers, S. (2014) 'Global civil society as megaphone or echo chamber? Voice in the international disability rights movement'. *International Journal of Politics, Culture and Society* 27, 459–476.

Meyers, S. (2016) 'NGO-ization and human rights law: the CRPD's civil society mandate'. *Laws* 5 (2), 21.

Mikkelsen, B. (2005) *Methods for Development Work and Research: A New Guide for Practitioners*. London: Sage.

Oliver, M. (1983) *Social Work with Disabled People*. Basingstoke: Macmillan.

Oliver, M. (1990) *The Politics of Disablement*. Basingstoke: Macmillan.

Rehabilitation International (1980) 'Rehabilitation International's Charter for the 80s'. *American Journal of Occupational Therapy* 34, 645–647. Retrieved on 11 June 2017 from http://ajot.aota.org/article.aspx?articleid=1890015

Slim, H. (2002). 'Making moral low ground: rights as the struggle for justice and the abolition of development'. *The Fletcher Journal of Development Studies* Praxis XVII: 1–5.

Stein, M. and Lord, J. (2012) 'Forging Effective International Agreements: Lesson for the UN Convention on the Rights of Persons with Disabilities'. In Heymann, J. and Cassola, A. (Eds.) *Making Equal Rights Real: Taking Effective Action*. Cambridge: Cambridge University Press, 27–50.

Thomas, P. (2005) *Disability, Poverty and the Millennium Development Goals: Relevance, Challenges and Opportunities for DFID*. DFID Knowledge and Research Programme. Retrieved on 5 May 2017 from http://digitalcommons.ilr.cornell.edu/cgi/viewcontent.cgi?article=1257&context=gladnetcollect

United Nations (2006) *Convention on the Rights of Persons with Disabilities and Optional Protocol*. Washington, DC: United Nations.

United Nations (2011) *Best Practices for Including Persons with Disabilities in All Aspects of Development Efforts* Washington, DC: United Nations. Retrieved on 14 November 2016 from www.un.org/disabilities/documents/best_practices_publication_2011.pdf

Uvin, P. (2002) 'On moral high ground: the incorporation of human rights by the development enterprise'. *The Fletcher Journal of Development Studies* Praxis XVII: 1–11.

WHO (World Health Organization) and World Bank (2011) *World Report on Disability*. Geneva: WHO. Retrieved on 22 October 2016 from http://whqlibdoc.who.int/publications/2011/9789240685215_eng.pdf

Yeo, R. (2005) *Disability, Poverty and the New Development Agenda*. London: DFID. Retrieved on 4 May 2016 from www.dfid.gov.uk/r4d/PDF/Outputs/Disability/RedPov_agenda.pdf

Young, R., Reeve, M. and Grills, N. (2016) 'The functions of disabled people's organisations (DPOs) in low and middle-income countries: a literature review'. *Disability, CBR and Inclusive Development* 27(3), 45–71.

6 Disability, health and rehabilitation

Health is defined in the constitution of the World Health Organization (WHO) as 'a state of physical, mental and social well-being and not merely the absence of disease and infirmity' (WHO, 1948, p. 1). As this holistic definition suggests, there are numerous factors that may have an impact on a disabled person's health status. These include personal characteristics, such as age, gender, type and severity of impairment, past experiences, behaviour patterns and family circumstances. They also include a wide range of environmental influences, such as living and working conditions, cultural beliefs and practices, the strength of community support networks and the availability of affordable and accessible healthcare services.

Rehabilitation is defined in the *World Report on Disability* as 'a set of measures that assist individuals who experience, or are likely to experience, disability to achieve and maintain optimal functioning in interaction with their environments' (WHO and World Bank, 2011, p. 96). This broad definition encompasses rehabilitation measures that are designed to support disabled people to carry out various everyday activities (such as reading, writing or climbing the stairs) and to promote their full participation in society, as well as measures that are simply designed to improve bodily functioning.

Disabled people have a right to access health and rehabilitation services on an equal basis with others. This is an important theme of the Convention on the Rights of Persons with Disabilities (CRPD), which contains separate articles on health and rehabilitation, as summarised in Box 6.1.

Box 6.1 Health and rehabilitation in the CRPD

The CRPD recognises four key factors that are crucial to meeting the health and rehabilitation needs of disabled people:

- Accessibility
- Affordability
- Availability
- Quality.

(continued)

(continued)

Article 25 calls on governments to ensure that disabled people can access the highest standards of health services (including health and life insurance), without discrimination. It recognises that disability itself may be linked to specific health needs, which should be addressed. It also calls for the provision of health services close to people's own communities, particularly in rural areas.

Article 26 underlines the importance of rehabilitation services in enabling disabled people to maximise their independence and participate in society as fully as possible. It calls on governments to ensure the non-discriminatory provision of rehabilitation services in health, employment, education and social services. Article 26 stresses that rehabilitation services should be voluntary, tailored to individual needs and strengths, provided at the earliest possible stage and close to people's communities. It also recognises the need for ongoing professional training within rehabilitation services, and for the awareness and use of assistive devices and technologies to be promoted.

This chapter first explores the linkages between disability and health, and then discusses how the concept of rehabilitation has evolved in recent years, partly in response to criticisms from disabled people. This is followed by a discussion around some of the main barriers to the provision of appropriate health and rehabilitation services, in the four key areas of accessibility, affordability, availability and quality. Various strategies, designed to address these barriers and support disabled people to live full, active and healthy lives, are examined. The final part of the chapter focuses on the concept of community-based rehabilitation (CBR), a term that is widely used to describe strategies that are designed to harness the potential of local communities to support and empower disabled people.

Disability and health

There is some evidence to suggest that disabled people are more vulnerable to ill-health than the general population, for a variety of reasons. They may be more likely to adhere to certain behavioural patterns, for example, as illustrated by a study in Rwanda (Amosun *et al.*, 2005) involving 300 people with lower limb amputations, which found that participants were less likely to exercise and more likely to consume alcohol and recreational drugs than the general population, with negative health consequences. Another health risk factor commonly associated with disability is the increased exposure of disabled people to the risk of physical violence and psychological abuse, such as isolation, or even confinement, and being made to feel guilty or inadequate (Elwan, 1999). Disabled people are also believed to be at greater risk of sustaining injuries due to burns, falls and accidents associated with the use of assistive devices (WHO and World Bank, 2011). Finally, some disabled people may be vulnerable to early ageing, and thus more susceptible to health conditions that are more common in older age. Research has shown, for example, that people with Down syndrome over the age of 55 are far more likely to develop Alzheimer's disease than the general population (Connolly, 2006).

Despite being vulnerable to ill-health, disabled people are often unable to access appropriate healthcare services. Strong evidence of a close association between disability and unmet health needs was provided by the *World Health Survey*, a multi-national household survey involving face-to-face interviews conducted across 70 countries (WHO, 2002–04), in which disabled people reported not receiving adequate healthcare more frequently than non-disabled people across all age groups, particularly in low-income countries. Unmet health needs can limit the extent to which disabled people are able to take advantage of educational and livelihood opportunities, thus reinforcing the vicious cycle of poverty and disability (DFID, 2000).[1]

This section has identified certain health risks that are associated with disability, as well as highlighting an apparent disparity between disabled people and the general population in terms of unmet health needs. It is important, however, not to automatically equate disability with poor health. Many disabled people are in perfectly good health, and it can be offensive to assume otherwise.

Disability and rehabilitation

Historically, rehabilitation services have been rooted in the medical model, which views disability as arising from impairment and thus underlines the importance of medical solutions to the problems associated with disability. Resulting practices have sometimes involved considerable pressure being placed on disabled people (often children) to undergo intensive physical therapy in order to achieve relatively minimal improvements in bodily functioning, often within a segregated environment away from their homes and communities. This has led to much criticism from within the disability movement, with Oliver (1996) describing many traditional rehabilitation practices as 'oppressive to disabled people and an abuse of their human rights' (p. 107).

In more recent times, the term 'rehabilitation' has broadened to cover a wide range of responses to disability, from medical interventions designed to improve body function and independence to more comprehensive community-based strategies, designed to increase activity levels and promote fuller participation within society. Rehabilitation strategies may thus cover areas such as health, communication, mobility, self-care, education, employment, recreational activities, social interaction and quality of life. This shift is consistent with the rights-based perspective, which views disabled people as potential contributors to society. However, the persistence of a charity model outlook in many countries (Lang *et al.*, 2011), often reinforced by NGOs that use charitable images of disability as they seek to raise funds, can be a hindrance to the adoption of rehabilitation strategies that are designed to promote inclusion and participation.

The WHO's (2001) International Classification of Functioning, Disability and Health (ICF),[2] provides a useful conceptual framework for viewing the range of rehabilitation needs that a disabled person may have and systematically identifying corresponding goals, while recognising the various facilitating factors and disabling barriers that may impact on the achievement of those goals. A rehabilitation programme based on the ICF would focus not just on a person's medical condition, but also on the activities that he or she is able to carry out and aspects of the physical and social environment that may potentially be adapted in order to increase his or her participation in society (Shakespeare, 2014). Case Study 6.1 illustrates the use of the ICF as a basis for a rehabilitation assessment.

Case study 6.1   Using the ICF to guide a rehabilitation assessment

The value of the ICF as a framework to support holistic rehabilitation assessment is demonstrated in the case of a 13-year-old girl, named 'Michelle', from Burkina Faso. Michelle had meningitis when she was younger, resulting in a right hemiplegia, which causes stiffness and lack of control in the right side of the body. While she is able to carry out most everyday activities with ease, her parents had withdrawn her from school due to concerns over bullying, partly attributed to impairment-related differences in her appearance and movement, and consequently she had not learned to read or write. Michelle enjoys household tasks and has aspirations to become a housemaid in the future, but her fear of bullying could discourage her from accessing community services, such as healthcare services and vocational training centres, while her illiteracy could limit her awareness of job opportunities. Rather than focusing entirely on Michelle's medical needs and physical abilities, an ICF-guided assessment of Michelle's rehabilitation needs would thus identify factors such as social stigma, illiteracy and inaccessible service provision, within the education and employment sectors as well as the health sector, as potential barriers to the fulfilment of her aspirations. Resulting strategies might include, for example, confidence building, support to develop literacy skills and awareness-raising initiatives designed to reduce stigma within the local community.

Source: Adapted from MacLachlan *et al.*, 2016[3]

Rehabilitation processes tend to be multi-disciplinary and multi-sectoral, often involving the employment, education and social welfare sectors as well as the health sector. As well as providing a conceptual basis for a comprehensive rehabilitation assessment, the ICF supports the use of a common language for describing disability in terms human functioning[4] (Steiner *et al.*, 2002), thus promoting consistency and coordination among professionals working in different areas. The use of this common language also has the potential to enhance the international comparability of rehabilitation data, which is currently limited due to differing definitions of rehabilitation and varying perceptions of disability, as well as differing approaches to measuring disability (WHO and World Bank, 2011).

Disabled people themselves should be viewed as key decision makers within the rehabilitation process. They should be supported to identify their own priorities and objectives, so that rehabilitation strategies are designed to enable them to achieve their aspirations and empower them to take control of their own lives. Family members may also be able to make a valuable contribution to the assessment of rehabilitation needs and implementation of associated strategies, given the crucial role that they often play in providing care and support (McConkey, 2007).

Barriers to health and rehabilitation

As stated at the beginning of this chapter, the CRPD identifies accessibility, affordability, availability and quality as four key factors that are crucial to ensuring that disabled people are able to access appropriate health and rehabilitation services. This section examines the barriers that exist in each of these areas, as well as various strategies which potentially may help to overcome them.

Accessibility

The problem of accessibility was highlighted by a study on architectural barriers in basic healthcare units covering 41 Brazilian cities (Siqueira *et al.*, 2009), revealing that 60 per cent of the units did not allow adequate access to those with functional limitations. In order to make health and rehabilitation facilities fully accessible, it is necessary to ensure that disabled people can reach them, enter them and make full use of them. This can best be achieved in the longer term by taking account of the needs of disabled people when designing new health infrastructure projects. In the shorter term, however, alterations to buildings and equipment are often necessary to ensure that existing facilities are as accessible as possible.

Appropriate technology[5] can play an important role in enhancing the accessibility of built environments, including equipment and machinery, if it is used in a way that creates opportunities for disabled people, rather than placing restrictions on them (Albert *et al.*, 2004). The provision of appropriate assistive devices, for example, can be highly effective in empowering disabled people to live more independently and make better use of existing facilities. Manufacturing devices locally, using local materials, can save money, provide local employment opportunities and help to ensure that devices are appropriate to local conditions. The Association for the Physically Disabled of Kenya (APDK) has demonstrated this by employing disabled people to produce high-quality wheelchairs, tricycles and walking devices, specially designed to cope with African terrain, at its Kabete Wheelchair Workshop in Nairobi (Cobley, 2012).

Where disabled people have difficulty in reaching health and rehabilitation facilities, alternative models of service delivery may provide a solution. The *World Report on Disability* (WHO and World Bank, 2011) calls for the increased use of emerging information and communication technologies (ICTs), such as remote mobility assessments using teleconferencing equipment, in order to improve the accessibility and efficiency of health and rehabilitation services while also supporting disabled people to better manage their own conditions. Hospital or clinic-based services can be moved into communities, in order to integrate services and relocate equipment to where it is most needed. This would hopefully reduce patient waiting times and travelling distances, thus also addressing cost barriers, but may not be sufficient to ensure easy access for all. Research conducted by Jenny Hunt (2011), within deeply impoverished shantytowns on the outskirts of Lima, Peru, revealed that disabled people were often unable to reach local rehabilitation clinics on foot, due to the rough and steep terrain, and usually too poor to be able to hire motorised transportation. She proposes the setting up of a mobile rehabilitation service which would operate from different community buildings (making use of churches or soup kitchens, for example) on each day of the week, thus ensuring that most disabled people living within the community would be within relatively easy reach of services on at least one day of the week.

Communication barriers frequently reduce the accessibility of health and rehabilitation services. A lack of appropriate signage, for example, may disadvantage people with visual impairment, while sign language interpreters may not be available to support those with hearing impairments. People with intellectual impairments or mental health conditions are sometimes denied the additional consultation time that they may require due to work pressures within mainstream services (McConkey, 2007). The use of appropriate communication methods, taking account of individual impairment-based needs, is thus vital to the delivery of fully accessible health and rehabilitation services.

Affordability

Cost barriers reduce access to health and rehabilitation services for many disabled people, as well as reinforcing poverty. The *World Health Survey* (WHO, 2002–04) identified affordability issues (including transport costs) as the most significant barrier to accessing healthcare in low-income countries, with disabled people more likely than non-disabled people to sell items, borrow or rely on family members in order to pay for healthcare. This is consistent with the findings of a World Bank (2009) study based on rural village surveys conducted in the Indian states of Uttar Pradesh and Tamil Nadu, which identified cost, distance and inadequate transportation as the top three barriers to accessing health services, and also noted that many disabled people had to pay for their own assistive devices. Similarly, Grech's (2008) study on disability and poverty in Guatemala identifies widespread mistrust in doctors among disabled people, due to the high fees that they tend to charge, while a study in rural China (Sagli *et al.*, 2013) noted that high healthcare costs associated with the privatisation of healthcare tend to deepen poverty within households with disabled family members.

Reducing, removing or subsidising the fees charged by service providers is one obvious way of reducing financial hardship and encouraging disabled people to access services. The 2010 *World Health Report* (WHO, 2010a) claims that full access to healthcare services will only be achieved when governments cover the costs of healthcare for disabled people who cannot afford to pay. However, removing the cost barriers is only part of the solution. Even free healthcare services may not be used by disabled people if there are other barriers present.

Pro-poor health insurance schemes provide a means of protecting poor people from the impact of health and rehabilitation costs in the event of sudden shocks, such as illness of accident, and these are likely to be of particular benefit to disabled people, given their disproportionate representation among the poor. Sagli *et al.* (2013) examined the impact of one such scheme in China, implemented by the government in 2003 with the aim of reducing household poverty in rural areas. The scheme only covered certain healthcare costs, however, and payments were made on the basis of reimbursement, which meant that very poor households often had to borrow in order to afford the upfront costs. Another drawback of the scheme was that reimbursement rates were lower for outpatient expenses, which meant that those with long-term or recurring health issues not requiring hospital admission were disadvantaged. The researchers concluded that, while many of the study participants expressed satisfaction with the scheme, its impact in terms of breaking the cycle of poverty and disability had been rather limited.

Cash transfers are another common approach to overcoming the cost barriers associated with health and rehabilitation services. Many countries provide cash transfers (or income support) to poor people, and some target these at households with a disabled member, or directly at disabled people, in recognition of the additional costs and barriers that they face. This increases their disposable income, which they can use according to their own priorities. There has been a recent growth in conditional cash transfer schemes, where receiving cash benefits is conditional on participation in, for example, a healthcare programme. Evaluations of such schemes in several Latin

American countries indicate that many of them have been quite successful in terms of extending the coverage of both education and preventative health services (Fiszbein and Schady, 2009). However, conditional cash transfer schemes can only work effectively for disabled people if accessible and inclusive services are locally available (Mont, 2010; Palmer, 2013).

Availability

The poorest countries of the world bear the heaviest burdens of disease and injury, yet have the fewest resources to cope with them (Gottret and Schieber, 2006). As a result, the supply of health infrastructure in many countries of the Global South is woefully inadequate, with few services universally available (WHO, 2010a). In Malawi, for example, health clinics in poorer areas experience high staff turnover and often lack essential equipment and medicines (Ingstad *et al.*, 2012). Another problem is that services are often located far from people's homes, especially for those living in rural areas. In Brazil, for example, basic therapeutic services are not available in many rural areas (Siqueira *et al.*, 2009), while household surveys in the Indian states of Tamil Nadu and Uttah Pradesh (World Bank, 2009) revealed that over half of the respondents had reported that there were no healthcare facilities in their local area. The Indian surveys also revealed that a similar number of respondents were unaware of India's disability certification process, which disabled people must complete in order to access appropriate treatment and rehabilitation services.

A severe lack of skilled personnel limits the availability of health and rehabilitation services in many countries. It has been estimated, for example, that 'more than 75 per cent of developing countries have no prosthetics and orthotics training programmes, which leads to a poor coverage of prosthetics and orthotics services' (WHO, 2005, p. 8). The *World Report on Disability* (WHO and World Bank, 2011) calls for the expansion of educational and training programmes, in order to improve the supply of health and rehabilitation professionals, noting that some countries, such as post-conflict Vietnam, have responded to a chronic lack of rehabilitation workers by introducing shorter 'mid-level' training programmes.

One way of increasing the coverage of health and rehabilitation services is to develop specialist interventions, designed to fill in the gaps within mainstream provision. Targeted health promotion programmes, for example, can have a positive impact on knowledge, behaviour and lifestyle patterns among disabled people, thus reducing the occurrence of secondary conditions,[6] empowering disabled people to manage their own health more effectively, reducing medical costs and increasing community participation (Rimmer and Rowland, 2008). Such interventions may be specifically targeted at those who are particularly difficult to reach, such as people with mental health conditions and intellectual impairments, or at certain age groups, thus helping to reduce inequalities in healthcare provision. One such intervention, designed to raise awareness of issues around HIV/AIDS among young disabled people in Africa, is described in Case Study 6.2.

Case study 6.2   Preventing HIV/AIDS among young people with disabilities in Africa

In 1999, the international network Rehabilitation International began an HIV/AIDS project in Mozambique and the United Republic of Tanzania to promote the African Decade of Persons with Disabilities, and to provide HIV/AIDS leadership and training. The non-governmental organisations (NGOs) Miracles in Mozambique, the Disabled Organisation for Legal Affairs and Social Economic Development in the United Republic of Tanzania were local partners in the project, with support by the Swedish International Development Agency.

A baseline survey, carried out with 175 disabled people aged 12–30, revealed that knowledge about HIV/AIDS was low, there was a lack of health information available in accessible formats and health facilities were also often inaccessible.

The project developed educational materials on HIV/AIDS issues and rights for youths and young adults with disabilities, as well as for out-reach workers and peer educators working with this group. The materials included manuals in accessible formats, such as braille, and a DVD with sign language. Project materials were widely disseminated to HIV/AIDS and disability organisations. Four training workshops, delivered in Kiswahili and Portuguese to 287 participants, were later expanded to include people with disabilities in rural areas of Mozambique. Some participants trained to serve locally as HIV/AIDS educators. At the same time, a wide-ranging campaign used mass media, the Internet and seminars involving repre-sentatives of governments and NGOs to educate the public.

At the conclusion of the project, it was recommended that disability issues should be mainstreamed within HIV/AIDS educational programmes. The participatory and inclusive approach proved effective in training young people with disabilities as well as peer educators and outreach workers.

Source: Rehabilitation International, 2007, cited in WHO and World Bank, 2011, p. 74

Quality

Disabled people often receive poor or inappropriate services due to a lack of disability awareness and negative or discriminatory attitudes within health services, while important clinical decisions are sometimes affected by invalid assumptions. The common assumption that disabled people are not sexually active, for example, sometimes deters health professionals from offering sexual and reproductive health services (Drainoni *et al.*, 2006). The way that disability is understood by health sector providers can have a critical impact on the types of assistance and treatment that disabled people receive (Shakespeare, 2014). A recent qualitative study in Malawi (Braathen *et al.*, 2015)[7] revealed that, while qualified health service professionals generally attributed disability to medical causes, they were often supported by community health workers with less education and training who had not divorced themselves from spiritual or traditional perceptions, such as the belief that disability was sometimes associated with witchcraft. The study highlighted one particular case where such perceptions had been internalised by a disabled person, as well as her family, leading her to lose hope of ever leading a meaningful life. It should be noted that misconceptions about disability and disabled people are not confined to countries of the Global South, however, as highlighted by the following quotation from a disabled person's advocate who participated in a focus group discussion in Massachusetts, United States:

Misunderstandings of disability within health services

We hear frequently that people are terrified of going to the ER [emergency room], because their disabilities are misunderstood. People don't take the time to understand them and what they need. They're afraid of leaving the ER in worse shape than when they came in.
(Drainoni *et al.*, 2006, p. 109)

In order to ensure that disabled people are treated respectfully and receive appropriate treatment and support, there is clearly a need to sensitise those that provide health and rehabilitation services, in order to increase understanding of both the social and medical causes of disability, to promote positive, non-discriminatory attitudes and to develop the necessary skills and knowledge to enable them to meet the specific needs of disabled people. This will not be achieved, however, through the expansion of professional training programmes that simply focus on building medical knowledge and skills. Training programmes also need to raise awareness of disability as a human rights issue and take account of the various ways in which disability is reinforced through the interaction between people with impairments and the environment in which they live. Cornielje and Tsengu (2016) discuss this issue, noting that conventional training programmes often fail to adequately equip rehabilitation professionals with the necessary skills to work in poverty-stricken areas. In the African context, for example, they question the extent to which training programmes pay sufficient attention to the powerful influence of the religious model[8] on perceptions of disabled people, the role of traditional health remedies and the important contribution that family members can make to rehabilitation programmes.

Disabled people are experts by experience and uniquely positioned to share their knowledge of disabling barriers, which they encounter on a daily basis. They also tend to be frequent users of healthcare services, and thus potentially a source of valuable feedback on the quality of services. There is ample scope, therefore, for the involvement of disabled people, as well as their families, in the planning and delivery of services at all levels. At the policy level, resources should be set aside for the involvement of organisations that represent disabled people, on a collaborative basis, in the reform of policy and legislation (WHO and World Bank, 2011). At the local level, health providers can seek to raise the quality and inclusiveness of services by seeking the views of disabled people and their representative organisations. At the individual level, health and rehabilitation providers should aim to work in a collaborative way with disabled people by supporting them to manage their own conditions more effectively and to make informed decisions about their health. This may be quite a challenge, however, for professionals who have years of training and are used to making the decisions, rather than assuming the role of facilitator and putting their expertise at the disposal of others.

Those with complex health needs often receive fragmented services from different service providers, and may experience transitional difficulties when care is transferred from one service provider to another (for example, from child to adult services). This problem can only be addressed if service providers work together to coordinate services in a way that ensures that disabled people access appropriate services and resources at the right time, improving the efficiency and cost-effectiveness of healthcare services in the long-term as well as reducing anxieties for disabled people. One common approach designed to achieve this is CBR, in which locally based CBR workers work with disabled people and their families to develop individual rehabilitation plans and to help them to navigate the various services available. This approach will be further explored in the next section.

Reflection exercise 6.1

Imagine that you work for a disability organisation in a country that you are familiar with, and have been tasked with designing an advocacy campaign aimed at improving the accessibility, affordability, availability and quality of health and rehabilitation services for disabled people. Provide an outline of the main elements of your advocacy campaign, including approaches, methods of implementation and, where possible, evaluation measures.

Community-based rehabilitation

Local communities can potentially play an important role in supporting and contributing to rehabilitation programmes, particularly in settings where community interdependence is strong. This potential is recognised in the following bold statement from a document produced by the International Disability and Development Consortium (IDDC):

Harnessing community potential

80 per cent of (the) information, skills, resources that disabled persons need to enable them to fully participate and access their rights can be met within their local communities.

(IDDC, 2004, p. 4)

Many community-based schemes come under the umbrella of CBR, a catch-all term for strategies that involve decentralising rehabilitation services and building on local community resources. The concept has gradually evolved over the past half-century, from focusing quite narrowly on increasing the provision of basic medical rehabilitation services, particularly within rural areas, to encompassing a wide range of approaches designed to empower disabled people and promote their full inclusion in society. There are various definitions of CBR available, but perhaps the most widely recognised is the one set out in a joint position paper on CBR produced by the International Labour Organization (ILO), United Nations Educational, Scientific and Cultural Organization (UNESCO) and WHO:

Definition of CBR

CBR is a strategy within general community development for rehabilitation, equalization of opportunities and social inclusion of all children and adults with disabilities. CBR is implemented through the combined efforts of people with disabilities themselves, their families and communities, and the appropriate health, education, vocational and social services.

(ILO *et al.*, 1994, p. 1)

One significant aspect of this definition is the emphasis on CBR as a strategy *within* community development, which implies that CBR programmes should be sensitive to the local context, including social, cultural, economic

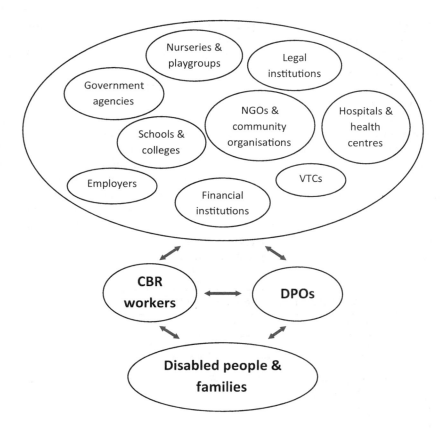

Figure 6.1 CBR stakeholder linkages

and political conditions, and aim to engage with a wide range of community stakeholders. Figure 6.1 highlights various stakeholder linkages that could potentially form part of a CBR initiative.

The main objective of CBR is to empower disabled people to take control of their own lives and access their rights to full participation, with the support of motivated community workers or 'CBR workers' who provide them with information and advocate for their inclusion, so that they can become 'active contributors' to their communities (ILO *et al.*, 2004). Although CBR workers often receive only basic training in rehabilitation, they are usually part of the community themselves and have a good understanding of local traditions and customs, which puts them in a strong position to gain the trust of disabled people and their families. This enables them to play a key role in the CBR process, as Figure 6.1 illustrates, by facilitating linkages between disabled people and the community stakeholders that can potentially support them to achieve their rehabilitation objectives. The diagram also highlights the important role that disabled people's organisations (DPOs), with their knowledge of local disability issues, can play in this process. DPOs are often well placed to make initial contact with disabled people and their families and may already have established strong links with some community stakeholders.

CBR is sometimes viewed as a relatively low-cost means of reaching out to disabled people on a wide scale and ensuring that they are able to make the best use of mainstream and specialist services that are available locally. The approach is often seen as particularly well suited to social and economic environments that are characterised by high levels of poverty, high unemployment rates and limited social services (Metts, 2000). However, as Ingstad (2001) points out, there is a danger in presenting CBR to governments of the Global South as a low-cost approach. For CBR to work effectively, it is vital that CBR workers receive the necessary training and support to carry out their pivotal role. They also require access to an infrastructure of mainstream and specialist services, so that they can make referrals to relevant professionals and services as required. In some settings, this may require considerable investment.

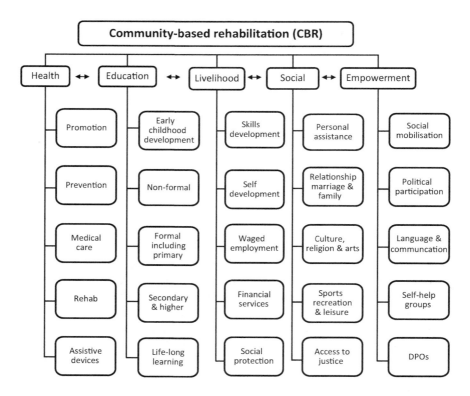

Figure 6.2 The CBR matrix

Source: Adapted from WHO, 2010b, p. 25

The CBR matrix

The CBR matrix, shown in Figure 6.2, displays the potential range and depth that is possible within a comprehensive, multi-disciplinary CBR programme. The matrix has five major components (health, education, livelihood, social and empowerment), each of which is split into five elements.[9] This provides a basic framework covering the various areas that a CBR programme may cover. However, each CBR programme is unique and will be influenced by a wide range of local contextual factors, as well as resource constraints. It follows, therefore, that some CBR initiatives may have a strong focus on certain areas identified in the matrix, while paying less or no attention to others. Case Study 6.3 describes a CBR initiative in Kenya that has successfully addressed a number of the areas covered by the matrix.

Case study 6.3   The Meru North District Disability Centre

This case study examines a multi-disciplinary CBR programme, aimed at promoting the empowerment and inclusion of disabled people across the vast rural district of Meru North, in Kenya's Eastern Province.

The scheme, which began in 1996, provides a range of home and community-based services, including vocational training and medical rehabilitation, as well as forming and strengthening DPOs within the district. Another primary objective is to promote disability rights through institutional and community awareness-raising, as well as providing information to disabled people on how to access specialist and mainstream services.

This latter objective was very much in evidence at two DPO meetings that I attended with the scheme's social worker, who repeatedly challenged members not to 'limit their aspirations' and encouraged them to take advantage of the services that were locally available. Family members present were also encouraged to air their concerns and participate in group decision making. At one of the meetings, held in the open air at the local chief's compound in the village of Machungulu, a special education teacher from a nearby school made an impassioned plea to the parents present to 'be at the forefront of promoting disability rights', and to take advantage of the special unit at the school. She emphasised the potential skills that an education can develop, and illustrated her point by asking one of her pupils, an eight-year-old child with paralysed hands who had

(continued)

(continued)

accompanied her to the meeting, to sign his name on my notepad by gripping a pen between his toes. Several group members present raised the issue of assistive devices, and some members, it was reported, had been unable to attend due to a lack of wheelchairs, braces or boots. In response to this, the DPO chairman was asked to provide the District Disability Centre with a list of all those in need of assistive devices, including artificial limbs, so that proper assessments could be carried out and arrangements made for appropriate aids to be supplied as necessary.

At the time of research, the scheme was providing loans to 60 DPOs, ranging in size from 15 to over 200 members. Most were running group income-generating projects, such as dairy goat farming or charcoal production, as well as supporting members in their own business enterprises. Eight of the groups had built up sufficient capital to access mainstream financial institutions. One issue recently identified, however, was that some of the poorest disabled people were excluded from joining DPOs, as they could not afford the weekly membership fee of Ksh20. In order to address this problem, groups had been encouraged to introduce multiple levels of membership, to allow for those who could only afford to pay Ksh10, or even Ksh5 per week. Each level within the group had its own secretary to keep records of member shares, loan disbursements and repayments. According to the social worker, this innovative approach had enabled the scheme to empower some of the very poorest people in the community.

In order to maintain contact with such a large number of people, many of whom live in isolated rural communities, the project relies on an extensive network of trained disability support volunteers who report back to professional staff at weekly meetings, held at the District Disability Centre in the town of Meru. At one of these meetings, at which I was present as an observer, several of the volunteers raised issues relating to individual households to which they were attached, such as the reluctance of a parent to send their disabled child to school or the identification of a disabled person in need of vocational training, an assistive device or professional counselling. In each case specific action was agreed on, in order to address the identified need. Whenever it was felt that an issue could not be addressed within the programme, arrangements were made to make a referral to local government authorities or other partner organisations within the district.

This scheme appears to have achieved significant success, in terms of addressing a wide range of disability issues and supporting disabled people across a vast rural area, including some who are so poor that they would normally be excluded from joining DPOs. It was interesting to note that high priority was given to medical rehabilitation. One of the scheme's medical specialists summed up the programme's holistic approach by asserting that 'economic empowerment aspirations cannot be achieved unless an individual's physical impairment needs are also met'.

Source: Adapted from Cobley, 2012

Reflection exercise 6.2

Analyse Case Study 6.2 in relation to the CBR matrix presented in Figure 6.2. Based on the information provided, to what extent does the programme cover each of the five major components of the matrix?

CBR issues and challenges

Despite the rapid spread of CBR across the Global South, there have been some criticisms of the way that the concept has been understood and implemented. Miles (1999), for example, argues that CBR initiatives are sometimes 'imposed' on communities, with little value placed on the knowledge and wishes of participants. She notes concerns, within the disability movement, that 'institutional practices and attitudes have, in some cases, simply been relocated to the community' (p. 14). Lang (1999) also acknowledges these criticisms, but claims that CBR has the potential to become a powerful tool for empowerment, as long as disabled people are made aware of what they themselves can achieve and supported, rather than led, along the road to empowerment by communities and professionals. The latest revision of the joint position paper (ILO *et al.*, 2004) reflects on these concerns and calls for the participation of disabled people in both the planning and implementation of CBR programmes.

Another important factor that may influence a CBR programme is the strength and cohesion of the local community. A study of CBR programmes in Ghana, Guyana and Nepal showed that outcomes were limited because governments rarely allocated resources to the programmes and anticipated community resources were not forthcoming (WHO and SHIA, 2002). As a result, CBR workers were often unable to make referrals for physical rehabilitation and assistive devices. Ingstad (2001) also points out that community participation is sometimes lacking, and the potential for volunteering may be overestimated. One of the biggest challenges facing any CBR programme is the need to overcome negative attitudes within communities. The potential scale of this problem was illustrated by an evaluation of a CBR initiative in Nigeria, where a restaurant owner was asked whether she would ever consider employing a disabled person. She replied that she would not, because 'they can't do anything right; besides, they will bring bad luck to my business' (Tsengu *et al.*, 2006, p. 55). Unfortunately, as Tsengu goes on to report, this view was shared by 80 per cent of private employers in the district!

Despite these challenges, the CBR approach has increasingly been recognised as an appropriate strategy for meeting the needs of disabled people and promoting their full inclusion in mainstream society, particularly in the Global South (Cornielje and Tsengu, 2006). Adequately resourced CBR strategies thus have the potential to play a vital role in supporting governments in working towards the full implementation of the CRPD.

Summary of key points

- Health and rehabilitation services can play a vital role in alleviating poverty, improving quality of life and promoting more inclusive societies.
- While disability should never be equated with poor health, disabled people are vulnerable to certain health risks and tend to have higher levels of unmet health needs than the general population.
- Traditionally rooted in the medical model of disability, the concept of rehabilitation has broadened to encompass a wide range of responses to disability, from medical interventions to more comprehensive community-based strategies designed to empower disabled people and promote their full participation.
- The ICF serves as a useful conceptual framework for guiding rehabilitation approaches, as well as supporting the use of a common language in relation to disability.
- The CRPD promotes the rights of disabled people to accessible, affordable and high-quality health and rehabilitation services within their own communities. However, a wide range of barriers frequently combine to prevent disabled people from accessing these rights. Strategies designed to address these barriers include making better use of appropriate technology, implementing alternative models of service delivery, reducing cost barriers, designing specialist interventions to fill the gaps in mainstream service provision and raising awareness of disability rights among professional staff and volunteers.
- The rapidly evolving concept of CBR encompasses approaches that attempt to harness the potential of communities to support disabled people and their families to make best use of existing mainstream and specialist services. The Meru North scheme provides an example of a comprehensive, coordinated and far-reaching CBR approach.

Discussion questions

1   Given the hierarchical nature of many societies in the Global South, how realistic is it to expect health and rehabilitation professionals to act as facilitators and for local disabled people to act as key decision makers?

2   How might a rehabilitation approach tackle the common community perception, often internalised by disabled people and their families, that disability is a sign of divine retribution for sins committed in the past?

3   Within many cultures of the Global South, community and family interdependence is very strong, with less importance attached to an individual's independence. How might health and rehabilitation programmes take account of this?

Notes

1   The vicious cycle concept is presented in Chapter 3.
2   The ICF is presented and discussed in Chapter 2.
3   See Suggested further reading.
4   In the ICF, functioning is viewed in terms of activity and participation levels, as well as bodily functioning.
5   'Appropriate technology' is a philosophy which stems from the radical thinking of E.F. Schumacher (1973), based on the principle that choices of technology should put people's needs first and should, wherever possible, be based on local skills, knowledge and resources.
6   Secondary conditions are health conditions or concerns, such as pressure sores, obesity, pain and fatigue, that occur after the onset of the primary condition that is the initial cause of disability. They are often preventable and sometimes attributable to certain behaviours or lifestyle patterns (Rimmer and Rowland, 2008).
7   See suggested further reading.
8   See Chapter 2 for an explanation of the religious model.
9   The WHO (2010b) has produced a set of detailed CBR guidelines, with separate chapters focusing on each of the five major components of the matrix. See Suggested further reading.

Suggested further reading

Braathen, S., Munthali, A. and Grut, L. (2015) 'Explanatory models of disability: perspectives of health providers working in Malawi'. *Disability and Society* 30(9), 1382–1396.

MacLachlan, P., Mannan, H. and McVeigh, J. (2016) 'Disability and Inclusive Health'. In Iriarte, E., McConkey, R. and Gilligan, R. (Eds.) *Disability and Human Rights: Global Perspectives*. London: Palgrave, 150–172.

WHO (World Health Organization) (2010b) *CBR Guidelines*. Geneva: WHO. Retrieved on 24 April 2017 from www.who.int/disabilities/cbr/guidelines/en/index.html

References

Albert, B., McBride, R. and Seddon, D. (2004) 'Perspectives on disability, poverty and technology'. *Asia Pacific Disability Rehabilitation Journal* 15(1), 12–21.

Amosun, S.L., Mutimura, E. and Frantz, J.M. (2005) 'Health promotion needs of physically disabled individuals with lower limb amputation in Rwanda'. *Disability and Rehabilitation* 27(14), 837–847.

Braathen, S., Munthali, A. and Grut, L. (2015) 'Explanatory models of disability: perspectives of health providers working in Malawi'. *Disability and Society* 30(9), 1382–1396.

Cobley, D.S. (2012) 'Towards economic empowerment: segregation versus inclusion in the Kenyan context.' *Disability and Society* 27(3), 371–384.

Connolly, B.H. (2006) 'Issues in aging in individuals with lifelong disabilities'. *Revista Brasiliera de Fisioterapia Sao Carlos* 10(3), 249–262.

Cornielje, H. and Tsengu, D. (2016) 'Equipping Professionals with Competencies to Better Support Persons with Disabilities'. In Iriarte, E., McConkey, R. and Gilligan, R. (Eds.) (2016) *Disability and Human Rights: Global Perspectives*. London: Palgrave, 246–258.

DFID (Department for International Development) (2000) *Disability, Poverty and Development*. London: DFID.

Drainoni, M.-L., Lee-Hood, E., Tobias, C. and Bachmann, S. (2006) 'Cross-disability experiences of barriers to health-care access; consumer perspectives'. *Journal of Disability Policy Studies* 17(2): 101–105, 107–115.

Elwan, A. (1999) *Poverty and Disability: A Survey of the Literature*. SP Discussion Paper No. 992 Washington, DC: World Bank.

Fiszbein, A. and Schady, N. (2009) *Conditional Cash Transfers: Reducing Present and Future Poverty*. Washington, DC: World Bank.

Gottret, P. and Schieber, G. (2006) *Health Financing Revisited: A Practitioners Guide*. Washington, DC: World Bank.

Grech, S. (2008) 'Living with disability in rural Guatemala: exploring connections and impacts on poverty'. *International Journal of Disability, Community and Rehabilitation* 7(2). Retrieved on 30 January 2017 from www.ijdcr.ca/VOL07_02_CAN/articles/grech.shtml

Hunt, J. (2011 *Situation Analysis of Disability Resources and Needs of Shantytowns Near Lima, Peru*. Student Publication. Dayton, Ohio: Wright State University. Retrieved on 2 June 2017 from http://corescholar.libraries.wright.edu/cgi/view-content.cgi?article=1054&context=mph

IDDC (International Disability and Development Consortium) (2004) *Inclusive Development and the UN Convention*. IDDC Reflection Paper. Retrieved on 30 March 2017 from www.un.org/esa/socdev/enable/rights/ahc3iddc.pdf

ILO, UNESCO and WHO (International Labour Organization, United Nations Educational, Scientific and Cultural Organization and the World Health Organization) (1994) *Community-Based Rehabilitation for and with People with Disabilities*. Joint Position Paper. Geneva: UN.

ILO, UNESCO and WHO (2004) *CBR A Strategy for Rehabilitation, Equalization of Opportunities, Poverty Reduction and Social Inclusion of People with Disabilities*. Joint Position Paper. Geneva: United Nations.

Ingstad, B. (2001) 'Disability in the Developing World'. In Albrect, G.L., Seelman, K. and Bury, M. (Eds.) *Handbook of Disability Studies*. London: Sage, 772–792.

Ingstad, B., Munthali, A., Braathen, S. and Grut, L. (2012) 'The evil circle of poverty: a qualitative study of malaria and disability'. *Malaria Journal* 11, 15.

Lang, R. (1999) 'Empowerment and CBR? Issues Raised by the South Indian Experience'. In Stone, E. (Ed.) *Disability and Development: Learning from Action and Research on Disability in the Majority World*. Leeds: The Disability Press, 130–148.

Lang, R., Kett, M., Groce, N. and Trani, J.F. (2011) 'Implementing the United Nations Convention on the Rights of Persons with Disabilities: principles, implications, practice and limitations'. *European Journal of Disability Research* 5(3), 206–220.

MacLachlan, P., Mannan, H. and McVeigh, J. (2016) 'Disability and Inclusive Health'. In Iriarte, E., McConkey, R. and Gilligan, R. (Eds.) *Disability and Human Rights: Global Perspectives*. London: Palgrave, 150–172.

McConkey, R. (2007) 'Community Based Services'. In Barron, T. and Amerena, P. (Eds.) *Disability and Inclusive Development*. London: Leonard Cheshire International, 21–68.

Metts, R. (2000) *Disability Issues, Trends and Recommendations for the World Bank*. World Bank. Social Protection Discussion Paper No. 0007. Washington, DC: World Bank.

Miles, S. (1999) *Strengthening Disability and Development Work*. BOND Discussion Paper.

Mont, D. (2010) 'Social Protection and Disability'. In Barron, T. and Ncube, J. (Eds.) *Poverty and Disability*. London: Leonard Cheshire International, 317–339.

Oliver, M. (1996) *Understanding Disability: From Theory to Practice*. Basingstoke: Macmillan.

Palmer, M. (2013) 'Social protection and disability: a call for action. *Oxford Development Studies* 41(2), 139–154.

Rehabilitation International (2007) *Final Technical Report: Raising the Voice of the African Decade of Disabled Persons: Phase II: Training Emerging Leaders in the Disability Community, Promoting Disability Rights and Developing HIV/AIDS Awareness and Prevention Programs for Adolescents and Young Adults with Disabilities in Africa*. New York, Rehabilitation International, 2007.

Rimmer, J.H. and Rowland, J.L. (2008) 'Health promotion for people with disabilities: implications for empowering the person and promoting disability-friendly environments.' *Journal of Lifestyle Medicine* 2(5), 409–420.

Sagli, G., Zhang, J., Ingstad, B. and Fjeld, H. (2013) 'Poverty and disabled households in the People's Republic of China: experiences with a new rural health insurance scheme'. *Disability and Society* 28(2), 218–213.

Schumacher, E.F. (1973) *Small Is Beautiful*. London: Blond and Briggs.

Shakespeare, T. (2014) *Disability Rights and Wrongs Revisited*. Second Edition. Abingdon: Routledge.

Siqueira, F.C., Facchini, L.A., da Silveira, D.S., Picchini, R.X., Thume, E. and Tomasi, E. (2009) 'Architectonic barriers for elderly and physically disabled people: an epidemiological study of health service units in seven Brazilian states.' *Ciencia and Saude Coletiva* 14(1), 39–44.

Steiner, W. Ryser, L., Huber, E., Uebelhart, D. Aeschlimann, A. and Stucki, G. (2002) 'Use of the ICF model as a clinical problem-solving tool in physical therapy and rehabilitation medicine. *Physical Therapy* 82(11), 1098–1107.

Tsengu, D., Brodtkorb, S. and Almdes, T. (2006) 'CBR and Economic Empowerment of Persons with Disabilities'. In Hartley, S. (Ed.) *CBR as Part of Community Development: A Poverty Reduction Strategy*. London: UCL, 49–63.

WHO (World Health Organization) (1948) *Constitution of the World Health Organization*. Geneva: WHO.

WHO (2001) *International Classification of Functioning, Disability and Health*. Geneva: WHO.

WHO (2002–04) *World Health Survey*. Geneva: WHO.

WHO (2005) *Guidelines for Training Personnel in Developing Countries for Prosthetics and Orthotics Services*. Geneva: WHO.

WHO (2010a) *The World Health Report – Health Systems Financing: The Path to Universal Coverage*. Geneva: WHO.

WHO (2010b) *CBR Guidelines*. Geneva: WHO. Retrieved on 24 April 2017 from www.who.int/disabilities/cbr/guidelines/en/index.html

WHO and SHIA (Swedish Organizations of Disabled Persons International Aid Association) (2002) *Part One. Community-based Rehabilitation as We Experienced It . . . Voices of Persons with Disabilities*. Geneva: WHO.

WHO and World Bank (2011) *World Report on Disability*. Geneva: WHO. Retrieved on 22 October 2016 from http://whqlibdoc.who.int/publications/2011/9789240685215_eng.pdf

World Bank (2009) *People with Disabilities in India: From Commitments to Outcomes*. Human Development Unit, South Asia Region. Washington, DC: World Bank.

7   Access to education

All children are entitled to an education, as stated in Article 26 of the 1948 Universal Declaration of Human Rights (United Nations, 1948). However, despite international commitments to the principles of Education for All (EFA) and Universal Primary Education (UPE), many disabled children are still not able to access this basic human right. Evidence of lower participation rates in education emerged from the *World Health Survey* (WHO, 2002–04), which showed that disabled children, on average, spend significantly less time in school than non-disabled children, across all age groups and in both low-income and high-income countries, with disabled girls at a particular disadvantage. A statistical analysis of data from this survey, relating to 15 low-income countries, identified a significant association between disability and lower educational attainment in 14 of them, more than for any other indicator of multi-dimensional poverty (Mitra *et al.*, 2012). In terms of the wider picture, it has been estimated that a staggering '90 per cent of children with disabilities in the developing world do not go to school' (UNICEF, 2014, p. 6). While such estimates should be treated with caution, given the widely reported lack of reliable data on disability in general, and on the educational status of disabled children in particular (UNESCO, 2014), the available evidence clearly suggests that far too many disabled children remain excluded from education. Furthermore, those who do attend school are often excluded from classrooms and are far less likely to complete primary education than their non-disabled peers (UNESCO, 2015b).

This chapter begins by exploring the linkages between disability, education and poverty, and then considers three strategic approaches to the education of disabled children: special education, integrated education and inclusive education. A brief summary of relevant international agreements, from the 1989 Convention on the Rights of the Child to the Sustainable Development Agenda, is then presented, with a focus on their implications for the education of disabled children. Finally, with governments and development agencies increasingly embracing the concept of inclusive education, the chapter concludes with a discussion around some of the challenges facing policy makers and practitioners, particularly in the Global South, as they attempt to put inclusive education into practice.

Disability, education and poverty

Without schooling, disabled children are at far greater risk of poverty in their adult lives, and will almost certainly become an economic burden on their families and communities (Filmer, 2008; Groce *et al.*, 2011). As well as boosting potential earnings, education can have a positive impact on virtually all other dimensions of poverty. Improvements in women's literacy, for example, have been shown to enhance the health and survival chances of both mothers and their children (Stubbs, 2008). Furthermore, education can bring wider benefits to society in general.

> ## The wider value of education
>
> While education is an ongoing process of improving knowledge and skills, it is also – perhaps primarily – an exceptional means of bringing about personal development and building relationships among individuals, groups and nations.
>
> (UNESCO, 1996, p. 12)

As this statement implies, education is not just about equipping children with knowledge and skills. It can also play an important role in developing their personal qualities and building their confidence to embrace opportunities and tackle the challenges that they will face in life. Education thus has the potential to transform the lives of disabled children by preparing them to live full and meaningful adult lives within mainstream society, rather than lives characterised by dependency and isolation. However, in the context of poverty, social exclusion and powerlessness, in which many disabled people live, education alone may not be sufficient to bring about this transformation. Interviews conducted with disabled people living in an impoverished district of rural Guatemala (Grech, 2014)[1] revealed that many of them tended to reject the notion that education would automatically lift them out of poverty, due to the existence of a range of discriminatory barriers that hinder the transition from education to work. Furthermore, while participants recognised the benefits of education, particularly in terms of its 'symbolic value in poor close-knit communities' (p. 142), they also highlighted the difficult choices that often had to be made when sending children to school might lead to a loss of household income, often vital for meeting basic needs.

While the relationship between disability and poverty is highly complex,[2] exclusion from education is certainly one of the key mechanisms through which this relationship is reinforced. However, as Grech's study illustrates, it is far too simplistic to assume that facilitating access to education, without simultaneously addressing issues such as stigma around disability, discriminatory practices (particularly in the employment sector) and inequitable resource distribution, will necessarily alleviate poverty among disabled people and their families.

Three strategic approaches

This section outlines three strategic approaches to meeting the educational needs of disabled children, illustrated by Figure 7.1, and discusses some of the advantages and disadvantages associated with each of them.

Special education

This traditional approach views the disabled child as having 'special needs', which cannot, or should not, be catered for within the mainstream system. Thus disabled children are educated in special schools or at home. This approach reflects an individual model perspective on disability,[3] because individual differences associated with disabled children are viewed as a justification for their segregation within the education system. For example, they may be viewed as slow learners or needing specialist equipment, or specially trained teachers, in order to make progress, or they may have mobility or communication needs which would create difficulties for them within mainstream schools that have not been designed to accommodate them.

The special education approach, which has effectively led to the creation of a parallel education system for disabled children, is often criticised for reinforcing the segregation of disabled people from a young age, and for labelling disabled children, either by their impairments or as 'special needs children' (Miles, 2007). In the United Kingdom (UK), the 1944 Education Act categorised children with 'special education needs (SEN)' according to their types of impairment, with some even labelled as 'uneducable' or 'educationally sub-normal', and established the entitlement of many disabled children to 'special educational treatment' in separate schools (HCESC, 2006). The

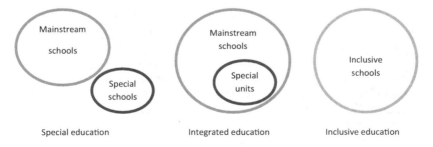

Figure 7.1 Three strategic approaches to school education

SEN concept was broadened following the release of the Warnock Report in 1978 to include children from poor and disadvantaged backgrounds, and the term is now generally understood as follows:

[handwritten: maybe be fix your school then :)]

Special educational needs

A child is commonly recognised as having special educational needs (SEN) if he or she is not able to benefit from the school education made generally available for children of the same age without additional support or adaptations in the content of studies.

(OECD, 2012, p. 1)

Internationally, it has been estimated that some 15–20 per cent of learners will have SEN at some point during the course of their education (OECD, 1999). It is important to emphasise, however, that not all children with SEN are disabled children, and that not all disabled children have SEN.

[handwritten: Classic hm]

The prevalence of special schools in many Northern countries has rapidly declined, as disabled children have increasingly been provided with the necessary support to enable them to attend mainstream schools. However, the special education model has been transferred to the Global South, where numerous special schools have been founded, particularly by colonial administrations and missionaries in the 1950s and 1960s (Kristensen *et al.*, 2006), with many remaining active today. These schools are often located in urban areas, whilst the majority of disabled people live in rural areas, so many of them are residential. This means, inevitably, that disabled children are frequently separated from their families and communities, at least during term-time, in order to attend. In many parts of the world, special schools continue to represent the dominant mechanism for meeting the educational needs of disabled children. For example, an analysis of special education services across 22 Arab countries of the Middle East and North Africa reveals that, despite many of these countries having ratified the Convention on the Rights of Persons with Disabilities (CRPD) and revised their educational policies to promote inclusive education, the segregation model remains 'the primary model used in the provision of special education services' (Hadidi and Khateeb, 2015, p. 520).

While special schools that continue to operate in high-income countries are often well resourced, with specialist facilities and teachers that are specially trained to work with disabled children, this is rarely the case in the Global South. While some receive donor funding, this is often time-limited and many special schools are poorly resourced once initial donor funding has stopped (Stubbs, 2008). This situation is only likely to get worse as Northern non-governmental organisations (NGOs) increasingly commit to the principle of mainstream inclusion, and many are now already 'extremely reluctant to fund segregated schools, vocational centres and residential facilities for people with disabilities' (LeFanu, 2014, p. 76).

The special education approach has received some criticism for its tendency to exert considerable pressure on children to achieve 'normal functioning', rather than accepting their physical and intellectual differences as a natural part of human diversity. As Stubbs (2008) points out, 'this can result in an inappropriate emphasis on making a child talk, or walk, when this is unrealistic and can cause undue pain' (p. 43). Oliver and Sapey (2006) go even further, referring to such practices as a form of emotional abuse, as they reinforce the notion that any form of impairment implies abnormality, rather than allowing disabled children the opportunity to form their own positive self-identities within a diverse society. They offer the example of deaf children that attend special schools that only allow lip reading, in order to conform to the hearing norms of society, thus denying them the opportunity to develop sign language skills that would enable them to 'become part of a linguistic culture' (p. 101).

Notwithstanding these criticisms, it should be noted that many disabled people's organisations (DPOs) continue to advocate for separate, specialist services, including special schools (Ainscow and Miles, 2008). In some cases, families may feel that their children will receive a higher quality and more specialised education in a segregated setting, particularly if mainstream schools are ill-equipped to meet the needs of disabled children. This was illustrated by research conducted in Botswana, for instance, which revealed that many families feel that sheltered environments, with smaller class sizes and specially trained teachers, offer a far more useful education than typically crowded mainstream classrooms, in which some parents fear that their children would be bullied by other children or even incur the wrath of their teachers for not being able to keep up in class (Ingstad, 2007).

While special schools may continue to play an important role in the education of disabled children, particularly in the Global South, for years to come, it seems inevitable that many will eventually close as mainstream systems gradually adapt and become more able to take account of diverse learning needs. However, the potential future role of special schools, in terms of filling the gaps in inclusive education and providing specialist support to inclusive schools, should not be ignored (Dyson, 2004). It is important to recognise that special schools are often a source of expertise and specialist knowledge, accumulated over many years, which can be a valuable source of support for disabled learners within the mainstream system, as well as helping to facilitate the changes that inclusive practice requires. They may be a valuable source of expertise in braille or sign language, for example, which mainstream schools could make use of in order to become more inclusive of children with visual or hearing impairments. In South Africa, the government has established an education structure that includes the 'special school as resource centre', offering 'on-site support for students with high-level learning needs, as well as providing support to neighbouring schools and communities' (Muthukrishna *et al.*, 2016, p. 139). A similar

not all
bad

approach has been implemented in South Korea, where the government has selected at least one special school in each district to partner a mainstream school, in order to promote inclusion (Kwon, 2005).

Integrated education

Integrated education, sometimes referred to as 'mainstreaming', involves supporting disabled children within mainstream schools, either through the provision of specialist support within mainstream classes or by setting up special classrooms or units within mainstream schools. This approach recognises that disabled children have a right to participate in mainstream education alongside their non-disabled peers. However, the focus remains on supporting the individual child within a system that is not designed to include them, rather than making fundamental changes to the system itself to make it more inclusive. As with special education, therefore, this approach tends to reflect an individual model perspective on disability, where the child, rather than the system, is seen as the problem that needs to be addressed. Kisanji (1998) raises this issue, describing the integration of disabled children as a 'process of consciously ignoring their specific learning needs and fitting them into existing educational structures and processes with cosmetic or no modification in an attempt to make them "normal"' (p. 65). A further criticism of the integrated approach is that it does not tend to foster 'team teaching', in that it reinforces the notion that disabled children can only be taught by 'special' teachers using 'special techniques', rather than encouraging teachers to work together to meet the learning needs of all children (Stubbs, 2008).

While integrated education may be viewed as similar to special education in terms of reinforcing segregation, there are also significant differences. Integration does aim to facilitate some socialisation between disabled children and their non-disabled peers, thus promoting social integration and perhaps moving a step towards full inclusion, while ensuring that disabled children can still learn at their own pace and receive the specialist support that they require. In resource-poor settings, however, special units often lack the specialist resources that teachers may have been trained to use, and they may sometimes be dependent on the support of parents, volunteers or older children. Nevertheless, a study of special units attached to mainstream schools in the Bushenyi district of Uganda (Miles *et al.*, 2011) identifies several advantages of the integrated approach over special schools, including reduced travelling time for children, due to wider coverage, and greater levels of engagement with parents and the local community.

Inclusive education

Inclusive education recognises that *all* children have a basic right to fully participate in mainstream education, irrespective of their individual differences and needs, and can be defined as follows:

Definition of inclusive education

> Inclusion is seen as a process of addressing and responding to the diversity of needs of all learners through increasing participation in learning, cultures and communities, and reducing exclusion within and from education. It involves changes and modifications in content, approaches, structures and strategies, with a common vision which covers all children of the appropriate age range and a conviction that it is the responsibility of the regular system to educate all children.
>
> (UNESCO, 2004a, pp. 12–13)

It is important to emphasise that inclusive education is not just about disability. It is about including all children, regardless of social differences. Children may be excluded from schooling, for example, on the basis of language, gender, ethnicity and economic circumstances, as well as disability. In fact inclusive education is sometimes viewed as part of a wider movement towards tackling the social exclusion of those children 'on the margins of society' (DFID, 2000, p. 12). For inclusion to work effectively, education systems need to be adapted in order to ensure that they meet the needs of all children and enable them to reach their educational potential. It is essential that all within the school environment, including pupils, teachers and administrators, buy into this principle, often requiring a fundamental change in ways of thinking that is unlikely to be achieved overnight. Developing fully inclusive schools may sometimes require a lengthy and ongoing process of sensitisation, which 'aims to enable both teachers and learners to feel comfortable with diversity and to see it as a challenge and enrichment in the learning environment, rather than a problem' (UNESCO, 2003, p. 7).

Box 7.1   Three-point justification for inclusive education

- There is an *educational justification*; the requirement for inclusive schools to educate all children together means that they have to develop ways of teaching which respond to individual differences and therefore benefit *all* children.
- There is a *social justification*; inclusive schools are able to change attitudes to difference by educating all children together, thereby forming the basis for a just and non-discriminatory society which encourages people to live together in peace.

(continued)

(continued)

- There is an *economic justification*; it is likely to be less costly to establish and maintain schools which educate all children together than to set up a complex system of different types of schools specialising in the education of specific groups of children. Inclusive schools offering an effective education to all of their students are a more *cost-effective* means of delivering Education for All.

Source: UNESCO, 2001, p. 20

The United Nations Educational, Scientific and Cultural Organisation (UNESCO) has strongly advocated for the worldwide adoption of inclusive education in a series of 'open file' documents, one of which presents the three-point justification shown in Box 7.1. Despite this strong case for inclusion, however, many disabled children continue to be educated in segregated or integrated environments. In fact, no country has a fully inclusive education system (WHO and World Bank, 2011).

Reflection exercise 7.1

Define 'inclusion' in your own words. Then think of a school, adult educational institution, workplace or other organisation that you are familiar with. To what extent does this institution or organisation reflect your definition? What changes could be made within this institution or organisation to make it more inclusive?

International agreements on disability and education

The agreements covered in this section have played a key role in encouraging governments and development agencies to reach out to all those children that are excluded from the education system, estimated to number around 58 million at primary school level and 63 million at lower secondary level (UIS, 2015). They have particular relevance for the disability sector, given that disability is one of the primary (and often neglected) causes of educational exclusion (UNESCO, 2013).

Convention on the Rights of the Child (CRC) 1989

The CRC (United Nations, 1989), which entered into force in September 1990, reinforces the rights of all children, irrespective of impairment or disability, to free primary education, which should develop each child's personalities, talents and abilities to the fullest (Article 29). Article 23 is particularly relevant, emphasising the need to 'ensure that the disabled child has effective access to and receives education, training, health care services, rehabilitation services, preparation for employment and recreation opportunities in a manner conducive to the child's achieving the fullest possible social integration and individual development' (Paragraph 3). Article 23 also recognises that, in order to achieve these objectives, disabled children may need 'special care' (Paragraph 2), which could be interpreted as recognition of the role of special education.

Jomtien Conference, 1990

This conference in Thailand, involving national governments, civil society groups, UNESCO and the World Bank, was the launching pad for an initiative known as 'Education for All' (EFA). The conference recognised that educational opportunities were limited for some children, while others were excluded altogether. In particular, the exclusion of girls, as well as other marginalised groups, was highlighted. The principles underpinning EFA, which was the internationally agreed response to this problem, are set out in the World Declaration on Education for All (UNESCO, 1990), which proclaims that 'every person – child, youth, adult – shall be able to benefit from educational opportunities designed to meet their basic learning needs' (Article 1(1)). The declaration also includes a commitment to reducing educational disparities and makes special mention of disability:

EFA and disability

> The learning needs of the disabled demand special attention. Steps need to be taken to provide equal access to education to every category of disabled persons as an integral part of the education system.
>
> (UNESCO, 1990, Article 3(5))

Salamanca Conference, 1994

The aim of this world conference was to further the objectives of EFA. The resulting *Salamanca Statement on Principles, Policy and Practice in Special Needs Education* (UNESCO, 1994) was instrumental in raising the profile of inclusive education within international development discourse, calling on governments to 'adopt as a matter of law or policy the principle of inclusive education, enrolling all children in regular schools, unless there are compelling reasons for doing otherwise' (Section 3). It was envisaged that regular schools would rise to this challenge by developing systems and child-centred teaching strategies aimed at meeting the diverse needs of children. One impact of the Salamanca Statement is that those involved in organising and delivering education have been encouraged to view changes made in order to meet the needs of those experiencing educational difficulties as potentially beneficial to all children, and therefore a stimulus to the development of richer and more child-friendly learning environments (Miles, 2007).

Millennium Development Goals (MDGs), 2000

The Millennium Declaration (United Nations, 2000) included the goal of achieving UPE by 2015,[4] so that 'children everywhere, boys and girls alike, will be able to complete a full course of primary schooling' (MDG Number Two). Although the MDGs make no mention of disability, it is now widely recognised that the goal of UPE cannot be achieved without taking steps to address the exclusion of disabled children from schooling.

World Education Forum for Action, Dakar, 2000

Also in 2000, the World Education Forum in Dakar reviewed progress on achieving EFA. This led to the release of the Dakar Framework for Action (UNESCO, 2000). While recognising 'significant progress' towards achieving EFA in many countries, the Framework noted that 113 million children still had no access to primary education. In order to address this, a set of new targets, compatible with the MDGs, was identified to accelerate progress towards the full achievement of EFA. There was no specific mention of disability, however, although it has since been estimated that 40 million of the 113 million excluded children were disabled children (Guernsey et al., 2006). Strategies identified for achieving the targets included national action plans on EFA, developing participatory and accountable school governance systems, enhancing the status of teachers and creating more inclusive and equitably resourced learning environments.

EFA Flagship on the Right to Education for Persons with Disabilities, 2004

The EFA Flagship (UNESCO, 2004b), developed by UNESCO in collaboration with international disability organisations, represented an attempt to address the lack of specific reference to the needs of disabled children in the Dakar Framework. This document stressed that the targets set out in the Framework could only be achieved if EFA was extended to disabled people. This would involve ensuring that public education systems were fully accessible and geared to meeting the needs of disabled children and adults.

Convention on the Rights of Persons with Disabilities, 2006

The CRPD calls on governments to 'ensure an inclusive education system at all levels' (United Nations, 2006, Article 24, Paragraph 1), clearly implying that education should be delivered to disabled children within fully inclusive mainstream schools. Article 24 also recognises that disabled children may require extra support, in order to benefit fully from inclusive education, calling on governments to ensure that 'effective individualised support measures are provided in environments that maximise academic and social development, consistent with the goal of full inclusion' (Paragraph 2(e)). Such measures could include the use of alternative communication systems, such as braille and sign language, and Article 24 goes on to emphasise the importance of ensuring that education is delivered in the 'most appropriate languages and modes and means of communication for the individual' (Paragraph 3(c)). Interestingly, this point could be used to support the argument that special schools may be more likely to offer an environment that maximises academic and social development, particularly for children with visual and hearing impairments, than mainstream schools. The World Federation for the Deaf (WFD) has advocated for special schools on this basis, pointing out that if deaf children are placed in regular schools, where many children and staff cannot use sign language, they are likely to be 'physically present but mentally and socially absent' (WFD, 2007, p. iii).

Sustainable Development Agenda

This new development framework (United Nations, 2015), built around the Sustainable Development Goals (SDGs), promises to 'leave no one behind'. Recognising that disabled people are among those that have frequently been left behind by development processes, the Agenda makes several references to disability,[5] which is treated as a cross-cutting issue. SDG Four is of particular relevance here, calling on governments to 'ensure inclusive and equitable quality education and promote lifelong learning opportunities for all'. As with all of the SDGs, this goal is accompanied by a set of targets, including the commitment to 'build and upgrade education facilities that are child, disability and gender sensitive and provide safe, non-violent, inclusive and effective learning environments for all' (Target 4a).

  With the SDGs likely to exert a strong influence on international development priorities until 2030, there is now a clear mandate in place to support the implementation of inclusive education across the globe. The next section focuses on this implementation process.

Inclusive education in practice

The task of effectively implementing inclusive education is far from straightforward, especially in resource-poor settings of the Global South. This section examines some of the common challenges that arise in four areas – accessibility, resources, teaching approaches and attitudes – and considers various strategies that may help to address these challenges.

School accessibility

Schools are not always fully accessible to disabled children. A lack of handrails and inadequate lighting or signage may create barriers for children with visual impairments, poor acoustics may disadvantage children with hearing impairments, while those with mobility impairments may have problems moving around the school and making use of facilities. Disabled children may also encounter significant barriers in getting to school, such as inaccessible or costly transport and uneven terrain. Disabled girls, in particular, are often at risk of exclusion due to fears for their safety when travelling unaccompanied over long distances or on public transport (WHO and World Bank, 2011).

Creating a learning environment that is welcoming, accessible and safe, as well as facilitating effective learning for disabled children, is vital to the success of inclusive education. Some improvements can be made to the physical accessibility of schools without incurring huge costs. For example, sensory indicators and colour contrasting can make the school environment safer and easier to navigate for children with visual impairments. The physical layout of classrooms can easily be changed to allow disabled children to participate as fully as possible in classroom activities. Children with mobility impairments, for example, may need extra space around them to allow them to move freely. It is also important to create a welcoming atmosphere, within the classroom, which encourages children to learn at their own pace and responds flexibly to individual needs. Large, noisy classes can present challenges to children with sensory or intellectual impairments, which may be reduced by allowing them to sit close to the teacher, or pairing them up with other children (or classroom assistants, where they are available) who can support them during lessons.

School resources

In many countries, class sizes tend to be very large, while resources to facilitate meaningful inclusion may not always be available. When UPE was first introduced in Uganda, for example, many schools were overwhelmed by a large influx of previously excluded children, including disabled children (Afako *et al.*, 2002). This reportedly had a negative impact on all students, leading to discipline problems and higher drop-out rates. More recently, UNESCO (2015) reports that pupil-to-teacher ratios are higher than 100 to one in certain countries, such as Guinea Bissau, Central African Republic and South Sudan. A lack of resources, such as school facilities, qualified teachers and learning materials, can make it very difficult to meet the diverse needs of all learners, a fundamental requirement for inclusive schools. In Tanzania, for example, where considerable progress has been made in terms of establishing inclusive primary schools, Opini and Onditi (2016) observe a 'lack of resources and support that is currently plaguing inclusive schools and affecting the quality of education students with disabilities receive' (p. 73). Teachers may not have the time, resources or skills necessary to provide the additional support that many disabled children need, especially when classrooms are overcrowded. However, strong community involvement and positive attitudes can help to compensate for resource constraints to some extent, as illustrated by Case Study 7.1.

Case study 7.1   Early years education in Dharavi, Mumbai

In Dharavi, India's largest informal settlement located on the outskirts of Mumbai, the National Resource Centre for Inclusion and UNICEF implemented a project to provide pre-school education to disadvantaged children, many of whom had previously been excluded from government education initiatives. The project reached more than 1,200 children in its first three years, including many disabled children, enabling them to follow an established early childhood curriculum, including personal hygiene, nutrition and English.

The first pilot project enrolled 432 children, including 43 disabled children, and employed local women, as well as involving community workers, helpers and parents. Research had established that many parents had previously opposed the inclusion of disabled children, so parent education sessions and focus groups were held to disseminate information and gauge changing attitudes. The pilot project also adopted an ecological curriculum, making use of teaching resources that had been creatively produced from recycled materials, such as plastic bottles, empty boxes and old clothes, with the help of volunteers and parents. The scheme was successful both in terms of enrolling disabled children, who showed more developmental progress than non-disabled children during the first six months of the project, and in terms of promoting more positive attitudes towards disability and inclusion within their own households and their deeply impoverished local communities.

Source: Adapted from Reiser, 2008

Another innovative strategy is the use of itinerant teachers, who can sometimes provide a cost-effective means of addressing teacher shortages and providing additional support to disabled children in areas such as communication, orientation and mobility. In Kenya, for example, itinerant teachers have played a crucial and wide-ranging role in promoting inclusive educational practices for children with visual impairment, providing regular visits to check on their progress within inclusive classrooms and supporting their transition from primary to secondary school, as well taking on a pastoral role, sometimes mediating between schools and families to resolve issues such as unpaid fees (Lynch *et al.*, 2011).

There is clearly a need for adequate funding to support the implementation of inclusive education, particularly in the Global South. The *World Report on Disability* (WHO and World Bank, 2011) acknowledges this, calling for funding mechanisms that are easy to understand, flexible, predictable and cost based. According to UNESCO (2003), inclusive education is most likely to succeed when school funding is decentralised, with budgets delegated to local authorities and funds allocated on the basis of performance indicators (such as enrolment figures). Funding can also sometimes be leveraged through collaborations with donor agencies. Schuelka and Johnstone (2012)[6] provide examples of North–South and South–South collaborations that have supported successful inclusive education initiatives in the Global South, while emphasising the importance of ensuring that such collaborations facilitate local decision making and empowerment.

Rigid teaching curricula and methods

Curricula and teaching methods are sometimes too rigid to meet the diverse needs of all children. Disabled children may be particularly disadvantaged where teaching materials have not been provided in alternative formats, such as braille or large print. Reports from several countries that participated in the Global Initiative on Out-of-School Children, launched by UNICEF and UNESCO Institute for Statistics (UIS) in 2010, revealed that school programmes and teaching materials were rarely adapted to meet the needs of disabled learners, and that teachers often received little or no training on inclusive teaching methods (UIS, 2015). Assessment methods may also be too rigid, focusing on academic performance rather than valuing the progress made by individual learners. In Uganda, for example, a study of three inclusive schools found too much emphasis on formal examinations and little evidence of adaptation for children with intellectual and hearing impairments enrolled at the schools, with some teachers showing 'little concern about different needs in their classes and negative opinions about children with disabilities' (Arbeiter and Hartley, 2010, p. 74). The *World Report on Disability* (WHO and World Bank, 2011) calls for individualised learning plans and greater use of information and communication technology, such as screen readers and braille, in order to create optimum learning environments for all children.

One innovative child-centred teaching strategy that has been adopted in many countries, particularly in the Global South, is the child-to-child approach. This strategy, developed in the 1970s by a group of health and education professionals, involves engaging children on health and social issues and encouraging them to disseminate their learning to other children, their families and the wider community. Child-to-child strategies have the potential to enrich the lives of disabled children, who are often socially isolated within their families and communities, by encouraging them to play and learn with their non-disabled peers and to share their learning with others, thus building their capacity to communicate, socialise and empathise. Activities can take place both inside and outside of the school environment, and may include informal sports or music groups, playgroups and summer camps. More focused child-to child strategies may include peer tutoring, twining (of a disabled and non-disabled child), community-based surveys and advocacy groups. While approaches may vary, the common aim is to encourage children to support each other, understand each other better and work together to share their knowledge. This can help to overcome social barriers between disabled and non-disabled children, as well as promoting positive attitudes to disability within the wider community. Case Study 7.2 provides an example of the child-to-child approach from Zambia.[7]

Case study 7.2   Child-to-child approach in Mpika, Zambia

In Mpika, Zambia, there is a very strong history of teachers communicating health education messages through child-to-child methods, and of the activities being incorporated into maths, English, geography and social studies lessons. In the mid-1990s they began to use the same methods to explore community attitudes to disability. School children were asked to conduct a community survey to identify those children who were 'out of school', and to find out why they stayed at home. This was very successful in raising awareness and in including children in school who would otherwise have remained at home. It was also a very effective way of encouraging the parents of some of the children to reduce their domestic workloads to enable them to attend school. A project was then developed to break down the social barriers which existed between the children being educated in the special unit and those in the main school. The focus was on developing friendships, travelling to school together, home visits at weekends, providing support with academic work etc.

Source: Miles, 2007, p. 85

Practical guidance on how to adopt child-centred approaches, in order to promote high quality inclusive education, can be found in UNICEF's (2009) *Child Friendly Schools Manual*.[8] This comprehensive guide promotes a rights-based, participatory approach and considers the 'whole child', taking into account their whole range of needs, including health and nutritional needs. The manual also argues that schools should promote the active involvement of the community, parents and children and proactively seek to identify and enrol excluded children.

Discriminatory attitudes

Disabled children are sometimes kept from attending school due to stigma and negative attitudes around disability, including the common misconception that it is not worth educating them because they are not capable of achieving anything worthwhile. Country reports on the 'Global Initiative on Out-of-School Children' have identified negative attitudes, such as the belief that disability is a punishment for past misdemeanours, often internalised by the parents of disabled children, as a 'major factor in whether children enrol or fail to complete their education' (UIS, 2015, p. 79). Those disabled children that do attend school may encounter discriminatory attitudes and a lack of disability awareness within classrooms, as highlighted by the mother of a ten-year-old boy with low vision who was attending an inclusive school in the Samar Province of the Central Philippines:

Lack of disability awareness in the classroom

He is made to sit at the back of the classroom, despite his sight problem, and he is sometimes bullied by the other children. His younger sister is in the same class and helps him with his work. If she is unwell, I keep them both at home.

(Cobley, 2015, p. 697)

Teacher attitudes are particularly crucial to ensuring that disabled children stay in school and are included in classroom activities, but some may feel that they should not be obliged to teach disabled children. In Zambia, for example, some teachers believe that conditions such as albinism are contagious (Miles, 2009).

Eliminating such misconceptions and raising disability awareness among school children and professional staff, as well as the wider community, is crucial to the successful implementation of inclusive education. The awareness-raising campaign that was incorporated into the early years education project in Mumbai (see Case Study 7.1) was of great importance in helping to ensure that community volunteers and parents fully understood the concept of inclusive education and recognised its potential benefits to their children. This enabled the project team to draw on their willingness to support the implementation of inclusive education, which they might otherwise have opposed. The UK Department for International Development (DFID) (2010, p. 11) recognises the key role that parents and communities can play, arguing that;

> a sustained and targeted awareness campaign can increase understanding that education is a basic human right, not only to encourage parents to send their children with disabilities to school, but to make the wider community aware that such children should attend school, and should be part of mainstream classes.

DPOs can play an important role in such campaigns, helping to challenge negative attitudes within communities and explaining the potential benefits of inclusive education, as they are often uniquely positioned to make contact with the parents of disabled children and to gain their trust.

Reflection exercise 7.2

Imagine that you are a teacher working at an inclusive primary school in a rural region of a low-income country. There are 60 children in your classroom between the ages of seven and ten.

A new child named Alice, who has cerebral palsy and low vision, has just been enrolled. Alice uses crutches and needs extra time and space for movement. She enjoys singing and drama, but often shuns affection and dislikes being touched.

Write down a list of the barriers to effective learning that Alice might encounter within your classroom. Then list the various types of preparation that you could make in order to help Alice to settle into the class.

Summary of key points

- Access to education is a basic human right and vital to the well-being of disabled children. Education can develop skills, knowledge and confidence in disabled people, preparing them for full participation in society and reducing the risk of them falling into long-term poverty.
- The special education approach, still dominant in many parts of the world, views disabled children as having 'special needs' and involves the segregated provision of education within special schools or at home.

- Integrated education involves supporting disabled children within regular schools, either within mainstream classes or separate on-site units. The onus remains on the individual child to adapt, rather than on the whole education system to become more flexible and responsive to the needs of all children.
- Inclusive education involves making changes to the whole school environment, including buildings, equipment, curricula, teaching methods and attitudes, in order to enable it to respond to the needs of all learners.
- A series of international agreements have reinforced the rights of all children to an education, introduced the EFA and UPE initiatives and increasingly advocated in favour of inclusive education.
- A wide range of challenges around the physical accessibility of schools, inadequate resources, rigid teaching approaches and discriminatory attitudes can hinder the effective implementation of inclusive education, particularly within resource-poor settings. Innovative strategies, such as making simple, low-cost accessibility improvements within schools, encouraging children to support each other and harnessing potential support within the local community, can help schools to rise to these challenges.

Discussion questions

1   How might local contextual factors, such as cultural beliefs, influence the implementation of inclusive education?
2   How might you support a family that was reluctant to send their disabled child to school?
3   How can inclusive schools make best use of the specialist knowledge and skills that can often be found within special schools?

Notes

1 See Suggested further reading.
2 See Chapter 3 for further discussion on the relationship between poverty and disability.
3 See Chapter 2 for an explanation of the individual model.
4 See Chapter 4 for a full list of the MDGs.
5 See Table 4.2, Chapter 4, for a full list of these explicit references.
6 See Suggested further reading.
7 Further information about Child-to-Child is available from www.childtochild.org.
8 See Suggested further reading.

Suggested further reading

Grech, S. (2014) 'Disability, poverty and education: perceived barriers and (dis)connections in rural Guatemala'. *Disability and the Global South* 1(1), 128–152.
Schuelka, M. and Johnestone, C. (2012) 'Global trends in meeting the educational rights of children with disabilities: from international institutions to local

responses'. *Reconsidering Development* 2(2). Retrieved on 22 November 2016 from http://pubs.lib.umn.edu/cgi/viewcontent.cgi?article=1009&context=recon sidering

UNICEF (United Nations Children's Fund) (2009) *Child Friendly Schools Manual*. New York: UNICEF. Retrieved on 13 November 2016 from www.unicef.org/ publications/files/Child_Friendly_Schools_Manual_EN_040809.pdf

References

Afako, R., Ojwang, P., Warimu, C. and Hartley, S. (2002) *Implementation of Inclusive Education in Uganda*. Based on collaborative research between the centre of International Child Health and the Uganda National Institute of Special Education. Paris: UNESCO.

Ainscow, M. and Miles, S. (2008) 'Making Education for All inclusive: where next. *Prospects* 38, 15–34.

Arbeiter, S. and Hartley, S. (2010) 'Teachers and pupils' experiences of integrated education in Uganda'. *International Journal of Disability, Development and Education* 49(1), 69–78.

Cobley, D.S. (2015) 'Typhoon Haiyan one year on: disability, poverty and participation in the Philippines'. *Disability and the Global South* 2(3), 686–707.

DFID (Department for International Development) (2000) *Disability, Poverty and Development*. London: DFID.

DFID (2010) *Guidance Note: Education for Children with Disabilities – Improving Access and Quality*. London: DFID.

Dyson, A. (2004) 'Inclusive education: a global agenda?'. *Japanese Journal of Special Education* 41(6), 613–625.

Filmer, D. (2008) 'Disability, poverty and schooling in developing countries: results from 14 household surveys'. *The World Bank Economic Review* 22(1), 141–163.

Grech, S. (2014) 'Disability, poverty and education: perceived barriers and (dis)connections in rural Guatemala'. *Disability and the Global South* 1(1), 128–152.

Groce, N., Kembhavi, G., Wirz, S., Lang, R., Trani, J.-F. and Kett, M. (2011) *Poverty and Disability: A Critical Review of the Literature in Low and Middle Income Countries*. London: Leonard Cheshire Disability. Retrieved on 22 December 2016 from www.ucl.ac.uk/lc-ccr/centrepublications/workingpapers/ WP16_Poverty_and_Disability_review.pdf

Guernsey, K., Nicoli, M. and Ninio, A. (2006) *Making Inclusion Operational*. Washington, DC: World Bank.

Hadidi, M. and Khateeb, J. (2015) 'Special education in Arab countries: current challenges. *International Journal of Disability, Education and Development* 62 (5), 518–530.

HCESC (House of Commons Education and Skills Committee) (2006) *Special Educational Needs*. Third Report of Session 2005–06, Volume 1. Retrieved on 10 November 2016 from www.publications.parliament.uk/pa/cm200506/ cmselect/cmeduski/478/478i.pdf

Ingstad, B. (2007) 'Seeing disability and human rights in the local context: Botswana revisited'. In Ingstad, B. and Whyte, S. (Eds.) *Disability in Local and Global Worlds*. Berkeley: University of California Press, 237–258.

Kisanji, J. (1998) 'The march towards inclusive education in non-Western countries: retracing the steps'. *International Journal of Inclusive Education* 2(1), 55–72.

Kristensen, K., Omagor-Loican, M., Onen, N. and Okot, D. (2006) 'Opportunities for inclusion? The education of learners with special educational needs and disabilities at special schools in Uganda'. *British Journal of Special Education* 33(3), 139–147.

Kwon, H. (2005) 'Inclusion in South Korea: the current situation and future directions'. *International Journal of Disability Development and Education* 52, 59–68.

LeFanu, G. (2014) 'International development, disability and education: towards a capabilities-focused discourse and praxis'. *International Journal of Education Development* 38, 69–79.

Lynch, P., McCall, S., Douglas, G. and Njoroge, M. (2011) 'Inclusive educational practices in Kenya: evidencing practice of itinerant teachers who work with children with visual impairment in local mainstream schools'. *International Journal of Educational Development* 31(5), 478–488.

Miles, S. (2007) 'Inclusive Education'. In Barron, T. and Amerena, P. (Eds). *Disability and Inclusive Development*. London: Leonard Cheshire International, 21–68.

Miles, S. (2009) 'Engaging with teachers' knowledge: promoting inclusion in Zambian schools'. *Disability and Society* 24(5), 611–624.

Miles, S., Beart, J. and Wapling, L (2011) 'Including deaf children in primary schools in Bushenyi, Uganda: a community-based initiative'. *Third World Quarterly* 32(8), 1467–1477.

Mitra, S., Posarac, A. and Vick, B. (2012) *Disability and Poverty in Developing Countries: A Multidimensional Study*. Washington, DC: World Bank. Retrieved on 17 March 2017 from www.addc.org.au/documents/resources/disability-and-poverty-in-developing-countries-a-multidimensional-study_578.pdf

Muthukrishna, N., Morojele, P., Naidoo, J. and D'amant, A. (2016) 'Access to education: experiences from South Africa'. In Iriarte, E., McConkey, R. and Gilligan, R. (Eds.) (2016) *Disability and Human Rights: Global Perspectives*. London: Palgrave, 133–149.

OECD (Organisation for Economic Co-operation and Development) (1999) *Inclusive Education at Work: Students with Disabilities in Mainstream Schools*. Paris: OECD.

OECD (2012) *CX3.1 Special Educational Needs (SEN)*. Paris: OECD. Retrieved on 23 June 2017 from www.oecd.org/els/family/50325299.pdf

Oliver, M. and Sapey, R. (2006) *Social Work with Disabled People*. Third Edition. Basingstoke: Macmillan.

Opini, B. and Onditi, H. (2016). 'Education for All and students with disabilities in Tanzanian primary schools: challenges and successes'. *International Journal of Educational Studies* 3(2), 65–76.

Reiser, R. (2008) *Implementing Inclusive Education: A Commonwealth Guide to Implementing Article 24 of the UN Convention on the Rights of People with Disabilities*. London: Commonwealth Secretariat.

Schuelka, M. and Johnstone, C. (2012) 'Global trends in meeting the educational rights of children with disabilities: from international institutions to local responses'. *Reconsidering Development* 2(2). Retrieved on 22 November 2016 from http://pubs.lib.umn.edu/cgi/viewcontent.cgi?article=1009&context=reconsidering

Stubbs, S. (2008) *Inclusive Education: Where There Are Few Resources*. Oslo: The Atlas Alliance.

UIS (UNESCO Institute for Statistics) (2015) *Fixing the Broken Promise of Education for All: Findings from the Global Initiative on Out-of-School Children*. Montreal: UNESCO Institute for Statistics.

UNESCO (United Nations Educational, Scientific and Cultural Organization) (1990) *World Declaration on Education for All and Framework for Action to meet Basic Learning Needs: Meeting Basic Learning Needs*. Adopted by the World Conference on Education for All in Jomtien, Thailand, 5–9 March, 1990. Paris: UNESCO.

UNESCO (1994) *The Salamanca Statement and Framework for Action on Special Needs Education*. Adopted by the World Conference on Special Needs Education, Access and Quality in Salamanca, Spain, 7–10 June, 1994. Paris: UNESCO.

UNESCO (1996) *Learning: The Treasure Within*. Report to UNESCO of the International Commission on Education for the twenty-first century. Paris: UNESCO.

UNESCO (2000) *The Dakar Framework for Action*. Adopted by the World Education Forum, Dakar, Senegal, 26–28 April, 2000. Paris: UNESCO.

UNESCO (2001) *Open File on Inclusive Education: Support Materials for Managers and Administrators*. Paris: UNESCO.

UNESCO (2003) *Overcoming Exclusion through Inclusive Approaches in Education: A Challenge and a Vision*. Paris: UNESCO.

UNESCO (2004a) 'An inclusive approach to EFA: UNESCO's role'. *Enabling Education* Issue 8. Manchester: EENET.

UNESCO (2004b) *The Right to Education for Persons with Disabilities: Towards Inclusion*. Retrieved on 29 March 2017 from http://unesdoc.unesco.org/images/0013/001378/137873e.pdf

UNESCO (2013) *Teaching and Learning: Achieving Equality for All*. EFA Global Monitoring Report 2013/14. Paris: UNESCO.

UNESCO (2014) *EFA Global Monitoring Repor – Teaching and Learning: Achieving Equality for All*. Paris: UNESCO.

UNESCO (2015) *Education for All 2000–2015: Achievements and Challenges*. EFA Global Monitoring Report 2015. Paris: UNESCO.

UNICEF (United Nations Children's Fund) (2009) *Child Friendly Schools Manual*. New York: UNICEF. Retrieved on 13 November 2016 from www.unicef.org/publications/files/Child_Friendly_Schools_Manual_EN_040809.pdf

UNICEF (2014) *Global Initiative on Out-of-School Children: South Asia Regional Study*. Kathmandu, Nepal: UNICEF. Retrieved on 10 January 2017 from www.unicef.org/education/files/SouthAsia_OOSCI_Study__Executive_Summary_26Jan_14Final.pdf

United Nations (1948) *Universal Declaration of Human Rights*. Retrieved on 28 January 2017 from www.un.org/en/documents/udhr/

United Nations (1989) *Convention on the Rights of the Child*. Retrieved on 22 February 2017 from https://downloads.unicef.org.uk/wp-content/uploads/2010/05/UNCRC_united_nations_convention_on_the_rights_of_the_child.pdf

United Nations (2000) *Millennium Declaration*. Retrieved on 13 February 2017 from www.un.org/millennium/declaration/ares552e.htm

United Nations (2006) *Convention on the Rights of Persons with Disabilities and Optional Protocol*. Washington, DC: United Nations.

United Nations (2015) *Transforming Our World: The 2030 Agenda for Sustainable Development*. Retrieved on 21 March 2017 from www.un.org/pga/wp-content/

uploads/sites/3/2015/08/120815_outcome-document-of-Summit-for-adoption-of-the-post-2015-development-agenda.pdf

World Federation of the Deaf (2007) *Education Rights for Deaf Children: A Policy Statement of the World Federation of the Deaf*. Retrieved on 12 December 2016 from www.wfdeaf.org/wp-content/uploads/2011/03/EducationRightsforDeafChildren_July-2007.pdf

WHO (World Health Organization) (2002-04) *World Health Survey*. Geneva: WHO.

WHO and World Bank (2011) *World Report on Disability*. Geneva: WHO. Retrieved on 22 October 2016 from http://whqlibdoc.who.int/publications/2011/9789240685215_eng.pdf

8   Pathways to economic participation

Economic participation can play a crucial role in lifting people out of poverty, as well as boosting self-esteem and creating a sense of fulfilment and purpose in life. Due to the existence of a wide range of barriers to training and employment, however, disabled people are far less likely to be economically active than the general working-age population (WHO and World Bank, 2011). The removal of these barriers is vital to reducing the dependence of many disabled people on welfare benefits and their extended families, and to facilitating their participation in the economic mainstream, thus helping to foster more just and inclusive societies. In the words of the late Paul Abberley (1999), a highly influential disability activist and academic, the social exclusion of disabled people is 'intimately related to our exclusion from the world of work' (p. 5).

Increasing the economic participation of disabled people can also bring significant economic benefits to society as a whole. Disabled people represent a sizeable pool of labour which can be utilised to boost overall productivity. Furthermore, increased earnings enable disabled people to spend more, thus creating extra demand for goods and services produced by others (Powers, 2008). The overall economic impact may be even greater if family members are released from some of their caring responsibilities and able to return to the labour market themselves. A desk-based analysis by Buckup (2009) uses data on disability prevalence rates and employment rates from ten low and middle-income countries, across Asia and Africa, to show that economic losses resulting from the exclusion of disabled people from work ranged from 3 per cent of gross domestic product (GDP) in Malawi and Vietnam to 7 per cent of GDP in South Africa. These findings should be treated with some caution, given the questionable reliability of disability prevalence rates,[1] but they do provide some idea of the potentially significant macroeconomic costs of excluding disabled people from work.

This chapter first reviews a series of relevant international agreements, which clearly establish that disabled people have a right to economic participation on an equal basis with others. This is followed by a discussion around the various environmental factors that may determine the types of economic opportunities that are open to disabled people, within a given context, as well as influencing the extent to which they are able to take advantage of these opportunities. The remainder of the chapter draws on several case studies to examine three pathways to economic participation – vocational skills development, waged employment and self-directed employment.

Relevant international agreements

The international agreements discussed in this section reinforce the rights of disabled people to economic participation, as well as providing some guidance as to how governments can tackle discrimination in this area and support disabled people to be economically active.

ILO Employment (Transition from War to Peace) Recommendation No. 71, 1944

In 1944, the International Labour Organization (ILO) declared that 'Disabled workers, whatever the origin of their disability, should be provided with full opportunities for rehabilitation, specialised vocational guidance, training and retraining, and employment on useful work' (ILO, 1944, general principles (X)). This Recommendation, adopted at the end of the Second World War to promote employment creation during the transition from war to peace, goes on to stipulate that 'wherever possible, disabled workers should receive training in company with able-bodied workers, under the same conditions and same pay' (Article X, 42(1)), thus promoting the principles of inclusion and equality. The Recommendation also recognises the role of specialised training centres for 'those disabled persons who require such special training' (Article X, 42(5)).

ILO Recommendation No. 59, 1955

This Recommendation, which places a strong emphasis on vocational training and equal pay, builds on the provisions of Recommendation No. 71. There is recognition of the rights of all disabled people to vocational training, as long as they have 'reasonable prospects of securing and retaining suitable employment' (ILO, 1955, Article II(2)), and the processes involved in providing vocational training are set out in detail. While primarily promoting mainstream training and employment opportunities, the Recommendation acknowledges that specialist facilities, such as sheltered workshops, may also be needed. This agreement formed a basis for national legislation and practice, in relation to the training and employment of disabled people, for the following 30 years (O'Reilly, 2007).

ILO Convention No. 159, 1983

Prior to the Convention on the Rights of Persons with Disabilities (CRPD), this was perhaps the most significant international agreement in relation to disability and economic participation, presenting a new set of international standards aimed at promoting equality of opportunity and the integration of disabled people into mainstream employment. Convention No. 159 also introduced the idea of 'special positive measures', which 'shall not be regarded as discriminating against other workers' (ILO, 1983, Article 4). This was an important statement, as it paved the way for affirmative measures, such as quota schemes and incentives for employers to recruit disabled people, to be included in national policies, as they are in many countries today.

ILO Code of Practice for Managing Disability in the Workplace, 2001

In 2001, following consultations with governments, employers' organisations and workers' organisations, the ILO (2001) produced its Code of Practice for Managing Disability in the Workplace. The Code provides detailed guidance on a wide range of employment-related issues, such as recruitment processes, workplace accessibility and adjustments, provision of training opportunities, career development, communication and awareness raising. Guidance on workplace accessibility, for example, encompasses the provision of accessible toilets and washrooms, workplace instructions and equipment, as well as appropriate signage and emergency evacuation plans. While not a legally binding instrument, the Code serves as a good practice guide for employers throughout the world, supporting them to 'utilise the skills and potential of people with disabilities within existing national conditions' (Preface). While aimed primarily at employers, the Code was also intended to assist public sector agencies (in forming the necessary policies for promoting disability employment rights), workers' organisations (in representing the interests of disabled workers) and disabled people's organisations (DPOs) (in promoting employment opportunities for their members) (Section 1.3).

Convention on the Rights of Persons with Disabilities, 2006

Economic participation is an important theme of the CRPD. Article 27, entitled 'Work and Employment', recognises that disabled people should have 'the opportunity to gain a living by work freely chosen or accepted in a labour market and work environment that is open, inclusive and accessible to persons with disabilities' (United Nations, 2006, Paragraph 1). It goes on to outline several state responsibilities in this area, such as enabling disabled people to access vocational and continuing training, promoting self-employment and the development of cooperatives, employing disabled people in the public sector and promoting private sector employment opportunities. In relation to this last responsibility, Article 27 specifically calls for 'appropriate policies and measures, which may include affirmative action programmes, incentives and other measures' (Paragraph 1 (h)), thus reinforcing ILO Convention No. 159. While Article 27 is of most direct relevance, several other parts of the CRPD also emphasise the importance of economic participation. Article 28, for example, highlights the close relationship between poverty and disability,[2] recognising the rights of disabled people to 'an adequate standard of living for themselves and their families' (Paragraph 1), while Article 8, on awareness-raising, calls on State Parties 'to promote recognition of the skills, merits and abilities of persons with disabilities, and of their contributions to the workplace and the labour market' (Paragraph 2(a)).

Sustainable Development Agenda, 2015

This new agenda for action (United Nations, 2015), which is likely to dominate international development discourse for years to come, embraces the concept of decent work. This concept, which had previously been promoted in several documents produced by the ILO, is explained below:

Decent work

Decent work sums up the aspirations of people in their working lives. It involves opportunities for work that is productive and delivers a fair income, security in the workplace and social protection for families. Decent work means better prospects for personal development and social integration, and freedom for people to express their concerns, organise and participate in the decisions that affect their lives.

(ILO, 2007, p. 4)

Within the Sustainable Development Agenda, decent work is seen as crucial to the promotion of sustainable economic growth, poverty eradication and reducing the inequalities that often lead to disharmony and conflict in the world. The eighth Sustainable Development Goal (SDG), entitled 'Economic Growth and Decent Work', is accompanied by the following target, which recognises that disabled people are often denied decent work opportunities:

Sustainable Development Agenda, Target 8.5

By 2030, achieve full and productive employment and decent work for all women and men, including for young people and persons with disabilities, and equal pay for work of equal value.

The Sustainable Development Agenda is thus consistent with previous international agreements in framing the economic participation of disabled people as a rights issue, but perhaps goes further in emphasising the need for employers to treat disabled workers fairly, ensuring that they have reasonable working conditions, fair remuneration and the same career development opportunities as other employees.

Environmental factors

A wide range of environmental factors can potentially hinder or help to facilitate the economic participation of disabled people. These include, for example, the workings of local and national institutions, such as government authorities, the judiciary, financial institutions, the education system, the media and all organisations that employ people. Where these institutions and organisations work in ways that promote the economic inclusion of disabled people, they are likely to create opportunities, while discriminatory ways of working will create barriers. The media, for example, may promote economic inclusion by highlighting the achievements of disabled people who have enjoyed career success, thus helping to establish positive role models, or it may reinforce stigma by portraying disabled people as suffering victims. Employers may promote economic inclusion by establishing non-discriminatory recruitment procedures, making their workplaces accessible and recognising the career potential of disabled employees.

Social structures and processes can also exert a strong influence that may be negative or positive. Cultural and religious belief systems that foster negative perceptions of disabled people as needy recipients of charity typically fail to take account of their productive and creative capabilities. Such beliefs are often internalised by disabled people and their families, lowering their own expectations and leading to an 'accumulation of negative self-belief and lack of confidence that is inculcated from a lifetime of being denigrated' (Albu, 2005, p. 11). Conversely, a growing awareness of the social causes of disability in many countries has engendered more positive identities of disabled people as citizens with equal rights, thus highlighting the need to combat discrimination and provide opportunities for disabled people to fulfil their economic ambitions.

Characteristics of the local economy, including the types of products and services that are in demand and the skills needed to produce or supply them, as well as the types of jobs that are available and the skills or qualifications needed to perform them, will to some extent determine what kind of economic opportunities are open to disabled people. These characteristics are constantly changing, and opportunities often arise through new developments, such as the growth of new industries, the opening of new product markets or the creation of new services. Seasonal or temporary jobs may also provide short-term opportunities. One particularly important characteristic is the balance between the formal and informal sectors, concepts which are explained in Box 8.1.

Box 8.1 Formal and informal sectors

The formal sector of the economy consists of 'regular, stable, and protected employment and of legally regulated enterprises' (ILO, 2002a, p. 12). Formal enterprises may exist within the public and private sectors, with the public sector tending to dominate in most low-income countries, especially in Africa (Coleridge, 2006). Formal sector workers are usually entitled to certain benefits, such as a minimum wage, written contracts, pensions, paid holidays and trade union membership. In countries of the Global South, however, formal sector jobs are 'often more scarce and subject to intense competition' (Powers, 2008, p. 7).

The concept of an 'informal sector', which relates to small-scale, unregulated enterprises falling outside of the formal sector, was initially referred to in a research project (ILO, 1972) on the conditions facing poor workers in Kenya. The study concluded that the relative ease of entry, low capital costs, small scale of operation and absence of formal education skills, which typically characterise the informal sector, make this the most realistic choice for many poor people in low-income countries. The concept was broadened following the 2002 International Labour Conference (ILO, 2002b), during which an expanded conceptual framework was presented. This new understanding encompassed informal enterprises, as before, but also included informal employment *outside of* informal enterprises, such as domestic workers and temporary or casual workers.

While the idea of distinct formal and informal sectors is quite convenient conceptually, it is important to recognise that there are some grey areas and linkages between the two. Many formal sector jobs are low-waged, for example, and workers often move frequently between formal and informal jobs. A report by the ILO (2002c), entitled *Decent Work and the Informal Economy*, highlights the close relationship that often exists between the two sectors, concluding that 'formal and informal enterprises and workers coexist along a continuum, with decent work deficits most serious at the bottom end, but also existing in some formal jobs' (p. 4).

It is important to understand how the formal and informal sectors operate locally, in order to enable disabled people to take advantage of the economic opportunities that each sector may offer. Many economies of the Global South are characterised by strong informal sectors, particularly in terms of employment. One analysis, based on data from 185 countries, concludes that 'the informal sector accounts for 30–40 per cent of total economic activity in the poorest countries, and a higher share of employment. This falls to something closer to 15 or 20 per cent in the richest quartile countries' (La Porta and Shleifer, 2014, p. 111). Where a large informal sector exists, it is likely to be the main source of employment opportunities for many disabled people, particularly those without formal qualifications.

The strength of the local disability sector is another significant environmental factor. DPOs are often a direct source of economic opportunities for disabled people, through the provision of services such as business support, financial services or group income-generating projects. They can also play an important role in providing information on training and employment opportunities, as well as encouraging community stakeholders, such as employers, to adopt more inclusive practices. Disability-focused non-governmental organisations (NGOs) can play a similar role in supporting economic participation. Leonard Cheshire Disability, for example, has established Livelihood Resource Centres in several countries across Asia and Africa which serve as an 'information gateway', providing advice and guidance to disabled people and their families, as well as working closely with training institutions, employers, government agencies, microfinance institutions and other stakeholders to facilitate the economic inclusion of disabled people.

Reflection exercise 8.1

Make a list of the environmental factors that are likely to hinder or help to facilitate the economic participation of disabled people within a country or community that you are familiar with. How might these factors vary between urban and rural areas?

Vocational skills development

Vocational skills development programmes can enable trainees to acquire the skills and personal attributes that support economic participation. However, disabled people are often faced with a range of barriers to accessing vocational training. Many have been denied a basic education (UNICEF, 2014), so may fail to meet the entry requirements for mainstream training courses. Training institutions may be distant or physically inaccessible, and courses may not be designed in a way that is flexible enough to meet the specific needs of disabled people. Attitudinal barriers within families, training institutions and the wider community, as well as a lack of confidence and low expectations among disabled people themselves, may also hinder vocational skills development.

A wide range of vocational skills are essential to many types of work that people engage in. Before examining different approaches to vocational skills development, it is worth considering the various types of skill that may actually be required by disabled people in a given context. Four important skill areas, often key elements of a comprehensive vocational skills development programme, are outlined in Box 8.2.

Box 8.2   Vocational skill types

Basic skills

Many disabled people lack basic skills, such as numeracy and literacy, due to past exclusion from education. While years of missed schooling cannot be easily compensated for, some basic skills training aimed at improving reading, writing and arithmetic can provide a significant boost to the employability or business potential of a trainee.

Personal or life skills

Personal or life skills training may include guidance on specific tasks, such as writing CVs, applying for jobs and succeeding at interviews, or more general guidance on developing the personal attributes that are necessary to succeed in business or employment. These may include, for example, timekeeping and time management skills, reliability, flexibility, interpersonal skills, team working and the ability to take responsibility, think creatively and solve problems. The incorporation of a life skills component within a training programme can help to build self-confidence and self-esteem, thus enabling trainees to present themselves more positively.

Technical skills

Technical skills enable people to perform specific tasks competently. These may include skills needed in manual occupations, such as farming, carpentry, tailoring, construction, plumbing and electrical work, as well as service occupations, such as bicycle or vehicle repair, hairdressing, sales, marketing and secretarial work. Virtually all types of work require some technical skills and, with increased dependency on technology, the need for relevant training is likely to increase in the future.

Entrepreneurial skills

Entrepreneurial or business skills can play a vital role in supporting disabled people to start new enterprises, or enhancing the profitability of existing enterprises. The specific skills required by an individual will depend on the type of business they are interested in and prior business experience, but are likely to include business planning, organisational skills, record-keeping, marketing, risk assessment, problem solving and making use of financial services.

Historically, vocational training for disabled people has tended to be based in segregated institutions, such as vocational training centres and sheltered workshops. While such schemes may provide some disabled people with their best chance of being productive and earning income (Powers, 2008), they have attracted much criticism for reinforcing the charity model ethos and isolation of disabled people from the rest of society (WHO and World Bank, 2011). They have also been criticised for failing to provide the accredited learning or employability skills that are necessary for participation in the labour market and for reinforcing stereotypical or outdated occupational roles, often quite menial in nature, such as carpentry for deaf trainees or basket making for blind trainees (Ransom, 2010). However, there are some positive examples of segregated training initiatives that have managed to avoid many of these pitfalls and serve as a valuable stepping stone to mainstream inclusion.

Case study 8.1   Technical Training Institute and Computer Training Centre in Bangalore

The Technical Training Institute (TTI) in Bangalore, run by the National Association for the Blind (NAB) and established in 1982, is a specialist training centre providing courses in general mechanics to trainees with visual impairment. Courses last for two years, leading to Government Trade Certificates, and trainees are also provided with basic skills and mobility training to supplement the technical skills. The NAB site also offers hostel accommodation and job placement services, and has recently opened a computer training centre in order to take advantage of opportunities arising within Bangalore's booming information technology sector.

The TTI has been designed to replicate a mainstream workplace. Trainees are taught skills that are required by modern-day industry and trained on regular industrial machines fitted with simple adaptations for training purposes, so that they will be able to adapt to ordinary workplaces.

(continued)

(continued)

For example, various parts of a standard pillar drill machine were connected, using pieces of string, to a braille information board explaining how each part should be used.

The computer training centre is similarly geared to the requirements of mainstream employment, with students being trained on open-source software so that employers would not need to purchase software licences in order to accommodate them. According to one trainee, regular visits from company representatives had helped to instil confidence that their skills were needed in the commercial world.

On graduation, trainees from both centres are referred to the job placement service, as they make the transition from training to mainstream employment. This service provides successfully placed candidates with a three-day orientation programme and regular follow-up visits, designed to resolve any difficulties arising in the early months of employment and to foster positive relationships between NAB and local employers. According to NAB's chief executive officer, this process of building rapport was vital to the ongoing success of the scheme. The TTI superintendent estimated that around 90 per cent of the trainee mechanics were successful in finding employment, usually within local factories. Similarly, the head of Computer Studies reported that demand for computer graduates was extremely high, within both the corporate and government sectors.

Source: Adapted from Cobley (2013a, pp. 447–448) and research notes

The scheme highlighted in Case Study 8.1 appears to have achieved considerable success, in terms of promoting economic participation, due to its provision of accredited training courses and close links to local employers. The approach of preparing trainees to adapt to the requirements of regular workplaces, described by one staff member as 'meeting society halfway', may seem to be at odds with the demands of many social model advocates for society itself to adapt to the needs of disabled people, rather than the other way around. In resource-poor settings, however, where mainstream employment opportunities are often extremely scarce, this is perhaps a realistic strategy for maximising the employment prospects of disabled trainees.

In general, the increasingly widespread adoption of a rights-based perspective on disability has led to a gradual transition from segregated institutions to the inclusion of disabled people within mainstream training programmes. This transition has been much slower in many countries of the

Global South, however, for reasons such as the 'physical inaccessibility of training centres, distant or inconvenient location of training, courses which are not relevant, inadequate transportation, unavailability and/or cost of child care, little flexibility in course design or delivery' (O'Reilly, 2007, p. 84). In Nigeria, for example, it has been noted that the few inclusive training centres that do exist 'do not have appropriate curricula for the special needs of people with disabilities' (Tsengu et al., 2006, p. 53).

One inclusive strategy, designed to ensure that the content of training is matched to local work opportunities, is to involve employers directly in the provision of training opportunities through apprenticeships. While the quality of such training may vary, many trainers will have vast experience in their particular trades and the skills acquired are likely to be highly marketable. Trainees are also likely to gain valuable work experience, often involving direct contact with the general public. Additionally trainers may be able to provide long-term job opportunities themselves, or at least to provide work recommendations on completion of training. Albu (2005)[3] reports on an enterprise-based scheme, involving 103 training placements, implemented between 2001 and 2004 in a conflict-torn area of Uganda. Only 60 of the training placements were completed, but at least 38 of those completing placements were already productively employed by 2004, including several that had been taken on by the employers that had provided their placements. One criticism of apprenticeship training is that informal training will not lead to formal accreditation (Coleridge, 2007), although this weakness could potentially be overcome if college placements were incorporated into apprenticeship schemes, as they are in many Northern countries.

There are some disabled people who, due to the nature and severity of their impairments, are likely to be excluded from even the most inclusive of vocational training programmes, due to their lack of realistic employment prospects. However, even people with the most profound and complex impairments can make a valuable contribution to household livelihood strategies if they are supported to develop skills that reduce their dependence on others. Case Study 8.2 focuses on a scheme in Kenya which recognises the potential of deaf-blind trainees to make just such a contribution, and even to generate income for their families.

Case study 8.2   Brian Resource Centre in Nairobi

The Brian Resource Centre provides training on small-scale agri-business and resource management skills to a small group of young deaf-blind trainees. The centre is located at the Nairobi home of the scheme's founder,

(continued)

(continued)

Joseph Shiroko, who set up the project in 2006 after becoming frustrated by the lack of local facilities for Brian, his deaf-blind son. The project trains students to utilise the natural resources that are readily available to them, in order to generate income through various agri-business activities, from kitchen gardens to animal husbandry. Families are encouraged to visit, and even undergo training themselves so that they can see how the skills being taught can be put to productive use, and how deaf–blind people can, with appropriate support, make a valuable contribution to family liveli- hood strategies. As Shiroko explained:

> The family is a 'key institution' in Kenya. When students graduate, we visit the families every three months to monitor progress, and to ensure that former trainees are using their skills. Without the support of families, the project would be doomed to failure. For example, a sewing machine given to a scheme graduate could be sold by the family for a quick profit.

The centre provides two-year training programmes for up to four train- ees at a time. Of the 12 that had completed the programme since the project's inception, three were employed at the centre as instructors. The others, according to Shiroko, had received business start-up kits and were contributing to family businesses or running their own income- generating projects.

This is a largely self-sufficient scheme, with training fees sup- plemented by a range of income-generating activities, such as rabbit breeding and the sale of charcoal bricks produced on-site. The govern- ment also provides some support, by seconding an agriculture extension worker to advise on the innovative farming and conservation methods in use, and a locally based NGO had provided business start-up kits.

Although small and segregated, this scheme demonstrates how it is possible to support people with multi-sensory impairments to engage in sustainable income-generating activities and to make a productive contribution to their households, and even their communities, within the Kenyan context. One interviewee, an NGO community worker who regularly visited the Centre, felt that key strengths of the project were its ability to adapt and evolve, in order to survive, and the strong commit- ment from families, who 'even push the founder to do more!'.

Source: Adapted from Cobley, 2012, p. 377, and research notes

Waged employment

Obtaining waged employment often represents a huge challenge for disabled people, particularly in the Global South context. Even those with appropriate qualifications are likely to encounter a wide range of barriers, including discriminatory recruitment procedures, inaccessible workplaces and transport difficulties, as well as negative attitudes among employers, who may view them as 'low achievers' and 'unproductive'. Such misconceptions are often reinforced by a lack of knowledge of the kind of adaptations which could make their workplaces more accessible and help to facilitate the productive employment of disabled people (WHO and World Bank, 2011). However, increased international recognition of disability rights, the spread of pro-disability employment legislation and the rise of corporate social responsibility have helped to create a more level playing field.

There is a growing international consensus that disabled people should not be excluded from waged employment, a trend that is clearly reflected in the international agreements described earlier. Many countries have responded by introducing affirmative measures designed to increase the labour market participation rates of disabled people, such as employment reservations or quotas schemes, usually in the public sector, and incentives for private sector employers. In Uganda, for example, the 2006 Persons with Disabilities Act (Government of Uganda, 2006) allows for a 15 per cent annual tax reduction for private employers who employ ten or more disabled people. In general terms, however, the impact of pro-disability employment legislation appears to have been very modest, with many disabled people feeling that legislation is either not mandatory or has ineffective enforcement mechanisms and inadequate penalties for non-compliance (Dube *et al.*, 2005). This lack of impact is illustrated by a study in India (World Bank, 2009), where the 1995 Disability Act established a 3 per cent disability employment reservation in the government sector. By 2003, only 0.44 per cent of government posts had been filled by disabled people, partly because the vast majority of posts had been identified as unsuitable for disabled people.

There is clearly a need for anti-discrimination legislation to be implemented more effectively, in order to increase labour market participation rates among disabled people. However, as O'Reilly (2007) suggests, there may also be a role for non-obligatory measures, based on persuasion or self-regulation, to be used in addition to legislation. For example, government agencies, employer associations or disability organisations could make awards to employers for offering employment opportunities to disabled people. With a growing awareness of corporate social responsibility placing increased pressure on multinationals to adopt more ethical recruitment practices, such schemes could play a valuable role in recognising companies that have been particularly proactive in this area. In India, for example, the National Centre for the Promotion of Employment of Disabled People (NCPEDP), a cross-disability advocacy organisation based in Delhi, introduced the Helen

Keller Award Scheme in 1999 to recognise individuals and companies that had shown active commitment to promoting equality at work. The Award Scheme was discontinued in 2013, but was then reintroduced in 2015 due to popular demand from within the disability movement and the corporate sector (NCPEDP website, undated).

While the desire to promote a positive company image may be prompting some companies to employ more disabled people, there is also encouraging evidence to suggest that others are now starting to recognise a business case for including disabled people in the workplace. ITC-Welcomgroup, a luxury hotel chain in India which has employed over 300 disabled people,[4] has produced an excellent *Disability Handbook for Industry* which claims that disabled employees 'tend to have better attendance records, stay with employers longer and have fewer accidents at work' (ITC-Welcomgroup, undated, Section 1.2). The handbook also observes the positive impact on staff morale when employers are seen to promote equal opportunities and provides a wealth of advice for employers on how to accommodate disabled employees and support them to reach their full potential.

Case study 8.3   Jobs fairs in Chennai

[Employability Jobs Fairs] started in 2004 and have become increasingly popular, now attracting up to 75 companies and 800 graduate-level candidates from across India each year. Participants at a staff focus group discussion estimated that around seven per cent of these candidates obtain jobs. In order to reach out to candidates in other states, who often travel huge distances to attend, the Ability Foundation recently organised additional jobs fairs in the northern cities of Delhi and Guwahati. The deputy director explained how the fairs work:

> They last for two days, with the first day involving screening, written tests and job matching, which helps to ensure that candidates only apply for those jobs that interest them and match their abilities. The aim is to set a high benchmark, so that employers know that they will recruit high quality candidates and candidates know that they have a good chance of success.

One beneficiary attended the 2008 Jobs Fair and was selected for a job by Standard Chartered Bank, for whom he now works as a customer services executive in Jaipur. As with many of the scheme beneficiaries that were interviewed for this study, he is grateful for the opportunity to lead an independent life and would like to help others to do the same. His ambition is to set up a rural organisation in Rajasthan, providing IT training to disabled people with little or no education.

Source: Cobley, 2013b, pp. 287–288

Jobs fairs, organised specifically for disabled job seekers, can be an effective way of enabling candidates to meet with a large number of potential employers that are likely to have a positive attitude towards disability employment by virtue of their attendance. Several disability-focused organisations in India have adopted this innovative strategy in recent years, including the Ability Foundation in Chennai, as described in Case Study 8.3. While these jobs fairs appear to have achieved notable success, this is partly due to their focus on graduate-level candidates, which effectively excludes the vast majority of disabled people. However, supporting those with appropriate academic qualifications to forge successful careers is one way of establishing role models that can challenge discriminatory attitudes and demonstrate that disabled people can succeed at the highest levels.

Self-directed employment

The term 'self-directed employment' refers to individuals running their own businesses, either individually or in collaboration with others (Neufeldt, 1995). As well as business ventures run by disabled individuals, this may encompass family businesses, worker cooperatives or group income-generating activities, such as those that are often set up by DPOs and self-help groups, and is thus a broader concept than self-employment. While self-directed employment may not offer the security and stability of waged employment, it does offer the flexibility of being able to work at one's own pace, which may well suit many disabled people. Business ventures of this type are most likely to operate in the informal sector, at least initially, and hence may provide some of the best employment opportunities for disabled people in countries where the informal sector dominates (Coleridge, 2007). Self-directed employment is by no means an easy option though. The business world can be fiercely competitive and many enterprises fail before they even get off the ground.

Successful entrepreneurs require confidence and self-belief, qualities that many disabled people lack due to overprotective families, negative community attitudes and a lack of exposure to the realities of working in a competitive environment. Overcoming the fear of failure and taking a step out of one's comfort zone may be the first hurdle that needs to be faced. Being one's own boss can be a liberating experience but also quite isolating, with many entrepreneurs working from home. The support and encouragement of family members and friends can reduce that feeling of isolation, as well as helping to instil the confidence needed to overcome the inevitable business setbacks that will occur from time to time. Practical support may also be of vital importance, since disabled people may not be able to carry out every task associated with a business themselves. Family members and friends can help to plug gaps in the supply chain by carrying out these tasks, and it may sometimes be possible to form business linkages between disabled entrepreneurs in order to fill these gaps. Moodie (2010) notes the potential value of this type of linkage, offering the example of a disabled entrepreneur in South Africa who started a laundry business and was then able to link up with another disabled entrepreneur, who used his car to collect and deliver the laundry for her.

Access to finance

Disabled people often lack qualifications, business experience and financial assets, and thus may fail to meet the lending criteria set by financial institutions. Even microfinance institutions, which provide financial services designed to support micro-enterprises and poor families (Martinelli and Mersland, 2010), often fail to reach disabled people. In fact, a multi-country survey of over 100 microfinance providers found that, for most of them, disabled people make up less than 0.5 per cent of their clients (Handicap International, 2006). Cramm and Finkenflugel (2008), in their analysis of the exclusion of disabled people from microcredit in Africa and Asia, describe how microcredit programmes often demand entry fees, collateral and prior business experience, all of which tend to exclude the poorest members of society, among whom disabled people are disproportionately represented. They also provide evidence to suggest that the perceived risks of providing loans to disabled people are often inflated by negative perceptions among loan or credit officers, some of whom feel that disabled clients are 'problematic and will create increased work burden' (p. 3). Given these barriers to microfinance, it is perhaps not surprising that many disabled entrepreneurs rely on their own personal savings and personal support networks to fund new businesses. This was illustrated by a survey of 841 disabled entrepreneurs in Uganda, which revealed that the vast majority of respondents had either used their own personal assets or relied on family and friends to make their initial business investments (Beisland and Mersland, 2012). Interestingly, however, this survey also revealed that 89 per cent of the entrepreneurs had made use of at least one type of microfinance service, usually once they were economically active. Many of them had managed to access less formal financial institutions, such as rotating savings and credit associations (ROSCAs), which are commonplace in Uganda.

Group enterprises

Group enterprises often have a greater chance of success than individual ventures, as they are able to tap into a diverse range of skills, attributes and resources. They may also find it easier to access business finance, since they are able to pool resources to build capital. Another advantage of group enterprises is that they can draw on the strength of peer support that often exists between members. In the South Indian state of Tamil Nadu, for example, numerous self-help groups formed by disabled people have launched successful business enterprises, often with the support of government agencies and locally based NGOs that have provided entrepreneurial skills training and helped to facilitate links with financial institutions (Cobley, 2013a).[5] The value of peer support was highlighted during an interview conducted with a bank manager, based in the Nagapattinam District, who had approved loans to several local self-help groups. He explained that 'peer pressure within the groups creates solidarity, which leads to good repayment rates. The disability self-help groups are now seen as a good banking investment' (p. 450).

The potential of disabled people to develop successful group business ventures, with appropriate support, has also been recognised in the Philippines, where the 1999 Economic Independence of Disabled Persons Act requires the government to procure 10 per cent of its furniture requirements from business cooperatives comprised of disabled people. One such cooperative is described in Case Study 8.4.

Case study 8.4   Business cooperative in the Philippines

In the rural district of Santa Fe, members of a DPO were engaged in the production of hollow blocks and school furniture. Many of the workers lived on-site through the week, returning to their homes at weekends. The cooperative benefited from the government's pro-disability procurement policy, which virtually guaranteed a continuing stream of furniture orders. Three members of the cooperative were interviewed, and all of them spoke of their pride at being able to work for a living and support their families, rather than relying on government or NGO 'handouts'. Interestingly, they also expressed a strong preference for working alongside other disabled workers within the communal setting. As one member put it, 'here we look out for each other and nobody looks down on us'.

The project had received various forms of business support from two locally based NGOs, including the provision of transport for delivering furniture and enabling workers to access medical services. A representative from one of these NGOs highlighted the importance of adopting a twin-track approach to promoting the economic participation of disabled people

(continued)

(continued)

in a resource-poor setting, by campaigning for mainstream inclusion while simultaneously supporting more focused initiatives such as the Santa Fe cooperative. As he explained: 'We are striving for full inclusion in the mainstream, but this will take a long time. In the meantime, we recognise that, for some, their best prospects of employment are within the cooperatives'.

Source: Adapted from Cobley, 2015

Business development support (BDS)

BDS services, such as those provided to the self-help groups in South India and the Santa Fe cooperative in the Philippines, may be designed to support both existing and potential entrepreneurs, either individually or collectively. Potential entrepreneurs can be supported to draw on their own interests, capabilities, knowledge, social contacts and resources, including personal attributes such as creativity and determination, in order to develop a viable business plan, which is usually the starting point for a new enterprise. Even if a formal business plan is not required, it is important to have a clear idea of what is required in order for a business to succeed. Those already engaged in business may benefit from BDS services designed to support them in strengthening and further developing their enterprises.

BDS services can play an important role in bringing together the various forms of support that disabled entrepreneurs may need, in order to give them the best chance of succeeding in business. It may sometimes be necessary to address medical rehabilitation needs, for example, in order to ensure that a disabled person is fit and well enough to fully benefit from a training course or to engage in business activities. The need for a holistic approach was highlighted by an international comparative study on economic inclusion conducted by Handicap International (2006), based on field visits to seven countries in Asia and East Africa. The study report concludes that successful strategies for promoting self-employment among disabled people require 'complementary activities in multiple sectors' (p. 24). As well as developing business skills and facilitating access to financial services, these activities included physical rehabilitation, building self-esteem, raising disability awareness and advocacy services. The most cost-effective way of providing such comprehensive support, the report concludes, is to establish partnerships between organisations working in different domains. BDS services should therefore aim to foster links between the various community stakeholders that could potentially support disabled entrepreneurs to develop their businesses.

Reflection exercise 8.2

Make a list of the organisations, agencies and individuals, within a city, town or rural district that you are familiar with, that may be a potential source of support for a disabled entrepreneur. How can a disability service provider engage with these stakeholders effectively, in order to provide a comprehensive, coordinated and cost-effective package of BDS services to disabled entrepreneurs?

Summary of key points

- Economic participation can play a vital role in reducing poverty among disabled people and their families, as well as promoting more just and inclusive societies. Supporting disabled people to be economically active can also have significant economic benefits for society as a whole.
- A wide range of environmental factors, including the workings of local and national institutions, social structures and processes, characteristics of the local economy and the strength of the disability sector, exert an influence on the range and types of economic opportunities that are available to disabled people.
- Skills development strategies should be based on matching the interests and abilities of individual trainees to the needs and characteristics of the local market, and not limited by preconceived ideas and assumptions about the types of work that disabled people can or should do.
- Job placement schemes can help to smooth the transition from training to employment, particularly when close links are established between training institutions and employers.
- Despite increased international awareness of disability rights and the spread of pro-disability employment legislation, disabled people are still grossly under-represented in waged employment. Opportunities do exist, however, and many disabled people value the stability, security and career development prospects that waged employment can offer. Innovative strategies, such as setting up jobs fairs, can support disabled job-seekers to take advantage of these opportunities.
- Self-directed employment represents the most realistic route to economic participation for many disabled people. BDS services should aim to support disabled entrepreneurs, both individually and collectively, to achieve their business ambitions, building on the personal resources that they already have and bringing together the various forms of support that may be necessary to enable them to succeed.

Discussion questions

1   Given the drive towards mainstream inclusion and participation, rein-forced by the CRPD, what do you see as the future role, if any, of segregated training institutions and sheltered workshops?
2   How can training providers ensure that the content of vocational skills training programmes for disabled people reflects the career aspirations of trainees themselves and is matched to the requirements of the local economy?
3   How can mainstream employers be supported to make their workplaces and working practices more disability-inclusive?

Notes

1 See Chapter 2 for a discussion around the difficulties in measuring disability prevalence.
2 See Chapter 3 for further discussion on the relationship between poverty and disability.
3 See Suggested further reading.
4 Research interview conducted with ITC's general manager, Welcomenviron Initiatives, on 18 February 2011.
5 See Case Study 5.2, Chapter 5, for a description of the self-help group movement in South India.

Suggested further reading

Albu, M. (2005) *Economic Empowerment of Disabled People: Lessons from Northern Uganda about Developing the Market for Enterprise-based Skills Development Services*. DFID APT Enterprise Development: Project Report. Retrieved on 28 May 2017 from www.value-chains.org/dyn/bds/docs/463/APT%20Uganda%20Disabled%20People%202005.pdf

Coleridge, P. (2016) 'Access to Livelihoods'. In Iriarte, E., McConkey, R. and Gilligan, R. (Eds.) (2016) *Disability and Human Rights: Global Perspectives*. London: Palgrave, 189–204.

References

Abberley, P. (1999) 'The Significance of Work for the Citizenship of Disabled People'. *Paper presented at University College Dublin on* 15 April 1999. Retrieved on 21 March 2017 from www.leeds.ac.uk/disability-studies/archiveuk/Abberley/sigofwork.pdf

Albu, M. (2005) *Economic Empowerment of Disabled People: Lessons from Northern Uganda about Developing the Market for Enterprise-based Skills Development Services*. DFID APT Enterprise Development: Project Report. Retrieved on 28 May 2017 from www.value-chains.org/dyn/bds/docs/463/APT%20Uganda%20Disabled%20People%202005.pdf

Beisland, L.A. and Mersland, R. (2012) 'The use of microfinance services among economically active disabled persons: evidence from Uganda'. *Journal of International Development* 24 (51), 569–583.

Buckup, S. (2009) *The Price of Exclusion: The Socio Economic Consequences of Excluding People with Disabilities from the World of Work*. ILO Working Paper No. 43. Geneva: ILO.

Cobley, D.S. (2012) 'Towards economic empowerment: segregation versus inclusion in the Kenyan context'. *Disability and Society* 27 (3), 371–384.

Cobley, D.S. (2013a) 'Towards economic participation: examining the impact of the Convention on the Rights of Persons with Disabilities in India'. *Disability and Society* 28 (4), 441–455.

Cobley, D. (2013b) *Disability and Economic Empowerment in Kenya and India*. Saarbrucken: Lambert Academic Publishing Ltd.

Cobley, D.S. (2015) 'Typhoon Haiyan one year on: disability, poverty and participation in the Philippines'. *Disability and the Global South* 2 (3), 686–707.

Coleridge, P. (2006) 'Disabled people and economic empowerment'. *Behinderung and Dritte Welt: Disability and International Development* 2, 4–10.

Coleridge, P. (2007) 'Economic Empowerment'. In Barron, T. and Amerena, P. (Eds.) *Disability and Inclusive Development*. London: Leonard Cheshire International, 111–154.

Cramm, J. and Finkenflugel, H. (2008) 'Exclusion of disabled people from microcredit in Africa and Asia: a literature study'. *Asia Pacific Rehabilitation Journal* 19 (2), 15–33.

Dube, A., Hirst, R., Light, R. and Malinga, J. (2005) *Promoting Inclusion? Disabled People, Legislation and Public Policy*. DFID Research Paper. London: DFID.

Government of Uganda (2006) *Persons with Disabilities Act 2006*. Retrieved on 21 May 2017 from www.ilo.org/wcmsp5/groups/public/---ed_protect/---protrav/---ilo_aids/documents/legaldocument/wcms_232181.pdf

Handicap International (2006) *Good Practices for the Economic Inclusion of People with Disabilities in Developing Countries*. London: Handicap International.

ILO (International Labour Organization) (1944) *Employment (Transition from War to Peace) Recommendation*. Recommendation No. 71 Geneva: ILO.

ILO (1955) *R99 Vocational Rehabilitation (Disabled) Recommendation*. Recommendation No. 99. Geneva: ILO.

ILO (1972) *Employment, Incomes and Equality: A Strategy for Increasing Productive Employment in Kenya*. Geneva: ILO.

ILO (1983) *C159 Vocational Rehabilitation and Employment (Disabled Persons) Convention*. Geneva: ILO.

ILO (2001) *Code of Practice on Managing Disability in the Workplace*. Geneva: ILO.

ILO (2002a) *Woman and Men in the Informal Economy: A Statistical Picture*. Geneva: ILO.

ILO (2002b) *Workers in the Informal Economy: Platform of Issues*. Geneva: ILO. Retrieved on 21 May 2017 from www.wiego.org/sites/default/files/resources/files/ILC02PlatforM.pdf

ILO (2002c) *Decent Work and the Informal Economy*. International Labour Conference, 90th Session. Geneva: ILO.

ILO (2007) *The ILO at a Glance*. Geneva: ILO. Retrieved on 18 December 2017 from www.ilo.org/public/english/download/glance.pdf

ITC-Welcomgroup (undated) *Disability Handbook for Industry*. Retrieved on 3 May 2017 from www.itchotels.in/Custom/Disability%20Handbook%20For%20Industry.pdf

La Porta, R. and Shleifer, A. (2014) 'Informality and development'. *Journal of Economic Perspectives* 28 (3), 109–126.

Martinelli, E. and Mersland, R. (2010) 'Microfinance for People with Disabilities'. In Barron, T. and Ncube, J. (Eds.) *Poverty and Disability*. London: Leonard Cheshire Disability, 215–254.

Mersland, R., Bwire, F.N. and Mukasa, G. (2009) 'Access to mainstream microfinance services for persons with disabilities – lessons learned from Uganda'. *Disability Studies Quarterly* 29 (591), 569–583.

Moodie, B. (2010) 'Self-employment for People with Disabilities'. In Barron, T. and Ncube, J. (Eds.) *Poverty and Disability*. London: Leonard Cheshire Disability, 261–285.

NCPEDP (National Centre for the Promotion of Employment of Disabled People) (undated) *The NCPEDP – Helen Keller Awards*. Retrieved on 26 January 2017 from .www.ncpedp.org/The_NCPEDP_Helen_Keller_Awards

Neufeldt, A. (1995) 'Self-directed Employment and Economic Independence in Low-income Countries'. In O'Toole, B. and McConkey, R. (Eds) *Innovations in Developing Countries for People with Disabilities*. Chorley, Lancs: Lisieux Hall, 161–182.

O'Reilly, A. (2007) *The Right to Decent Work of Persons with Disabilities*. Geneva: ILO.

Powers, T. (2008) *Recognising Ability: The Skills and Productivity of Persons with Disabilities*. Employment Working Paper No. 3. Geneva: ILO.

Ransom, B. (2010) 'Lifelong Learning in Education, Training and Skills Development'. In Barron, T. and Ncube, J. (Eds) *Poverty and Disability*. London: Leonard Cheshire Disability, 145–175.

Tsengu, D., Brodtkorb, S. and Almdes, T. (2006) 'CBR and Economic Empowerment of Persons with Disabilities'. In Hartley, S. (Ed.) *CBR as Part of Community Development: A Poverty Reduction Strategy*. London: UCL, 49–63.

UNICEF (United Nations Children's Fund) (2014) *Global Initiative on Out-of-School Children: South Asia Regional Study*. Kathmandu, Nepal: UNICEF. Retrieved on 10 January 2017 from www.unicef.org/education/files/SouthAsia_OOSCI_Study__Executive_Summary_26Jan_14Final.pdf

United Nations (2006) *Convention on the Rights of Persons with Disabilities*. Washington, DC: UN.

United Nations (2015) *Transforming Our World: the 2030 Agenda for Sustainable Development*. Retrieved on 21 March 2017 from www.un.org/pga/wp-content/uploads/sites/3/2015/08/120815_outcome-document-of-Summit-for-adoption-of-the-post-2015-development-agenda.pdf

World Bank (2009) *People with Disabilities in India: From Commitments to Outcomes*. Human Development Unit. Washington, DC: World Bank.

WHO (World Health Organization) and World Bank (2011) *World Report on Disability*. Geneva: WHO. Retrieved on 22 October 2016 from http://whqlibdoc.who.int/publications/2011/9789240685215_eng.pdf

9   Disability and disasters

The *World Disasters Report* (IFRC, 2016) recently revealed that forced migration due to conflict was at its highest levels since the Second World War, while the frequency and scale of disasters caused by natural hazards was also increasing. When the growing threat of terrorism is factored in as well, it becomes clear that the world is becoming increasingly volatile. Disasters tend to be most devastating in low-income settings, which are often characterised by weak infrastructure, poorly constructed houses and a lack of resources for immediate and longer-term recovery. Events such as the Haiti earthquake of 2010, which resulted in the deaths of over 200,000 people and displacement of more than two million people (DEC, 2013), and Typhoon Haiyan, which swept across the Central Philippines in November 2013, claiming 6,000 lives and leading to the displacement of over four million people (NDRRMC, 2014), provide examples of the catastrophic scenarios that can easily arise when disasters occur in countries that are ill-equipped to withstand their impact.

The distinction that is sometimes made between human and natural disasters is a slightly false one, given that disasters arising from natural hazards are often caused or exacerbated by human factors, such as growing levels of pollution and preventable climate change, as well as poor disaster planning and management. The destruction wrought by Hurricane Katrina in 2005, for example, was partly caused by the failure of the man-made levees to adequately protect the low-lying city of New Orleans. There are often strong linkages between disasters as well, whether they arise from human or natural causes. For example, armed conflict tends to damage infrastructure and weaken social structures, thus increasing the potential impact of natural hazards. Conflict may also lead to a loss of skilled personnel and other key resources, such as medical equipment, thus further reducing capacity to respond to (and recover from) future disasters. Disasters arising from natural hazards also tend to damage infrastructure and drain resources, as well as deepening poverty and inequality, thus reinforcing conditions that increase the risk of conflict (Collier *et al.*, 2003).

In this chapter, the term 'disaster' is used to refer to any major disaster that is caused by human factors, a natural hazard or a combination of both.

The chapter first looks at what is known generally about the impact of disasters on disabled people. The disaster management cycle is then introduced and used as a framework to guide the discussion that follows around the extent to which disability issues are adequately addressed during the disaster planning, response, long-term recovery and mitigation phases. The next section focuses on the increasingly important role of disabled people's organisations (DPOs), as representative organisations of disabled people, in contributing to disaster planning and management processes. Finally, the chapter concludes by providing a summary of international frameworks and guidance documents on disaster management, which are examined in terms of the extent to which they promote disability-inclusive approaches.

Impact of disasters on disabled people

It is widely acknowledged that disabled people tend to be disproportionately affected by disasters (IFRC, 2007; Wisner *et al.*, 2012). Following the 2011 earthquake and tsunami in Eastern Japan, for example, which resulted in over 15,000 deaths, the mortality rate among disabled people was found to be more than double that of the overall population (Government of Japan, 2012). The vulnerability of disabled people to the impact of disasters is typically reinforced by high levels of poverty, particularly in the Global South, combined with factors such as stigma, inaccessible infrastructure, inadequate disability data and a lack of participation in disaster planning processes (Smith *et al.*, 2012). Structural inequalities, such as these, were highlighted by a global survey that was recently conducted by the United Nations Office for Disaster Risk Reduction (UNISDR) with the participation of 5,450 disabled people representing 126 countries. The survey revealed that disabled people were 'rarely consulted about their needs, and only 20% could evacuate immediately without difficulty in the event of a sudden disaster event, the remainder could only do so with a degree of difficulty and 6% would not be able to do so at all' (UNISDR, 2013). Magareta Wahlstrom, the head of UNISDR, stated that:

> The results of this survey are shocking. It clearly reveals that the key reason why a disproportionate number of disabled people suffer and die in disasters is because their needs are ignored and neglected by the official planning process in the majority of situations. They are often left totally reliant on the kindness of family, friends and neighbours for their survival and safety.
>
> (UNISDR, 2013)

Disabled people themselves do not form a homogeneous group. As discussed in Chapter 3, they have diverse needs and capacities, as well as multiple identities. Some may be particularly disadvantaged through the intersection of disability with other social identities, such as gender, age and ethnicity. A study conducted in war-torn Afghanistan (Bakhshi and Trani, 2006), for example, revealed that disabled women were particularly vulnerable to poverty and inequality, with gender an even more significant exclusionary factor than disability. A recent report on the 2015 Nepal earthquake (Lord *et al.*, 2016), based on extensive field research conducted in the early recovery phase, reveals that 'the earthquake affected the socially excluded groups, namely Dalits, Jananatis and women, particularly those with disabilities, disproportionately' (p. 18). The 2007 *World Disasters Report* (IFRC, 2007), which includes a whole chapter on disability, provides further evidence of intersectional discrimination, noting that in disaster situations disabled women and children 'are particularly vulnerable to violence, exploitation and sexual abuse' (p. 91). Disaster planning processes and programmes frequently fail to take account of the diversity among disabled people, who are often simply labelled a 'vulnerable group' (Kett, 2010; UNHCR, 2007).

When communities have been torn apart due to the destruction of infrastructure and breakdown of services, as well as illness, loss of life and displacement, disabled people may be vulnerable to increased poverty, vulnerability and discrimination (Priestley and Hemingway, 2007). In Nepal, for instance, the vulnerability and exclusion of disabled people, arising from entrenched social hierarchies and environmental barriers within Nepalese society, was even greater following the 2015 earthquake (Lord *et al.*, 2016). Many disabled people were denied access to health services, for example, particularly in rural areas where damage to roads and trails made it even harder for those with mobility impairments to reach the health centres, which were mainly located in market towns. One key informant reported that 'people with disabilities have not received health services after the earthquake in our community' (p. 25).

Major disasters typically lead to steep rises in disability prevalence. It has been estimated, for example, that disability prevalence increased by 20 per cent across the Asia Pacific region in the aftermath of the 2004 Asian tsunami (World Bank, 2005). It can be useful to distinguish between those who became disabled as a result of disasters and those with pre-existing impairments, as their experiences may differ significantly. Post-disaster relief and development programmes, including health and rehabilitation services, often prioritise those seen as 'victims' of the catastrophic events that have recently occurred, such as ex-combatants (Kett, 2010). Hence those with pre-existing impairments may be regarded as 'lower priority', often leading to exclusion, isolation and deeper poverty. In Palestine, for example, people who have become disabled due to Israeli violence often gain martyrdom status and are provided with financial compensation by the Palestinian Authority, while those with impairments unrelated to the conflict tend to be marginalised and do not receive equivalent financial support (Burton *et al.*, 2013). It cannot be assumed, however, that this will always be the case. In Liberia, many young disabled people with visible impairments, assumed to be ex-combatants who 'got what they deserved', tend to be stigmatised and neglected, often ending up begging on the streets (IFRC, 2007).

The disaster management cycle

There are many different versions of the disaster management cycle, which shows how the various phases of disaster management link together in a cyclical manner. One such version is shown in Figure 9.1.

This diagram is something of an over-simplification, as the disaster management phases will not always be so clearly defined and will often overlap (Coppola, 2015). The actual occurrence of a disaster (referred to in the diagram as 'impact') may continue for several years and overlap with all phases of the cycle, particularly in areas affected by protracted or recurring conflict. Nevertheless, the diagram provides a useful analytical tool that will be utilised in this section to frame an analysis of disability issues during each of the four main phases of the cycle.

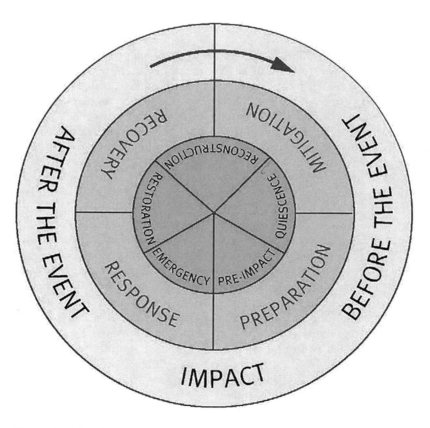

Figure 9.1 The disaster management cycle

Reproduced with permission from David Alexander's *Principles of Emergency Planning and Management*, 2002, p. 6

Preparation

This phase involves the implementation of processes and measures designed to minimise the impact of an impending disaster and increase the survival chances of those likely to be affected. Preparedness measures include the mapping of vulnerable households, implementing or improving early warning systems and putting into place evacuation plans. However, a lack of data on the prevalence, whereabouts and diverse needs of disabled people can seriously undermine the extent to which these measures are disability-inclusive (Smith *et al.*, 2012), as well as reducing opportunities for disabled people to actively participate in preparatory processes. The Sustainable Development Agenda (United Nations, 2015b) acknowledges the need for improved data collection on disability, calling on all nations to 'increase significantly the availability of high quality, timely and reliable data disaggregated by disability' (Target 17.18).

The 2007 *World Disasters Report* (IFRC, 2007) highlights the frequent failure of early warning systems and evacuation plans to take account of disability, pointing out that many lives were saved in the 9/11 attacks because the Associated Blind Organisation, which had offices on the ninth floor of the World Trade Centre, had worked with the Fire Department to develop an evacuation plan and regularly carried out drills. The Report recommends developing a range of impairment-specific early warning and communication systems, such as large print and braille materials for partially sighted and blind people, sign language captions on televisions for deaf people and face-to-face discussions with those who have intellectual impairments. There is also recognition of the importance of disability awareness training, particularly for emergency service and relief agency personnel, as an essential element of disaster preparation.

Response

The response phase normally occurs during or immediately after the occurrence of a disaster. It is during this phase that relief agencies intervene to rescue people and respond to their immediate needs. Kett (2010) observes that many agencies adopt a 'blanket' approach to meeting the basic needs of the most vulnerable people, including disabled people, who are often viewed as 'passive victims'. While the provision of basic requirements, such as food, shelter, water and sanitation, following a disaster is clearly an urgent priority, it is the failure on the part of many relief agencies to take account of disability, in terms of *how* these needs are provided for, that often puts disabled people at a disadvantage. A study conducted in the flood-prone coastal belt of Bangladesh (CSID, 2002), for example, revealed that disabled people often had difficulty in queuing for long periods at aid distribution points, so they would either send a child to collect a smaller ration or pay a neighbour to collect rations for them. While blanket approaches help to ensure that disabled people survive the immediate aftermath of a disaster, they may also reinforce vulnerability by failing to ensure that relief aid distribution processes are accessible and non-discriminatory.

Displacement, when it occurs, can exacerbate the problems that disabled people face following the occurrence of a disaster. When communities are displaced, the rights and needs of disabled people that are forced to migrate are often ignored, while others may simply be left behind or stranded during transit, leaving them with reduced family and community support and increased vulnerability to poverty, violence and exploitation (Berghs, 2015; Pisani and Grech, 2015; UNHCR, 2007). Research conducted in Northern Uganda (Businge, 2016), for example, reveals that disabled people were sometimes left behind when government forces moved people to protected villages in safe zones during the long-running conflict.

When disabled people do travel, they tend to face greater security risks than others, particularly if their journeys take longer due to mobility difficulties. Interviews with disabled people that fled from conflict in Sierra Leone revealed tremendous difficulties encountered during flight, with their survival often attributed to the support of family members, friends and even strangers (dos Santos-Zingale and McColl, 2006).[1] Journeys usually end up at temporary shelters or camps, which are often designed with little thought given to accessibility, even when accessibility guidelines and policies are in place (Priestley and Hemingway, 2006). In the Philippines, for example, the government constructed bunkhouses to accommodate some of those that lost their homes during Typhoon Haiyan. A visit to one of the bunkhouse complexes, which was still fully inhabited one year on from the disaster, revealed significant accessibility concerns (Cobley, 2015).[2] The bunkhouses were raised above the ground, due to the risk of flooding, with three steps leading to each entrance and no ramps, and the communal washrooms were far too cramped for easy access. One bunkhouse resident with a visual impairment revealed that he had injured himself several times because there were no handrails to assist him along the narrow concrete path between the bunkhouse and the toilet block.

Disabled people are often vulnerable to discrimination, stigma and even physical abuse while living in temporary shelters and camps. There is anecdotal evidence from the Dadaab refugee camps in Kenya, for example, of disabled refugees, especially children, suffering frequent physical and verbal abuse (WRC, 2008). They may also be disadvantaged in terms of access to relief aid, as illustrated by the following account of life in a temporary camp in Sierra Leone:

Disability discrimination within temporary camps

The most important activity, which disturbed me, was when I wanted to go to the toilet . . . You know a disabled person cannot squat unless they sit down and the toilet was not clean, people

> messed it up . . . It was very bad, I had no one to help me fetch water . . . When I wanted a child to help me, I had to pay him to fetch water, do laundry, you know, it was really difficult . . . There were NGOs who brought supplies, by the time they reached where we were, we did not get it. It is a hard fight to get the supplies and it is only possible through good connections. And I was not able to walk very fast when they told us we should form a queue for the supplies.
>
> (dos Santos-Zingale and McColl, 2006, p. 249)

When displacement becomes protracted, disabled people can end up living in such conditions for many years, facing challenges in all areas of life. While basic health care is sometimes available in temporary camps, access to specialist medical and rehabilitation services is often a problem. Even where such services are locally available, disabled refugees may be denied access due to a lack of accessible or affordable transport, complex referral processes or encampment policies that restrict freedom of movement (Mizra, 2015; Pearce, 2015). Livelihood opportunities may also be limited (UNHCR, 2007), while disabled children may be denied access to schooling, due to a lack of appropriate teaching methods and learning materials, as well as inaccessible school buildings and facilities (Shivji, 2010; WRC, 2008). Case Study 9.1 provides an example of a medical outreach programme designed to ensure that disabled children living in refugee camps received the specialist support that they required.

Case study 9.1   A model project: regular visits by disability workers in Nepal

A very successful component of Caritas Nepal's disability programme has been its community outreach work, funded by UNHCR. Disability workers visit the homes of children with disabilities on a daily basis to provide physiotherapy, counselling and occupational therapy.

The disability workers assess the physical needs of the children and provide cost-effective aids and appliances, such as special chairs, parallel bars and crutches. They provide materials to maintain the personal hygiene of children with mental disabilities and help teach children and their families about daily living skills.

(continued)

(continued)

In 2007, regular home visits were made to 116 refugees with disabilities in the camps. In addition, community workers provide respite care for children with cerebral palsy in the camps for a fixed period of time to give their mothers, or other caregivers, a much-needed break. 54 children with spastic cerebral palsy were benefiting from this programme in 2007 and it was considered one of the model programmes in the refugee camp.

Source: WRC 2008, pp. 20–21

Reflection exercise 9.1

Some governments and humanitarian agencies implement 'cash for work programmes' in response to disasters, in order to involve local people in disaster recovery work, such as the clearing of debris, and to provide a source of short-term income at a time when many will have lost their livelihoods. These programmes are sometimes criticised, however, for effectively discriminating against disabled people, due to their emphasis on hard physical labour (Kett, 2007). Consider how you might design a disability-inclusive 'cash for work' programme to be implemented during the response phase of a major disaster. Think about how you would recruit participants and how you would arrange the work programme to ensure that disabled workers were able to participate as fully as possible.

Recovery

There is often a gradual transition from the response phase to the recovery phase, in which services are gradually restored and those affected by the disaster are supported to rebuild their lives. During the recovery phase, which may last for several years, disabled people typically continue to face huge barriers to participation in areas such as employment, education, health care and community participation. In post-conflict Sierra Leone (dos Santos-Zingale and McColl, 2006), for example, disabled people revealed that they had experienced great difficulties in accessing various public and private services, including transportation and medical care, and also felt excluded from community meetings and activities. The sense that many felt excluded from their recovering communities was highlighted by one study participant:

Exclusion from community activities

Sometimes you want to go and watch sports. No sooner than you appear at the gate people will say 'go home, if anything happens here you cannot get out fast!'. I had to say to them 'We too are human beings we have our right and this is social business and it is the only social activity I like to be involved in'. Most of my fellow disabled were stopped. When they recognised me as the polio chairmen I tried to advocate on their behalf, but they (people at the gate) would not listen.

(dos Santos-Zingale and McColl, 2006, p. 250)

Reconstruction and recovery processes may provide opportunities for disabled people, as well as presenting challenges. If accessibility needs are taken into account as infrastructure is repaired or rebuilt, and services re-established, then more inclusive societies can be the outcome. Anti-discrimination disability legislation, where it exists, as well as local or external expertise on disability rights and disabling barriers, can be useful in guiding efforts to promote inclusivity (Priestley and Hemingway, 2007). There are also economic arguments in favour of accessible reconstruction, since the cost of making new buildings accessible is minimal, in comparison to the cost of making alterations at a later stage (Berman-Bieler, 2010). Accessibility requirements are sometimes ignored, however, as governments and donors rush to complete rebuilding programmes so that displaced people can return to their homes (IFRC, 2007).

Mitigation

Mitigation processes, which often overlap with long-term recovery processes, are designed to reduce the likelihood of a disaster occurring in the future, or to minimise the likely consequences of a future disaster. From a disability perspective, programmes and campaigns designed to raise disability awareness, reduce stigma and combat discrimination are important disaster mitigation processes that can play a crucial role in reducing the vulnerability of disabled people to the impact of future disasters. Increased understanding of disability within communities can help to raise the visibility of disabled people, thus facilitating the collection of more accurate data on their whereabouts and specific needs. The raising of disability awareness within humanitarian agencies is particularly important, since these agencies are usually at the forefront of disaster management. Many relief agencies lack knowledge and awareness as they consider disability to be a specialist field, so tend to refer disabled people that they come across to 'specialist' agencies (Kett *et al.*, 2005; IFRC, 2007; Mizra, 2011).

One example of a disability-inclusive approach to disaster mitigation is a project developed by the Centre for Disability in Development (CDD) in the flood-prone coastal areas of Bangladesh. This involved the establishment of Ward Disaster Management Committees (WDMCs), each including disabled representatives. Within each WDMC, five task forces were formed with various areas of responsibility (CDD, 2011). Project activities included disability and disaster awareness-raising programmes, such as street theatre (involving disabled people), the construction of an accessible rescue boat and training on the evacuation of disabled people for family members and neighbours. Case Study 9.2 also highlights the potential benefits of supporting and empowering disabled people to play an active role in disaster preparedness and mitigation processes.

Case study 9.2   Disability-inclusive disaster risk management in Vietnam

Despite many persons with disabilities being respected war veterans, impaired people in Vietnam tend to be viewed as victims in need of special assistance. When Malteser International and local DPOs launched a disaster risk management (DRM) project in the central province of Quang Nam, this perception began to change. Rather than being an afterthought to overall planning, persons with disabilities spoke up and contributed to a new DRM system that includes better disaster preparedness for all members of target communities. A new manual has been created in the process, providing step-by-step guidance for disability-inclusive DRM in Vietnam and beyond.

Just south of the city of Danang, Quang Nam province lies in Vietnam's central area that is frequently hit by typhoons, storms and floods. During the war, the province saw some of the heaviest fighting. High numbers of persons with disabilities are testimony to this past.

As Malteser International prepared a new project for community-based DRM, it collaborated closely with DPOs that had been established under the 2011 National Law on Disability. Together with Malteser International, the DPOs facilitated a thorough assessment of people with disabilities and their specific needs. They then followed a twin-track approach. Recognising prevalent stigma as well as a reluctance of many persons with disabilities to express specific concerns, the DPOs first worked exclusively with persons with disabilities (and their families) and built up capacity and self-confidence. Only afterwards did the project launch the second track, the overall assessment of disaster risks

and the development of village DRM plans. Persons with disabilities – 2,443 of whom were trained and 273 selected as representatives in DRM committees – were now confident to raise specific concerns and to contribute to the overall implementation. As Nguyen Van Quang, head of the Dien Ban DPO, explains: 'Earlier, we did not dare to call the President of the commune's People's Committee to talk. Now, we can come to the People's Committee and discuss our business with him face to face'. The result for the people in Quang Nam is both greater inclusion of people with disabilities as well as better preparedness, anticipation and response of floods and storms.

Source: Adapted from Handicap International, 2014, p. 18

The role of DPOs in disaster management processes

As Case Study 9.2 illustrates, DPOs can play a crucial role in disaster risk management processes. They are uniquely positioned to advocate and mediate on behalf of their members on specific issues, as well as raising the profile of disability and advising more generally on how to take account of disability rights and the priorities of disabled people. Priestley and Hemingway (2006) observe that, in emergency relief situations, DPOs and their close allies are more likely to advocate solutions based on rights-based and social model perspectives than mainstream relief agencies, thus underlining the importance of including them. However, as Kett (2010) observes, DPOs are rarely included in planning and coordination meetings, due to their limited capacity and lack of experience and knowledge of humanitarian interventions.

The strengthening of DPOs and their networks is vital, in order to enable them to engage with humanitarian agencies more effectively and to promote more inclusive approaches to disaster management. This was one of the objectives of the Earthquake Disability Project, implemented by the World Bank in response to the 2005 Pakistan earthquake, which included a capacity-building component designed to strengthen DPOs and enable them to work alongside the Pakistan government to develop a community-based rehabilitation[3] strategy. According to some beneficiaries, this inclusive project resulted in a marked increase in disability awareness across the wider community (World Bank, 2010).

As well as raising awareness of the wide range of disability issues that may arise in the post-disaster context and using their knowledge to contribute to disaster risk management plans, DPOs can also contribute to disaster management processes in more practical ways. This is illustrated by Case Study 9.3, which shows how a DPO in the Philippines was able to play a lead role in relief operations following Typhoon Haiyan.

Case study 9.3   Ageing and Disability Focal Points in the Philippines

A representative of the disability-focused NGO Christoffel Blinden Mission (CBM) described a project that had been implemented in Ilioilo Province in the Western Visayas, a region that was also in the path of Haiyan. CBM had supported a well-established local DPO, the Association of Disabled People Iloilo (ADPI), to set up and run its own relief operations. The group had carried out a range of activities from an initial mapping exercise and recruiting volunteers (many of whom were disabled) to organising the delivery of relief aid packages to nearly 4,000 vulnerable households, including many with disabled family members. Four months later, as the emergency relief phase drew to a close, ADPI set up two Ageing and Disability Focal Points, in response to a growing realisation that vulnerable people often did not know how to access mainstream services. The Focal Points provided an accessible point of contact and information, from where referrals could be made to existing services in areas such as health, assistive devices, shelter, education and livelihoods. According to one CBM representative, these Focal Points have developed strong partnerships with a range of local and international relief and development agencies, enabling them to advocate for greater inclusion of disabled people within mainstream services. He also highlighted the central decision-making role of the DPO, demonstrating that disabled people can be development planners and actors, as well as beneficiaries, in the recovery process: 'They worked harmoniously together during the relief phase, so we asked them how they would like to continue their work. They came up with the idea of the Focal Points themselves. The project has changed community perceptions and raised self-esteem among the group's members'. CBM has now committed to extending funding for a further two years, to enable ADPI to focus on longer-term development initiatives across four municipalities, in the areas of health and livelihoods.

Source: Adapted from Cobley, 2015

DPOs can also make an important contribution to peacekeeping and reconciliation processes in the post-conflict context, as illustrated by a recent study (Kandasamy et al., 2016)[4] conducted in Sri Lanka. The study focuses on the work of a local women's disability advocacy organisation which has provided advocacy support to rural disabled women, living in areas affected by the long-running civil war, who typically experience marginalisation and discrimination on the basis of disability, gender, rurality and poverty. According to many of the disabled women that were interviewed for the study, the emphasis on leadership training and raising their own awareness of disability rights had been effective in terms of empowering them to adopt more positive identities, to challenge discrimination and to participate more fully in their communities. Furthermore, the organisation had played a part in easing ethnic tensions by encouraging the development of cross-ethnic relationships between Tamil and Sinhala disabled women, many of whom would previously have avoided or even feared each other due to a lack of understanding and acceptance of cultural differences.

Reflection exercise 9.2

Make a list of the potential benefits that may arise from the implementation of disability-inclusive approaches to disaster management during each phase of the disaster management cycle. Then consider each of these potential benefits in terms of who they relate to. Do they relate to disabled people and their families only, or do they extend to others in the wider community?

International disaster management frameworks and guidance documents

This section reviews a series of international disaster management frameworks and guidance documents, reflecting a gradual trend towards increased recognition of the need to support the active participation of disabled people within disaster planning, response and recovery processes.

Hyogo Framework for Action (2005–2015)

This ten-year plan, adopted at the World Conference on Disaster Reduction in Hyogo, Japan, was designed to make the world safer from the impacts of natural disasters. The Framework (United Nations, 2005) provides broad guidance on building disaster resilience within vulnerable communities, including the identification of underlying risk factors and the use of 'knowledge, education and innovation to build a culture of safety and resilience at all levels' (Section III, B). Although the Framework pays little attention to disability specifically, it does state that 'vulnerable groups should be taken into account when planning for disaster risk reduction' (Section III, A (e)). The only explicit reference to disability calls for the 'implementation of social safety-net mechanisms to assist the poor, the elderly and the disabled' (Section III, B (g)).

Convention on the Rights of Persons with Disabilities (2006)

The CRPD calls on State Parties to take 'all necessary measures to ensure the protection and safety of persons with disabilities in situations of risk, including situations of armed conflict, humanitarian emergencies and the occurrence of natural disasters' (United Nations, 2006, Article 11). The CRPD also emphasises the rights of disabled people to access the physical environment, including all public facilities and services. This is a critical consideration for governments and humanitarian agencies, underlining the importance of inclusive recovery and reconstruction programmes. There is specific mention of the need to eliminate barriers to 'information, communication and other services, including electronic services and emergency services' (Article 9, paragraph 1b). While these references highlight the vulnerability of disabled people in disaster situations and recognise their rights to access relevant facilities and services, the CRPD fails to explicitly acknowledge the potential role of disabled people as active agents of disaster recovery. This is a surprising omission, given that 'full and effective participation and inclusion in society' (Article 3, (c)) is one of the eight general principles on which the Convention is based.

Women's Refugee Commission (2008)

The Women's Refugee Commission (WRC) (2008) has produced a report entitled *Disability Among Refugees and Conflict-affected Populations* examining the challenges facing disabled refugees. The report contains several case studies and is accompanied by a useful resource kit, designed specifically for fieldworkers.

Sphere Standards

This is an inter-agency set of common standards and principles, designed to support good rights-based practice in humanitarian work and to raise the accountability of governments and relief agencies towards beneficiaries and donors. The standards are contained within the *Sphere Handbook* which provides guidance on various aspects of disaster planning and management. Disability is treated as a cross-cutting theme in the latest edition (Sphere Project, 2011), and hence referred to in each of the technical chapters. There is also a new standard on the need to promote 'people-centred humanitarian response', which calls on agencies to provide mechanisms by which people affected by disasters can provide feedback and influence programmes. This implicitly includes disabled people and their representatives. The standards are non-mandatory, however, and focus mainly on

~~short-term~~ emergency response ~~measures~~, rather than longer-term recovery and reconstruction. They are currently under revision, with a new version of the *Sphere Handbook* due to be published in 2018.

United Nations High Commissioner for Refugees (2011)

The United Nations High Commissioner for Refugees (UNHCR) has produced a helpful guidance document entitled *Working with Persons with Disabilities in Forced Displacement* (UNHCR, 2011), which addresses a range of typical discrimination issues faced by disabled people in the refugee context. The document advocates a multi-sectoral approach to meeting the needs of disabled refugees, covering areas such as inclusive education, vocational training and accessible infrastructure. It also emphasises the importance of consulting with disabled refugees, enabling them to participate in decision making and supporting them to take on leadership roles.

Sendai Framework (2015)

The Hyogo Framework has now been replaced by the Sendai Framework (United Nations, 2015a), a new international blueprint for disaster management adopted at the 2015 World Conference on Disaster Risk Reduction in Japan. This blueprint, which will remain in place until 2030 and applies to disasters arising from both natural and man-made hazards, calls for a 'broader and more people-centred approach to disaster risk' (Preamble, Paragraph 7). This sets the tone for a far more rights-based and participatory approach to disaster planning than Hyogo. There are several explicit references to disability, including the following recognition of the potentially vital role of disabled people and their representative organisations as active contributors to disaster planning processes: 'Persons with disabilities and their organisations are critical in the assessment of disaster risk and in designing and implementing plans tailored to specific requirements' (Paragraph 36(iii)).

The Sendai Framework represents a significant commitment, on the part of governments and humanitarian agencies around the world, to prioritise the mainstreaming of disability and active involvement of disabled people themselves in disaster management processes.

International Federation of the Red Cross and Red Crescent Societies (2015)

The International Federation of Red Cross and Red Crescent Societies (IFRC), in collaboration with CBM and Handicap International, has produced a practical and detailed technical guide, entitled *All Under One Roof: Disability-Inclusive Shelter and Settlements in Emergencies* (IFRC, 2016), designed to support humanitarian agencies to deliver more inclusive and accessible disaster planning and response interventions.

Charter on Inclusion of Persons with Disabilities in Humanitarian Action (2016)

This Charter (United Nations, 2016), which aims to support the implementation of the Sendai Framework, was launched at the World Humanitarian Summit in 2016 and subsequently endorsed by over 140 stakeholders, including nation states, United Nations organisations and civil society organisations. The Charter reaffirms the importance of empowering disabled people and enabling them to meaningfully participate in all aspects of humanitarian planning and action.[5]

Summary of key points

- Disabled people are disproportionately affected by disasters. The particular vulnerability of disabled people to the impact of disasters arises from a range of factors, including poverty, inadequate data, inaccessible infrastructure, discriminatory attitudes and their lack of participation in disaster management processes.
- Disabled people form a heterogeneous group within society. Their experiences, priorities and needs in the post-disaster context may differ on account of a range of factors, including age, gender and whether or not they became disabled as a result of the disaster. Disaster management policies and programmes need to recognise and take account of the diverse needs, vulnerabilities, capabilities and priorities of disabled people.
- Displacement, when it occurs, often exacerbates the risks and hardships that disabled people face. They may be left behind, often with reduced levels of support, or forced to undertake treacherous journeys that lead them to temporary shelters or camps, where they often experience increased levels of discrimination.
- In the aftermath of disasters, when economies may have been decimated and resources are often scarce, disabled people typically face increased discrimination and often feel excluded from their recovering communities. However, the recovery phase of the disaster management cycle also presents an opportunity for inclusive reconstruction and community building.
- DPOs have a vital role to play in disaster management, in terms of identifying the specific needs of disabled people, challenging discrimination, advocating on behalf of their members and empowering disabled people to participate more fully in their recovering communities. They can also contribute in more practical ways, as illustrated by Case Study 9.3. DPO networks need to be supported and strengthened to enable them to fulfil these roles more effectively.

- As highlighted by the Sendai Framework, there is growing international awareness of the need for more inclusive and people-centred approaches to disaster planning, recognising the potential role of disabled people and the organisations that represent them as key partners in disaster management.

Discussion questions

1 To what extent do human factors reinforce the vulnerability of disabled people to the impact of natural hazards?
2 How can emergency response interventions ensure that basic needs are met in a way that takes account of the diverse vulnerabilities and capabilities of disabled people?
3 How can DPOs with limited experience of humanitarian interventions be supported to make more effective contributions to disaster planning and management processes?

Notes

1 See Suggested further reading.
2 See Suggested further reading.
3 See Chapter 6 for an explanation of community-based rehabilitation.
4 See Suggested further reading.
5 See http://humanitariandisabilitycharter.org for further information on this charter.

Suggested further reading

Cobley, D.S. (2015) 'Typhoon Haiyan one year on: disability, poverty and participation in the Philippines'. *Disability and the Global South* 2(3), 686–707.

dos Santos-Zingale, M. and McColl, M.A. (2006) 'Disability and participation in post-conflict situations: the case of Sierra Leone'. *Disability and Society* 21(3), 243–257.

Kandasamy, N., Soldatic, K. and Samararatne, D. (2016) 'Peace, justice and disabled women's advocacy: Tamil women with disabilities in rural post-conflict Sri Lanka'. *Medicine, Conflict and Survival* 32, 1–19. DOI: 10.1080/13623699.2016.1237101

References

Alexander, D. (2002) *Principles of Emergency Planning and Management*. Harpenden: Terra Publishing.

Bakhshi, P. and Trani, J. (2006) *Understanding the Vulnerability of Afghans with Disability: Livelihoods, Employment, Income–The National Disability Survey in Afghanistan 2005*. Lyon: Handicap International. Retrieved on 22 January 2017 from www.hiproweb.org/fileadmin/cdroms/biblio-reference-0912/documents/RRD-64-Understanding%20vulnerability%20of%20Afghans%20with%20disabilities.pdf

Berghs, M. (2015) 'Disability and displacement in times of conflict: rethinking migration, flows and boundaries'. *Disability and the Global South* 2(1), 442– 459.

Berman-Bieler, R. (2010) 'Inclusive Development: Paving the Way as We Walk'. In Barron, T. and Ncube, J. (Eds.) *Poverty and Disability*. London: Leonard Cheshire Disability, 373–402.

Burton, G., Sayrafi, I. and Srour, A. (2013) 'Inclusion or transformation? An early assessment of an empowerment project for disabled people in occupied Palestine'. *Disability and Society,*. 28(6), 821–825.

Businge, P. (2016) 'Disability and armed conflict: a quest for Africanising disability in Uganda'. *Disability and the Global South* 3(1), 816–842.

CDD (Centre for Disability in Development) (2011) *Project Experience. Disability Inclusive Disaster Risk Reduction Project*. Dhaka: CDD. Retrieved on 18 March 2017 from www.cbm.org/article/downloads/82788/Disability-inclusive_disaster_risk_reduction_Bangladesh_CBM.pdf

Cobley, D.S. (2015) 'Typhoon Haiyan one year on: disability, poverty and participation in the Philippines'. *Disability and the Global South* 2(3), 686–707.

Collier, P., Elliott, L., Hegre, H., Hoeffler, A., Reynal-Quenol, M. and Sambanis, N. (2003) *Breaking the Conflict Trap: Civil War and Development Policy*. A World Bank Policy Research Report. Washington, DC: World Bank and Oxford University Press. Retrieved on 8 May 2017 from http://documents.worldbank.org/curated/en/908361468779415791/310436360_200500070100031/additional/multi0page.pdf

Coppola, D. (2015) *Introduction to International Disaster Management*. Third Edition. Amsterdam: Elsevier.

CSID (Centre for Services and Information on Disability in Development) (2002) *Unveiling Darkness: The Situation Analysis on Disaster and Disability Issues in the Coastal Belt of Bangladesh*. Dhaka: CDD. Retrieved on 18 March 2017 from www.csid-bd.com/research/research01.pdf

DEC (Disasters Emergency Committee) (2013) *Haiti, Three Years On*. Retrieved on 19 January 2017 from www.dec.org.uk/articles/haiti-3-years-on

dos Santos-Zingale, M. and McColl, M.A. (2006) 'Disability and participation in post-conflict situations: the case of Sierra Leone'. *Disability and Society* 21(3), 243–257.

Government of Japan (2012) *Annual Report on Government Measures for Persons with Disabilities (summary) 2012*. Cabinet Office. Retrieved on 4 August 2017 from www8.cao.go.jp/shougai/english/annualreport/2012/pdf/s12.pdf

Handicap International (2014) *Empowerment and Participation: Good Practices from South and South-East Asia in Disability Inclusive Disaster Risk Management*. Retrieved on 13 April 2017 from www.preventionweb.net/files/38358_38358hie mpowermentandparticipationi.pdf

IFRC (International Federation of Red Cross and Red Crescent Societies) (2007) 'Disability and disasters: towards an inclusive approach'. In *World Disasters Report 2007: Focus on Discrimination*, 86–111. Geneva: IFRC.

IFRC (2015) *All Under One Roof: Disability-Inclusive Settlements and Shelters in Emergencies*. Geneva: IFRC. Retrieved on 13 June 2017 from www.ifrc.org/Global/Documents/Secretariat/Shelter/All-under-one-roof_EN.pdf

IFRC (2016) *World Disasters Report 2016 – Resilience: Saving Lives Today, Investing for Tomorrow*. Geneva: IFRC.

Kandasamy, N., Soldatic, K. and Samararatne, D. (2016) 'Peace, justice and disabled women's advocacy: Tamil women with disabilities in rural post-conflict Sri Lanka'. *Medicine, Conflict and Survival* 32, 1–19. DOI: 10.1080/13623699.2016.1237101

Kett, M., Stubbs, S. and Yeo, R. (2005) *Disability in Conflict and Emergency Situations: Focus on Tsunami-affected Areas*. IDDC Research Report. Disability Knowledge and Research Programme. Retrieved on 13 December 2016 from http://iddcconsortium.net/sites/default/files/resources-tools/files/kar_tsunami_paper_05.pdf

Kett, M. (2007) 'Conflict Recovery'. In Barron, T. & Amerena, P. (Eds.) *Disability and Inclusive Development*. London: Leonard Cheshire International, 155–186.

Kett, M. (2010) 'Disability and poverty in post-conflict countries'. In Barron, T. and Ncube, J. (Eds.) *Poverty and Disability*. London: Leonard Cheshire Disability, 341–371.

Lord, A., Sijapati, B., Baniya, J., Chand, O. and Ghale, T. (2016) *Disaster, Disability & Difference; A Study of the Challenges Faced by Persons with Disabilities in Post-earthquake Nepal*. Study for UNDP with the support of the National Federation of Disabled-Nepal. Retrieved on 2 August 2017 from www.un.org/disabilities/documents/2016/Disaster-Disability-and-Difference_May2016_For-Accessible-PDF.pdf

Mizra, M. (2011) 'Unmet Needs and Diminished Opportunities: Disability, Displacement and Humanitarian Healthcare'. In *New Issues in Refugee Research*, Research paper No. 212. Retrieved on 13 May 2017 from www.unhcr.org/4e0dbdb29.pdf

Mizra, M. (2015) 'Disability inclusive healthcare in humanitarian camps: pushing the boundaries of disability studies and global health'. In *Disability and the Global South* 2(1), 479–500.

NDRRMC (National Disaster Risk Reduction and Management Council) (2014) *NDRRMC Update: Sitrep 27 Effects of Typhoon 'Ruby' (Hagupit)*. Retrieved on 3 February 2017 from ="http://www.ndrrmc.gov.ph/attachments/article/1356/Sitrep_No_27_re_Effects_of_Typhoon_Ruby_as_of_19DEC2014_0600H.pdf

Pearce, E. (2015) '"Ask us what we need": operationalizing guidance on disability inclusion in refugee and displaced persons programs'. In *Disability and the Global South* 2(1), 460–478.

Pisani, M. and Grech, S. (2015) 'Disability and forced migration: critical intersectionalities'. In *Disability and the Global South* 2(1), 421–441.

Priestley, M. and Hemingway, L. (2006) 'Natural hazards, human vulnerability and disabling societies: a disaster for disabled people?'. In *Review of Disability Studies* 2(3), 57–67.

Priestley, M. and Hemingway, L. (2007) 'Disability and disaster recovery: a tale of two cities?'. In *Journal of Social Work in Disability and Rehabilitation* 5(3–4), 23–42.

Shivji, A. (2010) 'Disability in displacement'. In *Forced Migration Review* 35, 4–7.

Smith, F., Jolley, E. and Schmidt, E. (2012) *Disability and Disasters: The Importance of an Inclusive Approach to Vulnerability and Social Capital*. Haywards Heath: Sightsavers. Retrieved on 14 February 2017 from www.worldwewant2015.org/file/287097/download/311264

Sphere Project (2011) *Sphere Humanitarian Charter and Minimum Standards in Disaster Response*. Geneva: Sphere Project. Retrieved on 3 November 2016 from www.sphereproject.org/handbook/

UNHCR (United Nations High Commissioner for Refugees) (2007) *The Protection of Older Persons and Persons with Disabilities*. Executive Committee of the High Commissioner's Programme. Standing Committee 39th Session, EC/58/SC/

CRP.14.6. Geneva: UNHCR. Retrieved on 21 March 2017 from www.unhcr.org/excom/EXCOM/4666d9602.pdf

UNHCR (2011) *Working with Persons with Disabilities in Forced Displacement.* Geneva: UNHCR. Retrieved on 4 May 2017 from www.unhcr.org/4ec3c81c9.pdf

UNISDR (United Nations Office for Disaster Risk Reduction) (2013) 'UN global survey explains why so many people living with disabilities die in disasters'. Press Release. Retrieved on 14 July 2017 from www.unisdr.org/files/35032_2013no29.pdf

United Nations (2005) *Hyogo Framework for Action (2005–2015).* Report on the World Conference on Disaster Reduction, Kobe, Hyogo, Japan, 18–22 January 2005. Retrieved on 14 October 2016 from www.unisdr.org/2005/wcdr/intergover/official-doc/L-docs/Hyogo-framework-for-action-english.pdf

United Nations (2006) *Convention on the Rights of Persons with Disabilities.* Washington, DC: United Nations.

United Nations (2011) *Best practices for Including Persons with Disabilities in all Aspects of Development Efforts.* Washington, DC: United Nations.

United Nations (2015a) *Sendai Framework for Disaster Risk Reduction 2015–2030.* Retrieved on 9 May 2017 from www.preventionweb.net/files/43291_sendaiframeworkfordrren.pdf

United Nations (2015b) *Transforming Our World: The 2030 Agenda for Sustainable Development.* Retrieved on 21 March 2017 from www.un.org/pga/wp-content/uploads/sites/3/2015/08/120815_outcome-document-of-Summit-for-adoption-of-the-post-2015-development-agenda.pdf

United Nations (2016) *Charter on the Inclusion of Persons with Disabilities in Humanitarian Action.* Retrieved on 29 December 2016 from http://humanitariandisabilitycharter.org

Wisner, B., Gaillard, J. and Kelman, I. (2012) *Handbook of Hazards and Disaster Risk Reduction.* Abingdon: Routledge

World Bank (2005) *Overview of Disabled Persons Organizations (DPOs) Working in Tsunami-affected Areas.* Washington, DC: World Bank

World Bank (2010) *Pakistan Earthquake Disability Project. Implementation, Completion and Results.* Report No. ICR00001584. Washington, DC: World Bank.

WRC (Women's Refugee Commission) (2008) *Disability Among Refugees and Conflict-affected Populations.* New York: Women's Refugee Commission. Retrieved on 16 May 2017 from www.womensrefugeecommission.org/resources/document/download/609

10 Researching disability

There is growing international recognition of disability as a priority development issue. This is reflected in the adoption and widespread ratification of the Convention on the Rights of Persons with Disabilities (CRPD), which emphasises 'the importance of mainstreaming disability issues as an integral part of relevant strategies of sustainable development planning' (United Nations, 2006, preamble (e)). The Sustainable Development Agenda, which promises to 'leave nobody behind', contains explicit references to disability in targets relating to five of the Sustainable Development Goals (SDGs),[1] providing further evidence of the rising profile of disability as an issue of critical importance to development planners. It is widely recognised, however, that there remains a significant lack of empirical evidence on which to build the policies and programmes that are necessary to effectively address the concerns and priorities of disabled people, particularly those living in the Global South.

The *World Report on Disability* (WHO and World Bank, 2011), which aims to provide a comprehensive and detailed analysis of the best scientific evidence available on a wide range of disability issues, in order to support governments and civil society in their efforts to implement the CRPD, clearly highlights the need for more research. The Report observes a lack of internationally comparable data and major research gaps, often resorting to making fairly general recommendations in the absence of hard evidence. In response to this problem, the Report calls for data from a wider range of sources, including disabled people's organisations (DPOs), to support national policy making and, in particular, for more qualitative research on the 'lived experiences of people with disabilities' (p. 46). These calls are reflected in the final list of recommendations, as shown in Box 10.1.

Box 10.1   Research gaps identified in the *World Report on Disability*

Research is essential for increasing public understanding about disability, informing disability policy and programmes, and efficiently allocating resources. This Report recommends several areas for research on disability including:

(continued)

(continued)

- the impact of environmental factors (policies, physical environment, attitudes) on disability and how to measure it;
- the quality of life and well-being of people with disabilities;
- barriers to mainstream and specific services, and what works in overcoming them in different contexts;
- accessibility and universal design programmes appropriate for low-income settings;
- the interactions among environmental factors, health conditions, and disability – and between disability and poverty;
- the cost of disability and the cost-effectiveness of public spending on disability programmes.

Source: WHO and World Bank, 2011, pp. 267–268

While there is clearly a lack of research on disability in a number of areas, there is a particularly acute need for research that captures the voices of disabled people themselves, reflecting their own priorities, experiences and viewpoints rather than the priorities of research funding bodies and assumptions of researchers, however well intentioned they may be. This final chapter begins by highlighting concerns expressed by many from within the disability movement around the historical impact of disability research, which has often been perceived as negative and even harmful. The chapter then focuses on two particular research paradigms that have the potential to address these concerns to some extent: firstly, the now well-established paradigm of participatory research, which has its roots within general qualitative research methodology; secondly, a relatively new research paradigm, known as emancipatory research, which has emerged from within the disability movement itself.

Historical impact of disability research

There is a firm body of opinion, particularly among disabled people themselves, to suggest that carrying out research on disability can actually be oppressive and disempowering for those disabled people that are intended to benefit from the research, particularly if researchers view disability purely as a medical issue and adopt the objective and detached standpoint that is typically required by conventional research models. Dissatisfaction with traditional approaches can be traced right back to the 1960s, when residents at the Le Court Cheshire Home in Hampshire were the subjects of a three-year research project (Miller and Gwynne, 1972), examining various aspects of their daily lives. In what came to be regarded as a landmark moment in the history of the disability movement in Britain, the final report rejected the residents' complaints and reinforced institutional practices that were already in place, even though the researchers themselves had described institutional life as a 'living death' (Barnes and

Mercer, 1997, p. 2). The sense of betrayal that many of the residents felt was eloquently expressed by Paul Hunt (1981), who went on to become a founder member of the Union of Physically Impaired Against Segregation (UPIAS),[2] in an article entitled *Settling Accounts with the Parasite People*:

Researchers as parasites

Long before publication of their research findings . . . it was clear that we, the residents, had been conned. It was clear to us that [the researchers] were definitely not on our side. They were not really on the side of the staff either . . . They were in fact basically on their own side, that is the side of supposedly 'detached', 'balanced', 'unbiased' social scientists, concerned above all with presenting themselves to the powers-that-be as indispensable. Thus the fundamental relationship between them and the residents was that of exploiters and exploited.

(Hunt, 1981, p. 38)

Several others have commented on the negative impact of much of the research on disability that has been carried out in the past. Shakespeare (1996), for example, describes the frequent 'lack of fit' between disabled people's descriptions of their own experiences and the ways in which academic researchers articulate those same experiences. In a self-reflective examination of some of the typical dilemmas facing disability researchers, Moore *et al.* (1998) provide several examples from their own experiences that highlight the danger of allowing service providers and other non-disabled stakeholders to exert such an influence over research processes that the views of disabled people themselves are overshadowed, or even ignored altogether. They attribute this tendency to the 'minority status' afforded to disabled people within society, claiming that 'identification with minority and oppressed groups impinges on a person's right to be heard by the majority' (p. 36). Perhaps the most vociferous critic of conventional approaches to disability research, however, has been Mike Oliver:

Research as a violation

Disabled people have come to see research as a violation of their own experiences, as irrelevant to their needs and as failing to improve their material circumstances and quality of life.

(Oliver, 1992, p. 106)

Table 10.1 Individual versus social model as a starting point for research

Individual model	Social model
Disability is located within the individual	Disability is located within society
Focus on impairment	Focus on the environmental context
Functional deficiencies, related to impairment, are the problem	Societal discrimination and prejudice is the problem
Solutions are likely to focus on medical treatment and rehabilitation	Solutions are likely to focus on the removal of disabling barriers

Historically, the influence of the individual model[3] has heavily contributed to the oppressive nature of much disability research (Oliver, 1992). A classic example of this influence was a survey carried out by the Office of Population Censuses and Surveys, on behalf of the United Kingdom (UK) government, involving face-to-face interviews with over 2,000 disabled people, during which they were asked questions such as 'Can you tell me what is wrong with you?' (Martin and White, 1988). The fundamental design flaw here, as Abberley (1992) points out in a stinging critique of the survey, is that questions such as this reflect an 'individualistic "personal tragedy" approach to disability' (p. 154) rather than exploring the various ways in which *society* disables people with impairments. Swain and French (2004) claim that most disability research has tended to reflect this view of disability, which leads to questions being framed in such a way as to emphasise the tragic nature of disability, sometimes even calling on disabled people to question whether they feel that their lives are worth living at all. In a similar vein, Moore *et al.* (1998) contend that research based on the individual model will 'inevitably recycle individual-blaming images of disabled people' (p. 12). They conclude that disability researchers are justified in counteracting this bias by openly aligning themselves with the views of the disabled people who are intended to benefit from their research, and declaring from the outset that research is intended to promote disability rights.

Over the past decade, in particular, disability research has increasingly reflected an acceptance of the social model[4] as a starting point for research, with an emphasis on examining the disabling role of society, rather than focusing on the limitations of the individual body. As Oliver (1990) astutely points out, such an emphasis might lead to a question such as 'Can you tell me what is wrong with you?' being reframed as 'Can you tell me what is wrong with society'? (p. 8). Table 10.1 highlights some of the main differences between research based on the individual model and research based on the social model.

Participatory and action research

Participatory research is often associated with the interpretive social science paradigm, which rejects the notion of a fixed, independent or 'objective' social reality. Instead, social reality varies from one person to another, and the purpose of research is to uncover the varying ways in which people understand and experience the social world themselves. Participatory approaches seek to capture these subjective views and experiences by involving research participants as equal partners in the research process, requiring a fundamental shift in the location of power from researchers to participants. This relocation of power – a key feature that distinguishes participatory from conventional research methodologies (Cornwall and Jewkes, 1995) – is reflected in the use of the term *participants*, rather than *subjects*. Participatory research is carried out *with participants*, rather than *on subjects*, recognising that participants can potentially play an important role in terms of influencing the design of the research, the issues to be addressed and the uses to which research findings will be put, rather than simply being viewed as a source of raw data.

Participatory research methods have a number of advantages over conventional approaches. The active involvement of local people in analysing their own situations can help to break down the mystique surrounding research, as well as instilling a sense of self-confidence and self-reliance in participants (Chambers, 1997). It has also been argued that participatory research is more likely to identify appropriate solutions to problems than conventional research methods, since the knowledge and intelligence of those who really understand the issues is validated through the research process (Laws *et al.*, 2003). It is perhaps not surprising, therefore, that participatory research methods have increasingly been adopted by disability researchers seeking to break down the disabling barriers and personal inhibitions (often arising from the internalisation of negative attitudes and disability-related stigma) that limit opportunities for disabled people to share their real-life experiences, express their feelings and raise the issues that are of most importance to them. While not inherently associated with the social model, the participatory research paradigm fits nicely with ideas of inclusiveness that underpin the social model, as well as the familiar slogan of the disability movement – 'nothing about us, without us' (Charlton, 1998).

One particular branch of participatory research is 'action research', which involves 'researchers' and 'participants' working collaboratively to bring about some form of social change that is initiated by participants. A good example of action research in the development field is participatory rural appraisal (PRA), sometimes referred to as participatory learning and action (PLA), defined by Robert Chambers in his seminal work *Whose Reality Counts*:

Participatory rural appraisal

PRA is a growing family of approaches and methods to enable local people to share, enhance and analyse their knowledge of life and conditions, and to plan, act, monitor and evaluate.

(Chambers, 1997, p. 102)

PRA methods, which often involve the use of practical, analytical tools, such as mapping, ranking or scoring, have been widely implemented by governments and development agencies for several decades now, with the aim of drawing on the knowledge and experiences of local people and putting them at the centre of the development process right from the outset. In South India, for example, the World Bank supported the State Government of Tamil Nadu in launching a large-scale poverty reduction programme (known as 'Vazhndhu Kaattuvom'[5]) in 2005, for which potential beneficiaries were identified through a process known as 'participatory identification of the poor' (Cobley, 2013). This involved community members meeting together to map out whole villages, often drawn in the sand with sticks, so that they could identify the most vulnerable people, including chronically ill and disabled people. Communities would then elect a Village Poverty Reduction Committee, including at least one disabled representative, which would be responsible for allocating project funds in line with local needs and priorities. This programme, based on the principles of participation and empowerment, effectively enabled whole communities to take a measure of control over their own development by putting resources at their disposal and facilitating community decision making, with the active involvement of disabled people.

Another type of action research is participatory action research (PAR), which is typically practice-based and aims to transform both theory and practice in relation to each other (Kemmis and McTaggert, 2003). Researchers act as facilitators and enablers, with participants taking a lead role in directing the project from start to finish, as explained below:

Participatory action research

PAR aims to renegotiate the position of 'the researched' to one of co-researchers, involving participants in every stage of the research process from the design stage to the writing of the research results.

(Kitchen, 2001, p. 63)

Kitchin (2002) adopts the PAR method himself in three projects examining accessibility issues in Ireland. He acknowledges, however, that while the projects did achieve some successful outcomes, such as enabling disabled people that took part to learn new skills and contribute to wider debates, the goal of 'equal partnership' was not achieved. Participants were reluctant to fully commit themselves to the projects, for reasons such as lack of confidence and limited time available. Another problem identified by Kitchin was the minimal level of project funding, which did not allow for the support needs of disabled participants to be fully met. As a result, the three projects effectively became 'semi-PAR projects', with the involvement of disabled participants limited to the early stages of the process, including setting up the projects and data collection. Kitchin himself was left to do most of the analysis and writing up, and he concedes that 'almost inevitably, given my familiarity with various literatures and professional research experience, the projects have reflected and been shaped by my opinions' (p. 9).

Whichever approaches are adopted, it is important to ensure that participation is as meaningful as possible, rather than tokenistic. As Kitchin's honest and realistic account illustrates, some disabled people lack the confidence or motivation to take part in research, while others have impairment-based needs that may hinder their participation if they are not fully accounted for. The checklist provided in Box 10.2 identifies some of the issues that often need to be considered, in order to facilitate the full and meaningful participation of disabled people in a research project.

Box 10.2 Checklist for facilitating meaningful participation

- Clearly establish the nature and limits of participation, in relation to the research project.
- Ensure that information about the research project is provided in accessible formats, appropriate to the impairment-based needs of participants.
- Proceed only with fully informed consent, and on the understanding that participants can withdraw at any stage.
- Be wary of generating unrealistic expectations as to the expected outcomes of the research or the likely benefits of participation.
- Ensure that any facilities (e.g. rooms or equipment) to be used are physically accessible to all participants.
- Provide appropriate capacity-building support to facilitate full participation (such as confidence-building measures or training in research methods).
- Provide appropriate practical support to facilitate attendance and participation (such as assisting with transport arrangements for participants with mobility impairments, providing a sign language interpreter for participants with hearing impairments or simply allowing extra time for participants with intellectual impairments).
- Try to create a relaxed environment that encourages participants to feel at ease.
- Show respect for cultural traditions and practices.

Adherence to the final point on this checklist can create tricky dilemmas, as the author experienced while attempting to conduct research in a participatory way with disabled people that had been affected by Typhoon Haiyan, a powerful and devastating storm that engulfed several provinces of the Central Philippines in 2013. This dilemma is described in Case Study 10.1.

Case study 10.1   Research dilemma in the Philippines

[An] ethical issue arose around confidentiality, given the tendency of family members and friends to crowd around during interviews, and sometimes even to join in. This was an inevitable consequence of local contextual realities. Firstly, there was a lack of physical space to conduct interviews within local communities, particularly as many were still living in cramped temporary shelters. Available space was generally considered to be communal, at least for the family and often for neighbours as well, rather than private. Secondly, as in much of the majority world, where 'community is often regarded as more important than the individual' (IDDC, 2004, p. 4), community life in the Philippines is characterised by interdependence, rather than by notions of individual freedom and privacy. To insist on privacy in such a context could be viewed as inappropriate (Singal, 2010), or even culturally insensitive. Hence it was necessary to accept the presence of onlookers, while acknowledging the possible influence that they could have on the interview findings. It should also be noted, however, that my overwhelming impression was that interviewees did not appear to be at all inhibited by the presence of onlookers who, for the most part, simply listened in respectful silence. Most of the interviews were conducted in Filipino, and the presence of onlookers, some of whom had knowledge of English, may also have helped to militate against the risk of interview content being filtered by NGO field workers who were acting as interpreters.

Source: Cobley, 2015, p. 693

While the principles of participatory research would appear to have much in common with the aims of the disability movement, some critics have argued that participation alone does not go far enough, in terms of putting disabled research participants in control of the research process. Oliver (1997), for example, argues that 'participatory and action research is about improving the existing social and material relations of research production;

not challenging and ultimately eradicating them' (p. 26). He goes on to conclude that we, as researchers, 'remain on the wrong side of the oppressive social and material relations of research' (p. 26). Oliver is among those that advocate an even more radical research paradigm known as emancipatory research.

Emancipatory research

Emancipatory research aims to enable participants to take control of the *whole* research process, thus turning the balance of power between researchers and their subjects upside down. This concept, which has evolved from within the UK disability movement, really took shape in a special issue of the journal *Disability, Handicap and Society* (later renamed *Disability and Society*), which was published following a series of seminars and a national conference on researching disability in 1991. In one of the articles, entitled 'Changing the Social Relations of Research Production', Oliver (1992) argued that if the goal of researching disability is emancipation, in line with the objectives of the disability movement, then the balance of power between researchers and disabled research subjects needs to be radically altered. Writing in the same special issue, Zarb (1992) goes even further. He argues that, as well as changing the social relations of research, the *material* relations would need to be addressed in order for disability research to be truly emancipatory. In other words, disabled people would need to be enabled to take control of the resources required for research, such as research funding, and to determine how these resources should be utilised. Zarb's vision makes a clear distinction between emancipatory and participatory research, as highlighted in the quotation below:

Who is in control?

[S]imply increasing participation and involvement will never by itself constitute emancipatory research unless and until it is disabled people themselves who are controlling the research.

(Zarb, 1992, p. 128)

There has been much debate among academics within the field of disability studies as to how to actually go about conducting emancipatory research (see, for example, Stone and Priestley, 1996; Barnes and Mercer, 1997; French and Swain, 1997; Albrecht *et al.*, 2001). Stone and Priestley (1996) give perhaps the clearest guidance by outlining six core principles on which an emancipatory research project should be based. These principles are listed in Box 10.3.

Box 10.3   Six core principles of emancipatory research

1   The adoption of a social model of disablement as the epistemo-
logical basis for research production.
2   The surrender of claims to objectivity through overt political commitment to the struggles of disabled people for self-emancipation.
3   The willingness only to undertake research where it will be of
practical benefit to the self-empowerment of disabled people and/
or the removal of disabling barriers.
4   The evolution of control over research production to ensure full
accountability to disabled people and their organisations.
5   Giving voice to the personal as political, whilst endeavouring to
collectivise the political commonality of individual experiences.
6   The willingness to adopt a plurality of methods for data collection
and analysis in response to changing needs of disabled people.

Source: Stone and Priestley, 1996, p. 706

If a research project is to realise its emancipatory potential, then a further
essential requirement is for its findings to be disseminated as widely as possible. Barnes (2001) emphasises this point, providing several examples of
research projects that have adhered, at least in part, to the emancipatory
research paradigm, and from which the dissemination of findings have triggered significant outcomes. He claims, for example, that the widespread
dissemination of findings from a large-scale study conducted in 1989 by the
British Council of Disabled People, on various forms of institutional discrimination faced by disabled people in the UK, played a 'crucial role in getting
anti-discrimination legislation onto the statute books in the UK' (p. 15).

Full adherence to Stone and Priestley's rather daunting list of criteria for the
production of truly emancipatory research may seem an unrealistic proposition to many involved in researching disability. On the question of objectivity,
for example, declaring a political commitment to endorsing the views of the
disability movement could leave disability researchers vulnerable to accusa-
tions of subjectivity, or even bias (Barnes, 2001). However, as Barnes goes on
to point out, all judgements and interpretations of data made by social science
researchers are influenced by a variety of forces, such as personal experiences
and the political or cultural context. Kitchen (2002) makes an even stronger
defence of researchers adopting inclusive research methodologies, arguing
that these approaches may be even more academically rigorous than standard
'expert' methodologies, because research participants are encouraged to verify
findings, thus helping to ensure that both data and interpretations are valid.

Further dilemmas may arise where disabled research participants do not
themselves share the emancipatory objectives of the wider disability movement

or a commitment to the social model of disability. As Singal (2010) warns, for example, there may be a danger in placing too much emphasis on the social model in Southern contexts, where 'disability is most likely the result of disease, malnutrition or other treatable or preventable factors' (p. 422). Turmusani (2004) also questions the applicability of the emancipatory research paradigm in Southern contexts, pointing out that aspirations relating to individual or group liberation may be considered less important than the need for disabled people to contribute to the overall welfare of their families and communities. He goes on to argue that debates around researching disability need to 'become more accommodating to include other views on disability and also become culture sensitive' (p. 10). Stone and Priestley (1996) themselves concede that the imposition of Western conceptualisations may be 'condemned for irrelevance where disabled people's struggles revolve around daily survival rather than political emancipation' (p. 711).

The question of accountability is perhaps even more problematic. It is difficult to see how researchers can shift control of research production into the hands of disabled people and their organisations. Much academic research is ultimately controlled by the funding bodies, donor agencies and academic institutions that actually commission research, so it is only by gaining control, or at least significant influence, over these bodies that power can begin to change hands. Even if the funding bodies were to become more inclusive, however, there is no guarantee that those disabled people who were actually to find themselves in positions of power and influence would be truly representative of the wider community of disabled people who participate in research projects.

Even it were theoretically possible, as well as culturally appropriate, for a research project to strictly adhere to the criteria for emancipatory research, as articulated by Stone and Priestley, there is no guarantee that this would necessarily lead to emancipatory outcomes for disabled people. It is simply not possible to judge the emancipatory impact of a research project until sufficient time had elapsed for real and positive changes to disabled people's lives to become apparent. It is interesting to note that, five years after introducing the concept, Oliver (1997) himself acknowledges that 'One cannot "do" emancipatory research (nor write methodology cookbooks on how to do it), one can only engage as a researcher with those seeking to emancipate themselves' (p. 25).

Perhaps the best way to approach the challenge of confronting oppression within the research process is to focus on what is achievable, as well as appropriate, within the context of a particular research project. When Oliver (1992) first introduced the concept of emancipatory research, he highlighted three fundamental principles on which the new paradigm should be based. Firstly, 'reciprocity', which involves researchers being prepared to make themselves vulnerable and to conduct research in an open and empathetic manner, so that data collection effectively becomes a two-way process of mutual sharing, rather than a one-way process of extracting data. Secondly, 'gain', which raises the question as to who benefits from research, and how the benefits can be shared, rather than appropriated by the researcher. Thirdly, 'empowerment', which involves the creation of a research environment that supports and enables participants to take the practical steps which may help them to empower themselves. This final principle is perhaps the most difficult to put into practice, given that empowerment can only really come from within (Freire, 1972), but certainly requires a willingness on the part of researchers to put their skills and knowledge at the disposal of participants, rather than dictating how these attributes should be used. These three principles provide a simple framework that can be used to reflect on one's own research practice, one indeed that Oliver (1997) makes use of himself to reflect on one of his own studies (Campbell and Oliver, 1996) around issues facing the UK disability movement. More recently Amy Petersen (2011)[6] makes use of this framework to reflect on her study on the educational experiences of four young African American disabled women from economically disadvantaged backgrounds in the United States (US) – women with whom she initially felt that she had little in common, and little to offer in her role as a researcher. Her use of this framework to reflect on how her approach changed during the course of the study is summarised in Case Study 10.2.

Case study 10.2   Reciprocity, gain and empowerment

In a self-reflective article, Petersen (2011) examines her research study in relation to the principles of reciprocity, gain and empowerment:

Reciprocity

Petersen describes how she was able to develop a more productive and positive relationship with participants by abandoning her initial view of herself as an expert, independent and objective researcher in order to make herself vulnerable. She was able to find common ground with one participant by sharing her own traumatic experiences of childbirth, and to offer practical assistance to another on how she might go about resolving problems that she was having with public transport. In doing so, she felt that power shifted within the research relationship. Interviews became a 'reciprocal dialogue that unfolded with less and less preconceived intent on my part and a greater willingness to follow the lead of the women and the twists and turns that characterised our conversations' (p. 300)

Gain

Petersen describes how she had initially felt a sense of urgency to complete the study quickly, so that she could enjoy the potential benefits of a degree, a new job and a publication to her name. During the course of the study, however, she came to realise that research has the potential to be of benefit to participants as well, not least through the process of validating their own experiences. One participant confirmed the importance of telling her story by asserting that 'talking with you has helped me feel more confident about what I believe about myself and what is possible for me' (p. 300).

Empowerment

Petersen reflects on how the monosyllabic responses that characterised her initial interviews signified a refusal on the part of participants to engage with her methods and to accept the objective, closed and professional stance that she had adopted as the researcher. When she abandoned her checklist of questions, shared more of herself as a person and began to explore ways in which the research might be of benefit to participants, she began to 'create a context for empowerment' (p. 301). In other words, she was able to foster a more constructive atmosphere within which participants felt able to think more deeply about their own personal circumstances and to explore ways in which they might take action to improve these circumstances.

The three basic emancipatory research principles of reciprocity, gain and empowerment can equally be applied to disability research projects that are conducted in the Global South. Singal (2010), for example, reflects on a large-scale qualitative research study that explored the experiences, expectations and aspirations of young disabled people in India, involving interviews conducted by young, relatively inexperienced, local researchers.[7] She describes how many of the participants valued the opportunity to share their feelings and experiences with other young people. Perhaps even more importantly, participants were able to become 'agents of change' (p. 424) by revealing that they had interests and aspirations that did not reflect the tragic view of disability that many of the researchers had previously held, thus significantly altering those perceptions.

Reflection exercise 10.1

Think of a disability-focused research project that you have conducted, participated in or read about. Reflect on this project in relation to the three principles of reciprocity, gain and empowerment. How might the project have been conducted differently in order to more closely reflect these principles?

Summary of key points

- There is a need for more research on disability in numerous areas, in order to support policy makers and development actors to address the needs of disabled people, promote their rights to full participation in society and to fully implement the CRPD. There is a particular need for research that gives voice to disabled people themselves, capturing their views, priorities and real-life experiences.
- Historically, much of the research that has been conducted on disability has been criticised for framing disability as an individual or medical issue, and for failing to give sufficient weight to the views of disabled research participants.
- In response to these criticisms, disability researchers have increasingly adopted more inclusive or participatory research methodologies, which aim to create greater equality within the research process and to validate the subjective experiences of research participants.
- The emancipatory research paradigm, closely associated with the UK disability movement, goes beyond participatory research in that it aims to turn over control of the entire research process to disabled people and the organisations that represent them. There is much debate, however, as to how emancipatory research can be put into practice, particularly in Southern contexts where the emancipatory goals of the worldwide disability movement may conflict with local priorities.
- While there are some significant differences between the participatory and emancipatory paradigms, there is no doubt that several key principles are common to both. In particular, the need to listen carefully to the views of disabled participants, to learn from their experiences and to allow them, where possible, to exert a guiding influence on the research agenda, so that research findings reflect their true priorities and realities.

Discussion questions

1   To what extent is it possible, or desirable, to remain objective when conducting research with disabled people?
2   How does the way in which interview or survey questions are framed influence a research project?

3 How might disabled research participants be encouraged and supported to participate in the early stages of a research project, when the objectives are shaped, and in the later stages, when data is analysed and findings are disseminated?
4 To what extent does the emancipatory research paradigm provide a useful basis for conducting research on disability in the Global South?

Notes

1 See Table 4.3, Chapter 4.
2 See Chapter 2 for an explanation of the key role played by UPIAS in laying the foundations for the Social Model of Disability.
3 See Chapter 2 for an explanation of the individual model.
4 See Chapter 2 for an explanation of the social model of disability.
5 Vazhndhu Kaattuvom is a Tamil expression meaning 'let's show how to live'.
6 See Suggested further reading.
7 See Suggested further reading.

Suggested further reading

Petersen, A. (2011) 'Research with individuals labelled "other": reflections on the research process'. In *Disability and Society* 26(3), 293–305.
Singal, N. (2010) 'Doing disability research in a Southern context: challenges and possibilities'. In *Disability and Society* 25(4), 415–426.

References

Abberley, P. (1992) 'Counting us out: a discussion of the OPCS disability surveys'. *Disability and Society* 7(2), 139–155.
Albrect, G., Seelman, K. and Bury, M. (Eds.) (2001) *Handbook of Disability Studies*. London: Sage.
Barnes, C. (2001) '"Emancipatory" Disability Research: project or process?'. Public Lecture at City Chambers, Glasgow, on 24 October 2001. Retrieved on 10 March 2017 from http://disability-studies.leeds.ac.uk/files/library/Barnes-glasgow-lecture.pdf
Barnes, C. and Mercer, G. (1997) 'Breaking the Mould? An Introduction to Doing Disability Research'. In Barnes, C. and Mercer, G. (Eds.) *Doing Disability Research*. Leeds: The Disability Press, 1–14.
Campbell, J. and Oliver, M. (1996) *Disability Politics in Britain: Understanding Our Past, Changing Our Future*. London: Routledge.
Chambers, R. (1997) *Whose Reality Counts*: Rugby: ITDG Publishing.
Charlton, J. (1998) *Nothing About Us Without Us*. Berkeley: University of California Press.
Cobley, D.S. (2013) 'Towards economic participation: examining the impact of the Convention on the Rights of Persons with Disabilities in India'. *Disability and Society* 28(4), 441–455.
Cobley, D.S. (2015) 'Typhoon Haiyan one year on: disability, poverty and participation in the Philippines'. *Disability and the Global South* 2(3), 686–707.
Cornwall, A. and Jewkes, R. (1995) 'What Is Participatory Research?'. *Social Science and Medicine* 41(12), 1667–1676.

Freire, P. (1972) *Pedagogy of the Oppressed*. Harmondsworth: Penguin.

French, S. and Swain, J. (1997) 'Changing disability research: participating and emancipatory research with disabled people'. *Physiotherapy* 83(1), 26–32.

Hunt, P. (1981) 'Settling accounts with the parasite people'. *Disability Challenge* 2, 37–50.

IDDC (International Disability and Development Consortium) (2004) *Inclusive Development and the UN Convention*. IDDC Reflection Paper. Retrieved on 30 March 2017 from www.un.org/esa/socdev/enable/rights/ahc3iddc.pdf

Kemmis, S. and McTaggert, R. (2003) 'Participatory Action Research'. In Denzin, N.K. and Lincoln, Y.S. (Eds.) *Strategies of Qualitative Enquiry*. Second Edition. Thousand Oaks, CA: Sage Publications, 559–604.

Kitchin, R. (2001) 'Using participatory action research approaches in geographical studies of disability: some reflections'. *Disability Studies Quarterly* 21(4), 61–69.

Kitchin, R. (2002) *Towards Emancipatory Disability Research: Reflections on Three Participatory Action Research Projects*. Maynooth: National Institute of Regional and Spatial Analysis, National University of Ireland. Retrieved on 13 March 2017 from http://sonify.psych.gatech.edu/~walkerb/classes/assisttech/pdf/ kitchin (2002).pdf

Laws, S. with Harper, C. and Marcus, R. (2003) *Research for Development: A Practical Guide*. London: Sage.

Martin, J. and White, A. (1988) *OPCS Surveys of Disability in Great Britain Report 2: The Financial Circumstances of Disabled Adults Living in Private Households*. London: HMSO.

Miller, E.J. and Gwynne, G.V. (1972) *A Life Apart*. London: Tavistock.

Moore, M., Beazley, S. and Maezler, J. (1998) *Researching Disability Issues*. Maidenhead: Open University Press.

Oliver, M. (1990) *The Politics of Disablement*. Basingstoke: Macmillan.

Oliver, M. (1992) 'Changing the social relations of research production'. *Disability, Handicap and Society* 7(2), 101–114.

Oliver, M. (1997) 'Emancipatory Research: Realistic Goal of Impossible Dream?'. In Barnes, C. and Mercer, G. (Eds.) *Doing Disability Research*. Leeds: The Disability Press, 15–31.

Petersen, A. (2011) 'Research with individuals labelled "other": reflections on the research process'. *Disability and Society* 26(3), 293–305.

Shakespeare, T. (1996) 'Rules of engagement: doing disability research'. *Disability and Society* 11(1), 115–119.

Singal, N. (2010) 'Doing disability research in a Southern context: challenges and possibilities'. *Disability and Society* 25(4), 415–426.

Stone, E. and Priestley, M. (1996) 'Parasites, pawns and partners: disability research and the role of non-disabled researchers'. *British Journal of Sociology* 47(4), 699–716.

Swain, J. and French, S. (2004) 'Researching Together: A Participatory Approach'. In French, S. and Sim, J. (Eds.) *Physiotherapy: A Psychosocial Approach*. Third Edition. Oxford: Butterworth-Heinemann, 317–332.

Turmusani, M. (2004) 'An eclectic approach to disability research: a majority world perspective'. *Asia Pacific Disability Rehabilitation Journal* 15(1), 3–11.

United Nations (2006) *Convention on the Rights of Persons with Disabilities and Optional Protocol*. Washington, DC: United Nations.

WHO (World Health Organization) and World Bank (2011) *World Report on Disability*. Geneva: WHO. Retrieved on 22 October 2016 from http://whqlibdoc. who.int/publications/2011/9789240685215_eng.pdf

Zarb, G. (1992) 'On the road to Damascus: first step towards changing the relations of disability research production'. *Disability, Handicap & Society* 7(2), 125–138.

Index

PGMO 08/14/2018